Environmental Law in Poland

Environmental Law in Poland

Barbara Kowalczyk
Rafał Mikowski
Łukasz Mikowski

This book was originally published as a monograph in the International Encyclopaedia of Laws/Environmental Law.

Founding Editor: Roger Blanpain
General Editor: Frank Hendrickx
Volume Editor: Kurt Deketelaere

Wolters Kluwer

Published by:
Kluwer Law International B.V.
PO Box 316
2400 AH Alphen aan den Rijn
The Netherlands
E-mail: international-sales@wolterskluwer.com
Website: lrus.wolterskluwer.com

Sold and distributed in North, Central and South America by:
Wolters Kluwer Legal & Regulatory U.S.
7201 McKinney Circle
Frederick, MD 21704
United States of America
Email: customer.service@wolterskluwer.com

Sold and distributed in all other countries by:
Air Business Subscriptions
Rockwood House
Haywards Heath
West Sussex
RH16 3DH
United Kingdom
Email: international-customerservice@wolterskluwer.com

Printed on acid-free paper

ISBN 978-94-035-0950-1

e-Book: ISBN 978-94-035-1000-2
web-PDF: ISBN 978-94-035-1044-6

Printed and bound by CPI Group (UK) Ltd, Croydon, CR0 4YY

The Authors

Barbara Kowalczyk graduated from the Faculty of Law, Administration and Economics at the University of Wrocław. She received her PhD in Law (specialization in Administrative Law) from the same institution. She is, presently, an Assistant Professor at the Institute of Administrative Science, the Section of Comparative Public Administration (formerly, the Section of Environmental Protection Law and Comparative Administrative Law), Faculty of Law, Administration and Economics, University of Wroclaw and also a Visiting Professor at the Faculty of Law of the Masaryk University in Brno (Czech Republic). She is the Deputy Editor and Administrative Science and Law Section Editor for the Board of Editors of Wroclaw Review of Law, Administration & Economics.

Barbara's research interests include: Legal Comparative Studies; Comparative Administration; European Administrative Law; Europeanization of Administrative Law; Administration of the European Union (EU). She is the author of books and dozens of articles, *inter alia* the monograph *Polski system azylowy* (*Polish asylum system*, 2014), co-author of the book *Prawo administracyjne Unii Europejskiej* (*Administrative law of the EU*, eds R. Grzeszczak, A. Szczerba – Zawada, 2016), co-editor (with J. Supernat) of the book *Kodeks postepowania administracji Unii Europejskiej* (*Code of administrative proceedings of the EU administration*, 2017). She is an attorney-at-law of the Wroclaw Bar Association.

Rafał Mikowski is an Assistant Professor at the Section of Administrative Law, Institute of Administrative Science, Faculty of Law, Administration and Economics of the University of Wroclaw. He received his PhD in 2010 with specialization in Administrative Law, awarded by the same institution. He is, presently, also a Lecturer at the Department of Social Sciences of Jan Wyzykowski University in Polkowice. He is an attorney-at-law of the Wroclaw Bar Association – Mikowscy & Partners Law Firm of Attorney-at-Law Dr Rafał Mikowski.

Rafał is the author and co-author of various publications in the field of administrative law, mostly related to the protection of information, including protection of information in the environmental law and has also co-authored textbooks and tutorials in administrative law. He is a member of the Public Administration Education Association (SEAP).

Łukasz Mikowski received his LLM from the Faculty of Law, Administration and Economics of the University of Wroclaw. He received his PhD in 2010, with specialization in Administrative Law, awarded by the same institution. He is presently employed as a Senior Lecturer at the Institute of Socio-Legal Studies of the Angelus Silesius University of Applied Sciences in Wałbrzych, as a Lecturer at the Department of Social Sciences of Jan Wyzykowski University in Polkowice and as a Lecturer at the Institute of Administrative Sciences at the Faculty of Law, Administration and Economics of the University of Wroclaw. He is an attorney-at-law of the Wroclaw Bar Association – Mikowscy & Partners Law Firm of Attorney-at-Law Dr Łukasz Mikowski.

Łukasz is the author and co-author of numerous publications in the field of administrative law, including environmental protection law. He is a member of the Public Administration Education Association (SEAP).

Table of Contents

Table of Contents

List of Abbreviations

CAP	Code of Administrative Proceedings
CC	Criminal Code
CCP	Code of Criminal Proceedings
Dz.U.	*Dziennik Ustaw* (Journal of Laws)
EU	European Union
GMO	Genetically Modified Organisms
SAC	Supreme Administrative Court
SFNFH	State Forests National Forest Holding

List of Abbreviations

General Introduction

§1. General Background

I. Geography and Population

A. Geography

1. Poland is a large country situated in Central Europe, on the Baltic Sea.[1] Warsaw (Warszawa) is the capital city. As of 1 January 2018, the total area of the country, according to administrative borders,[2] amounts to 312,679 km^2 and includes a land area (including inland waters) of 311,888 km^2 as well as internal waters measuring 791 km^2. Countries sharing a border with Poland comprise Germany (467 km), the Czech Republic (796 km), Slovakia (541 km), Ukraine (535 km), Belarus (418 km), Lithuania (104 km) and Russia (210 km). The sea border measures 440 km. The eastern border of Poland constitutes part of the European Union's (EU's) external border.

2. Poland is a low-lying country with 75% of its territory located below 200 MAMSL (0.2% of which lies below sea level), nearly 22% at 200–500 MAMSL, almost 3% above 500 MAMSL and just 0.2% above 1,000 MAMSL. Poland's highest point is the summit of Mt. Rysy (2,499 MAMSL) in the Carpathians (located in the south of the country), while its lowest point is in the voivodeship of Warmia-Masuria (-1.8 MAMSL). Its longest rivers are the Vistula (1,022 km in length, with a river basin area of 168,868 km^2) and the Oder (the length of the Polish segment is 726 km, with a river basin area of 106,043 km^2). Other significant rivers include the Warta, Bug, Narew and San. The largest lakes are located in the north-eastern portion of the country, in Warmia-Masuria voivodeship: Śniardwy (113.4 km^2) and Mamry (102.8 km^2). Poland's climate is moderately warm, transitioning from a marine climate in the west to a continental climate in the east.

3. The majority of the country's surface area (60%) is used for agricultural production, including arable land, orchards, meadows and pastures which occupy

1. All information from *Concise Statistical Yearbook of Poland 2018* (Statistics Poland, Warsaw) and published report on the results of the 2011 National Census of Population and Housing (Warsaw 2012).
2. The entire surface area amounts to 322,575 km^2, with a land area (including inland waters) of 311,888 km^2, internal waters of 2,005 km^2 and a territorial sea of 8,682 km^2.

approximately 18.8 million ha; the remaining portion is composed of built-up arable land. Forests and wooded lands occupy 30% of the country's surface area. Built-up and urbanized areas (including residential, industrial, recreational and transport infrastructure) constitute slightly over 5%. Ecologically classified lands comprise an area of 43,000 ha.

4. Areas under legal protection of particularly valuable natural attractions occupy 10.175 million ha, 32.5% of the country's area. This includes 23 national parks, 122 landscape parks, 1,498 nature reserves, 386 protected landscape areas and other protected regions.

5. As of 31 December 2017, the Natura 2000 network, established in compliance with EU regulations, included 145 Special Protection Areas, covering a total of 5.56 million ha (of which 649,000 ha on the Baltic Sea) and 849 Special Areas of Conservation, covering a total of 3.851 million ha (of which 360,000 ha on the Baltic Sea). Approximately 11% of Poland's surface area constitutes a Natura 2000 zone. Both types of areas protected under Natura 2000 can overlap with each other and with other forms of nature protection, either in part or in whole.

6. Poland also contains such natural resources as black coal, brown coal, oil and natural gas; metals such as zinc and lead ore as well as copper ore; chemical raw materials such as sulphur and rock salt and also rock raw materials (clay, sand, stone, etc.)

B. Population

7. According to the 2011 National Census of Population and Housing, the population of Poland amounts to 38,511,800 people, of which 60.8% live in urbanized areas, while 39.2% live in rural areas. Population density is 123 people/km^2. Men make up 48.4% of the population, women 51.6%. Average life expectancy as of 2017 is 78 years (around 74 for men and 82 for women).

8. The estimated population as of 31 December 2017 is 38,434,000 people, which includes actual population growth (natural increase and net of international migration for permanent residence). Significant negative population growth is forecast for next years: in 2030 – 37,185,000 and in 2050 – 33,951,000.

II. Legal and Political Structure

9. Poland's legal and political structure is set forth in the Constitution of 2 April 1997.[3] Poland is a republic (Article 1). She is a unitary state (Article 3), which thus implies uniform citizenship. The primary administrative division of the country is a tripartite structure: commune (the basic territorial entity), county and voivodeship

3. Dz. U. 1997, No. 78, item 483 with amendments.

(roughly equivalent to a region). Other divisions are applied for the performance of particular tasks (e.g., military administration, mining, maritime matters), as are supporting entities (in communes). The capital (Warsaw) has been given special status associated with its role.

10. The primary principle of the Republic of Poland's political structure is the principle that it is a democratic state ruled by law (Article 2). This serves as the basis for a number of more detailed principles, such as the investiture of supreme power in the nation and that of democratic representation (Article 4), the tripartite separation and balance of powers (Article 10) and associated burden of cooperation placed on public authorities, the principle of subsidiarity (expressed in the Preamble to the Constitution), the principle of decentralization (Article 15, Article 16(1) and Article 164) and the principle of substantial exercise of public power by local government (Article 16(2)).

11. In accordance with the tripartite separation of powers, legislative power is exercised by the *Sejm* (lower house) and Senate, executive power is vested in the President of the Republic of Poland and the Council of Ministers and judicial authority belongs to courts and tribunals. The model system of parliamentary cabinet governments is complemented by the so-called rationalized parliamentary system.

12. The *Sejm* is composed of 460 deputies, while the Senate has 100 senators. They are chosen in direct elections, and their term of office is 4 years. Parliament (the *Sejm*) performs two primary functions: legislative and oversight.

13. The dualism of the executive branch – the President of the Republic of Poland and the Council of Ministers – assumes the structural and functional independence of both authorities: a collegial government – the Council of Ministers headed by the of Prime Minister, responsible for carrying out state policy, and the head of the State – the President. These bodies are endowed with general powers and are superior to other institutions involved in the exercise of executive authority. These entities can be categorized into three segments: state administration, government administration and local government administration.

14. The President is elected by the nation for a five-year term of office and is the supreme representative of the state as well as guarantor of the continuity of state authority. The President ensures the observance of the Constitution, safeguards the sovereignty and security of the state as well as the inviolability and integrity of its territory. The President's *strict* executive authority is limited.

15. The central governmental authority is the Council of Ministers (cabinet), which conducts both internal affairs and foreign policy. The Constitution establishes the following presumptions concerning this body: it is responsible for all matters of state policy that are not reserved for other state or local government authorities. The Council of Ministers is composed of the Prime Minister and other ministers who are responsible for supervising the work of bodies of State administration (ministries) or for performing other tasks as appointed by the Prime Minister. One or more Deputy Prime Ministers may be appointed.

16. The Council of Ministers manages government administration, which is composed of specialized central organs of state administration typically under the authority of one minister. The central government is represented in voivodeships by the institution of Voivode, which is an organ of unified administration and superior to other organs comprising this administration, i.e., directors of unified services and inspectorates. Government administration is also performed by specialized organs of non-unified administration.

17. Local government is comprised of three divisions: commune, county and voivodeship. Local government units have legislative and oversight bodies selected through direct elections, as well as executive authorities elected directly at the commune level. Local government bodies are equipped with the authority to pass laws whose binding force extends to the territory they operate in (local law). They are subject to oversight exercised by government administration authorities based on the principle of legality. The independence of local government bodies is protected by the administrative court system, which serves as a venue for pursuing complaints against oversight activities.

18. Local government bodies perform a significant portion of public tasks. In respect of the commune, there is a statutory presumption of competence. The commune is the basic unit of local government, whose scope of activity encompasses all public matters of local significance not reserved by statute for other bodies. There is a degree of overlap between the subjective spheres of competence enjoyed by communes and counties in respect of local matters, such as social infrastructure, technical infrastructure, public order and safety, spatial management and land-use management. The tasks assigned to the county are of a complementary nature to those of the commune, observing the principle of subsidiarity. The functions of the county government should be complementary and compensatory in respect of the public functions performed by the commune government. What is more, the county carries out tasks to satisfy the needs of all communities in communes within its borders (specialized services). Tasks exceeding the capacity of the commune, extending beyond its boundaries or ones which by their nature are not divisible have been assigned to the county. Such tasks are those that require greater financial outlays and organizational engagement, professional knowledge and specialized procedures.

19. The scope of activity engaged in by voivodeship government does not infringe on the independence of the county and commune. Regional authorities are primarily responsible for their region's civilizational and economic development.

20. Units of local government at all levels have the right to cooperate with one another, allowing them to jointly carry out their activities as well as to assign tasks for performance. They can also perform assigned tasks falling under the scope of government administration. Local government bodies of all levels have the right to enter into international (cross-border) cooperation arrangements.

21. Judicial power is vested in courts and tribunals. The Constitution lists the Constitutional Tribunal and the Tribunal of State. The Constitutional Tribunal is a particular kind of court whose role is to perform judicial oversight in respect of the constitutionality of the law, making it 'the court over the law'. It adjudicates in matters concerning the conformity of statutes and international agreements to the Constitution, the conformity of a statute to ratified international agreements whose ratification required prior consent granted by statute and the conformity of legal acts issued by central state organs to the Constitution, ratified international agreements and statutes. It is also authorized to review the conformity to the Constitution of the purposes and activities of political parties, to hear constitutional complaints and to settle disputes over authority and jurisdiction between central constitutional organs of the state. Judgements of the Constitutional Tribunal are of universal binding application and are final.

22. The Tribunal of State is the venue before which constitutional accountability is adjudicated for violations of the Constitution or of a statute committed by individuals performing the most important state functions, such as the President, the Prime Minister and members of the Council of Ministers.

23. The justice in Poland is performed by the Supreme Court, common courts, administrative courts and military courts. Court proceedings are composed of no less than two instances. Administrative courts (the Supreme Administrative Court (SAC) and voivodeship/regional administrative courts) exercise control over the performance of public administration to the extent specified by statute. This judicial review, grounded in the principle of legality, encompasses the protection of subjective rights (grievances against administrative decisions, administrative inaction, etc.), as well as protection of the legal order (ruling on the conformity of laws established at a local level to statutes).

III. Economic Characteristics[4]

24. Poland's economic model is based on the concept of the social market economy (Article 20 of the Constitution). Poland is the 8th largest economy in the EU on the basis of Gross domestic product (GDP), and the 23rd largest in the world (as of 2018). In 2017 the Polish market has been upgraded from an emerging market to developed market status.

25. The largest component of Poland's economy is the service sector (62.3.%), followed by industry (34.2%) and agriculture (3.5%).

4. Sources of information: *Concise Statistical Yearbook of Poland 2018* and OECD, *Economic Surveys Poland March 2018 Overview.*

26. Over the last years, Poland's economic activity has been steadily on the rise. Economic growth is strong (GDP is about 5.1 in 2018). Rising social transfers and a booming labour market are underpinning rapid consumption growth. The unemployment rate is at a record low level (in 2018 – 5.8%). The minimum monthly wage as of 1 January 2018 is PLN 2,100. Average wages and salaries in enterprises sector amounted to PLN 4,778.

27. The currency is the Polish Zloty (PLN). The EUR exchange rate is approx. PLN 4.30 and the USD exchange rate is PLN 3.80. Inflation was 2.0%.

28. The income tax rates for natural persons are 18% and 32%, while for juridical persons (enterprises) it is 19% and 15% for small business and beginners (in the year of staring of business). The base value-added tax (VAT) rate is 23%, while other taxes generate much smaller income streams for the state budget.

29. The macroeconomic outlook is positive. Strong economic growth, stability of the financial sector and low unemployment were indicated.

IV. Social and Cultural Characteristics

30. Poland is inhabited by a population of overwhelmingly uniform Polish ethnic identity – approx. 94% of the total population. Around 2.2% of residents have both Polish and another national-ethnic identity. National minority status is enjoyed in Poland by Belarusian, Czech, Lithuanian, Armenian, Russian, Slovakian, Ukrainian and Jewish communities. Ethnic minorities include the Karaites, Lemkos, Romani and Tatars.

31. The dominant religion is Catholicism, with over 33,400,000 declaring membership in the Roman Catholic Church. Other faith communities include Old Catholic, Orthodox, Protestant and others.

32. The official language is Polish. National minorities have the right to use a minority language in conjunction with the performance of public tasks. In communes that fulfil statutory criteria, a minority or regional language may be used as a supporting language during contact with local administration. The rights of minorities in the public sphere also encompass for instance the right to use and write names and surnames in the minority language, including in civil register documents and identity documents.

33. Poland is perceived as an attractive tourist destination, including health spa tourism. Tourists are attracted to Poland by its rich history and natural virtues. The most commonly cited tourist attractions are Poland's cities, monuments and museums. Poland is also well known due to forests and national parks.[5]

5. Research conducted by the Polish Tourism Organization.

V. Main Environmental Problems

34. Under the previous political and economic regime Poland was among the most heavily-polluted countries. The industrialization and urbanization of Poland took place without respect for the principles of environmental and nature protection. The law was ineffective, while social and economic considerations triumphed over ecological ones.

35. Drivers of changes included association and later accession to the EU. The provisions of the Treaty of Accession established serious tasks to be carried out, with the general assumption that by 2015 Poland should fulfil all the same standards for environmental protection applicable to EU Member States.[6]

36. Among the most important issues in environmental protection are protection of the air from pollution and reduction in the emission of dust and gas into the environment, as – in comparison to the rest of the EU – the scale of these emissions remains significant. The total emission (in absolute values) of greenhouse gases in Poland, including carbon dioxide, is one of the highest among the EU countries. Per capita, annual greenhouse gases emission (as carbon dioxide equivalent) amounted in 2016 to 10.5 t for Poland and 8.7 t for the EU.[7]

37. One of the more difficult tasks facing Poland in the coming years is rational management of water resources, including renaturalization and permeability of rivers as well as protection of water from pollution. Poland is a country with a deficit of water resources. Poland's water resources are characterized by significant seasonal variability and uneven territorial distribution. The capacity of storage reservoirs in Poland is small, able to hold only 6% of the annual outflow of water, which does not provide adequate protection against periodic surpluses or deficits of water.[8]

38. For years, waste management was ignored, as was the education of society regarding sorting of household waste, as well as promotion and financial support of recycling. Key issues are ensuring effective enforcement of the new Waste Act (2012) and implementation of a new waste management system.

39. Mention should also be made of the continually low share of renewable sources in energy production.

40. Lastly, it is appropriate to discuss the effectiveness of legal regulations concerning strategic environmental impact assessments. The primary strategic objective of the country's ecological policy is to achieve a situation under which drafts of strategic documents from all sectors of the economy will, in compliance with the

6. *See* the section §3 'Historical Background'.
7. *Concise Statistical Yearbook of Poland 2018* (Warsaw), p. 39.
8. *Ibid.*, p. 31.

law, be submitted to an environmental impact assessment, and the results of that assessment will be taken into account in the final versions of those documents.

§2. Basic Principles of Environmental Law

I. Definitions and Notions

41. The conceptual and normative foundations for environmental law are provided in the Act of 27 April 2001 – Environmental Protection Act.[9] The legislature's initial intention was to perform a consolidation of regulations by creating a more general piece of legislation that would bring order to a diffuse system of laws and play the leading role in it. This was in line with the trend in Europe at the time to consolidate and codify environmental protection law. With time, however, the legislature began creating separate legislation regulating increasingly specific and separate issues, which is one of the reasons why the character of the general provisions contained in the Environmental Protection Act (presently Articles 5–8 and 12) is a subject of debate. The dominant view is that the Act contains provisions best understood as 'general principles' applying not only to that Act but also to all regulations concerning environmental protection.[10] They do not apply to spheres that have clearly been excluded from their jurisdiction, nor do they take precedence over the general principles contained in more specific statues regulating particular areas.

42. The general principles are universally binding normative regulations. Their specific role manifests itself by the manner in which they establish obligations to achieve particular desirable states and respect specific values; by the same token, they give direction to legislative processes, judicial and administrative processes, interpretive processes and processes associated with the exercise of individual rights.

43. The Act's regulations also serve to harmonize the foundations of Polish environmental law with regulations set forth in EU law, particularly with the provisions of Articles 11 and 191 TFEU. Among the principles shared by Polish and EU legislation are those of comprehensive protection, prevention, precaution, 'polluter pays' and the integration of environmental policy with sectoral policies. The principles of transparency and public participation were transferred from the Environmental Protection Act to the Act of 3 October 2008 on the Sharing of Information on the Environment and its Protection, Public Participation in Environmental Protection and Environmental Impact Assessments.[11] This has led to a clear weakening of the construction underpinning the general principles, which in turn demonstrates

9. Dz. U. 2018, item 799 with amendments.
10. J. Boć, *Wybrane zagadnienia prawnej ochrony środowiska,* 123 (Kolonia Limited 2013), also M. Górski, M. Pchałek, W. Radecki, J. Jerzmański, M. Bar, S. Urban, J. Jendrośka, *Prawo ochrony środowiska. Komentarz* (Legalis, CH Beck 2011).
11. Dz. U. 2017, item 1405 with amendments.

the legislature's lack of appreciation for the role played by the legal institution of 'general principles' in the system of regulations on environmental protection.[12] Principles which have not been expressly stated include the principle of a high level of protection (although it is indicated by some authors that the principle of comprehensive protection is associated in its substance with a 'high level of protection of the natural environment') and the principle of rectification at source (liquidated damages).

44. Article 4 of the Environmental Protection Act categorizes means of exploiting the natural environment and establishes clear boundaries for these means, providing for the acceptable scope of such exploitation and its legal basis. In declaring Article 4 as a 'general principle' as understood by legal theory, the subject literature defines it as 'the principle of legality of exploitation of the natural environment'.[13] The Act sets forth three means (legal forms) of exploitation of the natural environment. The statute endows everyone with the 'common use' right to exploit the natural environment without the application of technological installations for the satisfaction of personal needs and the needs of the household, including for recreational purposes and the practice of sport through: (1) introducing substances and/or energy into the natural environment; (2) other types of common use of waters as set forth in the Water Act. The scope of the concept 'common use' does not encompass other forms of statutorily permissible use, such as the exploitation of mineral or forest resources. These activities are regulated in other statutes, such as the Geological and Mining Act and the Forest Act.

45. Besides common use, the Act also differentiates exploitation of the natural environment exceeding the boundaries of common use, which takes two different forms: (1) use that does not require a permit (standard use), the scope of which is established by all other provisions of the Act, meaning that such use is regulated but by general provisions (statutes and secondary legislation) and (2) use which is only possible upon obtaining a permit (administrative decision) enumerating the scope and conditions of such use, issued by the competent environmental protection authority (special or regulated use).

46. The provisions contained in Article 5 of the Act introduced the principle of comprehensive protection of the natural environment (integrated protection),[14] giving voice to the idea of treating the natural environment as a whole. The present legal framework develops this concept through legal acts regulating the protection and management of particular elements of the environment in such statutes as the Water Act and the Act on the Protection of Nature. The principle assumes that such measures will be taken that, in protecting one aspect of the natural environment, also protect others, or at a minimum do not affect them adversely. In this context, the borders establishing where the application of this rule has effect are determined

12. Górski et al., *Prawo ochrony środowiska*.
13. *Ibid.* There is little clarity on this issue in the relevant doctrine.
14. 'Protection of one or several natural elements should account for protection of the remaining elements'.

by the scope within which particular elements of the natural environment have a mutual impact on one another.[15] Article 5 addresses not only elements of nature constituting the natural environment but also natural conditions afforded legal protection such as peace and quiet, biological diversity, absence of radiation and the non-occurrence of serious problems.[16] With regard to the implementation of the principle of comprehensiveness, one may draw attention to procedures associated with preventative protection of the natural environment, in particular proceedings involving environmental impact assessments of strategic documents and undertakings, as well as integrated permit proceedings.

47. The principles of prevention and precaution are set forth in Article 6 of the Act. Expression of the obligation to take preventative measures in respect of the natural environment is to be found in the duty borne by each individual engaging in an activity of a potentially negative impact on the environment to prevent such an impact. Those engaging in an activity whose negative environmental impact has not yet been fully established are obliged to observe the principle of precaution by undertaking all possible preventative measures. Putting into practice the principle of prevention generates a number of more detailed issues, associated *inter alia* with the concept of injury, the moment in which the principle should be applied, organizational and technical capacities and the spheres of its application linked with assessments of environmental impact and oversight by relevant administrative authorities.

48. The absolute binding force of the principle of precaution on all entities conducting an activity that may exert a negative impact on the environment adds to its significance, and what were, previously, recommendations have become duties in public law. The formulation of criteria for the application of the principle of precaution at the legislative level can take place using general indications of evidentiary standards. Mention may also be made of the precaution principle's mild version, which allows for consideration of such factors as parsimony, efficiency, the economic context, etc. when taking decisions as to protective measures. The principle's more stringent versions use the language of obligation (scientific uncertainty as to a potentially serious risk demands that protective measures be taken) and do not allow for consideration of other counterbalancing factors.[17]

Another provision establishes the 'polluter pays' principle – Article 7 of the Act declares that a party responsible for fouling the natural environment shall bear the costs of associated clean-up measures. Any party that might pollute the natural environment shall bear the costs of preventing such pollution. As J. Boć writes, the essence of this principle – developed especially for the purposes of environmental protection – is obvious, and indeed it permeates the entire construction of liability existent for centuries in civil law as well as in those provisions of administrative law that formulate the effects borne by a party whose actions result in damage or

15. J. Ciechanowicz-McLean, Z. Bukowski, B. Rakoczy, *Prawo ochrony środowiska*, 52–53 (Warszawa 2008).
16. J. Boć, K. Nowacki, E. Samborska-Boć, *Ochrona środowiska*, 135 (Wrocław 2008).
17. Górski et al., *Prawo ochrony środowiska* and literature cited therein.

loss.[18] This principle is complemented by the provisions of Article 7a, applied in situations defined under the criteria set forth in the Environmental Damage Prevention and Amelioration Act of 13 April 2007[19] as a direct threat of damage to the natural environment and/or damage to the natural environment. There is general agreement in the literature that the aforementioned Act neither excludes nor limits in any way administrative liability frameworks for exploitation of the natural environment, including those relevant to adverse environmental impact, whether set forth in the specific provisions of the Environmental Protection Act or in other statutes (e.g., the Water Act) but rather plays a complementary role. What is more, in no way does the Act run contrary to the principles of civil and criminal liability applicable in the entire system of environmental protection law but rather serves to supplement it.

49. As Article 8 declares:

> Policies, strategies, plans and programmes concerning but not limited to industry, energy, transport, telecommunications, water management, waste management, spatial management, forestry, agriculture, fishing, tourism and land use shall account for the principles of protection of the natural environment and of sustainable development.

This provision expresses the principle of integration of environmental protection with sectoral policies (principle of integration).[20] The list of areas here is not exhaustive but rather consists of examples; those named in the aforementioned provision have been recognized as having a particularly significant impact on the natural environment, which is why strategic documents associated with them are the subject of greater scrutiny. It should also be agreed that this principle encompasses all documents that indicate the substance of policies and action to be taken in a given area, taking into account its attributes and legal character rather than its name. The objective scope of the principle is defined in light of the obligation placed on public authorities to protect the natural environment (Article 74(2) of the Constitution). The fundamental procedural instrument for giving substance to this principle is the Strategic Environmental Assessment (SEA). It should be emphasized that when legal regulation concerning strategic assessments provide for a release from the duty to perform an assessment, authorities accepting those documents still remain bound by the duties resulting from the principle of integration set forth in Article 8.

50. The final general principle established in the Environmental Protection Act is the 'principle of comparability of results (surveys and measurements)', sometimes labelled as the 'principle of standardization' (Article 12).[21] Article 12(1)

18. Boć, *Wybrane zagadnienia*, 127.
19. Dz. U. 2018, item 954 with amendments
20. In respect of EU law. The relevant Polish literature uses the term the *planning principle*.
21. Górski et al., *Prawo ochrony środowiska*.

imposes the duty to apply methodology established in a manner determined by statute, which is addressed to state authorities and entities engaged in exploitation of the natural environment of whom it is required to conduct specified surveys and measurements. The primary objective behind introducing the requirement to apply referential methodologies is to achieve comparability of results but also to simplify oversight and inspection activities. The principle contained in paragraph 2 constitutes an exception, as it defines the conditions under which entities are exempted from applying an established referential methodology; these conditions are differentiated depending on the type of methodology concerned.

51. Another general principle of environmental protection law is that of transparency. The current legal framework contains this principle in the Act on the Sharing of Information on the Environment and its Protection, Public Participation in Environmental Protection and Environmental Impact Assessments. Article 4 states that everyone has the right to information about the natural environment and protection of it on such grounds as are set forth in statute. This is a statutory reference to the constitutional right to information about the condition of the natural environment and measures taken towards its protection (Articles 74(3) and 81). The importance of this issue has led to the introduction of a distinction between the general framework for access to public information and that which is applicable to the right of information on the natural environment. The limits of such are determined by references to regulations concerning the protection of confidential information.

52. The aforementioned Act also contains the principle of public participation (social engagement). In accordance with Article 5, everyone has the right under the conditions set forth by statute to participate in proceedings requiring the involvement of society. Everyone has the right to submit concerns and remarks in proceedings requiring the involvement of society. Such participation concerns procedures involving the issuance of (and changes to) decisions, as well as the development of drafts of (and changes to) documents. Participation of an entity so entitled can be grounded in both a legal and a factual interest.

II. Constitutional Provisions

53. The Constitution of the Republic of Poland (Constitution) of 1997 establishes the general legal framework for the protection of the natural environment and sustainable development in Poland. Article 5 makes direct reference to the issue of environmental protection, embedded in the portion of the Constitution dedicated to establishing the core values acknowledged by the Republic's social, political, economic and legal structure. This article declares that:

> The Republic of Poland shall safeguard the independence and integrity of its territory and ensure the freedoms and rights of persons and citizens, the security of the citizens, safeguard the national heritage and shall ensure the protection of the natural environment pursuant to the principles of sustainable development.

There is general acceptance of the view that in the Constitution, the concept of sustainable development functions independently of its obvious substantive association with the protection of the natural environment. The principle of sustainable development is an autonomous good and belongs to the sphere of social relations subject to continual development. It refers to those spheres in which the term 'development' is applicable, followed by 'sustainable development'. In the absence of specific justification, a given sphere of social relations may not develop through the retardation of development in another.[22] The essence of sustainable development is thus the 'equal treatment of social, economic and ecological considerations, which implies the necessity of integrating environmental protection issues with policies in individual sectors of the economy'.[23]

54. The principle of sustainable development has been acknowledged as the leading principle of public ecological policy, and one which should be complemented by a range of supplemental and specific principles.[24] The substance of this principle should be detailed in statutes and requires that mechanisms serving to realize it be defined. Article 3 of the Environmental Protection Act defines sustainable development as:

> social and economic development in which the process of integration of political, economic and social activities takes place, while observing a natural equilibrium and the sustainability of fundamental natural processes in order to ensure the capacity to satisfy the basic needs of communities and citizens of both current and future generations.[25]

55. The Constitution maintains a preference for expressing the issue of environmental protection in terms of the obligations of public authorities rather than of the subjective rights of individuals. The legislator did not include a 'right to the environment' in it,[26] rather establishing the right to information about the quality of the environment and its protection (Article 74(3)).

56. As regards constitutionally protected rights and freedoms of individuals and citizens, environmental protection is located among the particular values justifying the legislator's interference in this area. This is expressed in Article 31(3) of the Constitution, which establishes a general clause limiting the extent of permissible interference (only by way of statute) in the context of a general limitation on restricting the exercise of freedoms and rights while observing the principles of proportionality and of non violation of the essence of freedoms and rights.

---

22. W. Jakimowicz, *Wykładnia w prawie administracyjnym*, 78 (Wolters Kluwer Polska 2006).
23. II National Environmental Policy, adopted by the Council of Ministers in June 2000 and by the *Sejm* in August 2001.
24. *Ibid.*
25. Prior to introduction of the principle of sustainable development in the Constitution of 1997, the concept was used in a resolution of the *Sejm* in 1991, and later in the Forest Act (1991) and the Spatial Management Act (1994). It was also elaborated in the Act on protection and formation of the natural environment (1980), itself amended in 1998.
26. J. Jendrośka, M. Bar, *Prawo ochrony środowiska. Podręcznik*, 530 (Wrocław 2005).

57. The Constitution establishes a general and common responsibility in the area of environmental protection ('the principle of common responsibility for protection of the environment', Article 86): 'Everyone shall care for the quality of the environment and shall be held responsible for causing its degradation. The principles of such responsibility shall be specified by statute.' This implies neither definitive obligations nor responsibility but rather serves as the foundation for the statutory expansion of the 'polluter pays' principle. It is pointed out that this provision should be broadly interpreted, and its *ab initio* language refers to the need for active civic engagement in protecting the environment, something which itself is in the public interest.[27] Public authorities should support such activity, the responsibilities of whom are defined in Article 74. This is a fundamental constitutional regulation in respect of the duties borne by public authorities and is devoted in its entirety to matters of environmental protection. As set forth in paragraph 1, 'Public authorities shall pursue policies ensuring the ecological security of current and future generations' (also referred to as the 'principle of ecological security'). This is a different definition of the principle of sustainable development, one which accents the objective of public authorities' activities, and by the same token permits all legal means of accomplishing that objective.[28] Later this clause states that securing the environment is an obligation of public authorities, as is supporting the activities of citizens that aim to protect and improve the state of the environment. Article 74 also establishes a public subjective right to receive information about the quality of the environment and its protection (paragraph 3). Such rights may be pursued within the limitations set forth in statute.

58. Additionally, public authorities also have responsibilities related to environmental protection associated with the right to health. The principles of precaution and prevention, comprising the prevention of negative effects proceeding from degradation of the natural environment, place the burden on public authorities to undertake protective measures additionally when the harmfulness of particular activities to the natural environment is not demonstrated but is likely.[29]

59. Article 232 of the Constitution also directly addresses environmental protection, regulating the conditions under which the Council of Ministers may introduce a state of natural disaster. This exceptional state serves to mitigate the effects of natural disasters and technological accidents exhibiting similar characteristics as well as to negate them.

60. The Constitution also contains provisions indirectly concerning environmental protection, such as those establishing the system of sources of law, determining the functioning of public finances, and those protecting the freedoms and rights of citizens.[30]

---

27. *Ibid.*, 529.
28. Boć, *Wybrane zagadnienia*, 141.
29. *Ibid.*, 140–141.
30. Jendrośka, Bar, *Prawo ochrony środowiska*, 525.

§3. Historical Background

61. The beginnings of environmental protection law were linked with economic and commercial values. Among the first legal institutions designed to protect the natural environment was the royal hunting regalia, of which restrictions on hunting bison and auroch were particularly significant. Elements of protection of fish, trees and mineral deposits can be identified in other restrictions.

62. Regulations characteristic of a contemporary approach to protection can be observed from the moment when the primary motive for their implementation became so-called ideal values (scientific, aesthetic, historical, and natural values resulting from the threat to a species or area). One of the oldest Polish legal acts associated with protection of nature as an element of the environment is the Act of the National Parliament in Lwów of 10 July 1869 'forbidding the capture, extermination and sale of Alpine animals found in the Tatras, groundhogs and wild goats.' Protection activities along similar lines were continued after independence was restored in 1918. Examples include the decree of the Regency Council of the Kingdom of Poland of 31 October 1918 on the protection of monuments of art and culture. A subsequent act with a clear orientation on the environment was the Regulation of the Minister of Religious Faiths and Public Enlightenment of 16 September 1919 on the protection of some natural monuments. The concept of comprehensive nature protection was expressed in the Nature Protection Act of 10 March 1934, at the time held to be one of the world's most advanced pieces of legislation implementing the ideas of nature protection. Protection of nature's resources was also continued from the perspective of their management (forest, hunting and fishery management). A range of legal acts contained fragmentary regulation concerning particular elements of nature (e.g., the Water Act of 19 September 1922, the Regulation of the President of the Republic of Poland of 22 March 1927 on the law applicable to hunting, the Fishing Act of 7 March 1932).

63. After World War II, the next piece of legislation was adopted relatively quickly. This was the Nature Protection Act of 7 April 1949, constituting part of an entire complex of legislation from that period dealing with issues of using and protecting natural resources, part of the so-called planning trend. The innovation of the 1949 legislation consisted in its being the first act to apply its general assumptions to the entirety of the natural environment, in spite of the fact that the more detailed provisions were mainly regulations characteristic of conservatory protection. The Act established a framework for constructing and carrying out a comprehensive environmental protection policy. These concepts were, however, not truly implemented in practice owing to the ideological and economic reality of Poland in the 1950s.

64. In the mid-1960s, several pieces of legislation were passed in relation to the protection of the environment against pollution. Worthy of mention is the Clean Water Protection Act of 31 January 1961, later incorporated into the Water Act of 30 May 1962, whose assumptions were further elaborated in the Water Act of 24 October 1974. The Clean Air Protection Act of 21 April 1966 was another piece of legislation associated with pollution prevention measures. Issues of environmental protection also began to show up in regulations concerning other areas such as spatial management, building law, mining law and land-use law.

65. The next stage began with the Environmental Protection and Development Act of 1980, which was intended to systematize existing regulations. The intention of the legislator was that this Act would constitute a partial codification, containing general provisions applicable to all legal regulation addressing the issue of environmental protection and that it would address a wide range of more specific issues, making it the exclusive grounds for undertaking protective activities. This last category includes issues of protection of the air, protection against waste, vibrations and radiation, and protection from extraordinary threats. Common provisions were those concerning financing of environmental protection, issues of criminal liability and administrative financial penalties, and provisions addressing the structure of authorities and entities involved in environmental protection. The Act also was an attempt at constructing guidelines meant to function as general principles for the legal regime of environmental protection. In spite of attempts to comprehensively address the issue of environmental protection, the Act was drafted within the confines of a particular political and economic system and was riddled with flaws, particularly the excessively general character of many of its provisions. Another significant difficulty was effective implementation of regulations. As a result, attempts to prevent degradation of the environment in Poland largely failed.

66. The next stage in the development of environmental protection law is associated with the political transformation initiated in 1989. An expression of social and political change, as well as of the introduction of democratic governments and market principles in the economy, was the evolution of the Environmental Protection and Development Act of 1980 (amended thirty-three times in the period 1989–2001), bringing effectiveness to the system of legal protection for the environment. Among legislation enacted after 1989, mention should be made of the new Nature Protection Act and the State Environmental Protection Inspectorate Act, both of 1991. In 1997 the Waste Act was passed, removing that subject matter from the scope of general regulation. It should also be highlighted that 1990 saw the restoration of local self-government at the communal level, and in 1998 two more territorial divisions were introduced: the county and the voivodeship (province). Local authorities were entrusted with a significant portion of public tasks in respect of environmental protection. During this same period a new Constitution was also adopted, introducing fundamental regulations addressing issues of environmental protection.

67. In this period, the Europeanization of law exerted a strong and direct influence on the shape of Polish environmental protection law consisting in the obligation to adapt domestic law to the requirements of EU (then Communities) law. The influence of EU law on environmental protection law was itself dependent on the status of a given country in respect of the EU.

68. Obligations in respect of adaptation of the law during the pre-accession period were set forth in the Association Agreement concluded between Poland and the European Communities on 16 December 1991, which entered into force on 1 February 1993. Article 71 obliged Poland to 'ensure that environmental considerations are fully incorporated into policies from the outset'. In Articles 68 and 69, Poland obliged itself to undertake a gradual approximation of its internal law to that of the system in place in the Communities through the adoption of international environmental protection standards. The approximation of Polish law was realized in the years 1997–2004 and was comprised of processes referred to as 'harmonization' (in the 1990s), and later on, during a particularly intense period (1999–2001) 'adaptation'.[31] As a result, the Environmental Protection Act of 27 April 2001 was adopted, which at the time implemented around twenty acts of European law. It is emphasized in the doctrine that the regulation contained in this Act was not a simple mechanical transposition of European law onto domestic ground but, in fact, a successful effort at incorporating the requirements of European law into the Polish legal system in a manner compatible with its traditions.[32]

69. As an effect of Poland's accession to the EU on 1 May 2004, the scope of EU legal norms was automatically and instantaneously expanded by *ratione loci* and *ratione personae.* The requirement to fully and immediately adopt EU law was softened by negotiated derogation periods, which were at times quite long. One example is the implementation period for Directive 2001/80/EC of the European Parliament and of the Council on the limitation of emissions of certain pollutants into the air from large combustion plants in respect of some of the plants named specifically in the Treaty of Accession; the transition period for sulphur dioxide runs until 31 December 2015, for nitrogen oxide until 31 December 2017, and for dust emissions (municipal power stations) until 31 December 2017; these transition periods are dependent upon maintaining the total domestic emissions of substances at the levels set forth in the Treaty of Accession.

70. Accession to the EU determined the primary direction for the further development of Polish environmental protection law. The transposition process is a continual one, adapting Polish law to the dynamically evolving law of the EU. The Environmental Protection Act is held by doctrine to be a statute of general and horizontal character. The system of environmental protection law also encompasses dozens of additional statutes together with secondary legislation.

31. *Ibid.*, 504.
32. *Ibid.*

§4. THE ORGANIZATION OF ENVIRONMENTAL PROTECTION

I. Introduction: The Concept of 'Administrative Body' and 'Environmental Protection Body'

71. Factors which influence the administration of environmental protection in a given country include constitutional considerations, geographical conditions, issues arising out of the shaping (sectoral or comprehensive) of environmental protection law, the country's legal and administrative culture and its level of development.[33]

72. The position and tasks of public authorities bearing the burden of environmental protection are regulated in the provisions of statutes addressing both institutional (e.g., the Inspectorate for Environmental Protection Act, acts regulating local self-government) and jurisdictional/substantive matters (the Environmental Protection Act). This diffusion of institutional and jurisdictional legislation is characteristic of the system under which environmental protection is organized, as is the diffusion of authority and jurisdiction, rendering the structure of environmental protection administration in Poland complicated and opaque, often generating conflict. The proposed categories, often bleeding into one another, include: central and regional administration; state and local administration; and both unified (general) and non-unified (special) administration.[34] The majority of organs operate according to the fundamental territorial division of the country, while others function on the basis of geographical and ecological zones.[35]

73. The Environmental Protection Act contains definitions of the concepts 'administrative body' and 'environmental protection body'. The statutory definition of 'administrative body' is a functional one, encompassing both state administration (central and regional), as well as that of local self-governments (all levels) and other entities (including private ones) appointed on the basis of a statute or agreement to perform public tasks concerning the environment and environmental protection. This concept is referenced by the concept of an environmental protection institution. The provisions establish the organization and the tasks of a number of state organizational bodies, differentiated in character and mission but all associated with environmental protection, and gives them the name of environmental protection institutions. These are not the only such regulations, as other statutes are also relevant. It can thus be said that this is a broad category, encompassing all bodies performing any sort of task related to environmental protection, whether defined in the Environmental Protection Act or in other legislation.[36]

33. *Ibid.*, 108.
34. *Ibid.*, 541.
35. *Ibid.*, 543.
36. Other statutes, such as the Water Act and the Nature Protection Act, may establish specialized public administration bodies to handle matters as listed in those acts.

74. A qualified concept is that of 'environmental protection body' (*sensu stricto*). The Environmental Protection Act explicitly lists the following state and local governmental bodies, assigning the tasks and competencies set forth in that statute:

(1) Prefect (mayor).
(2) County commissioner.
(3) Provincial assembly.
(4) Provincial marshal.
(5) Voivode.
(6) Minister responsible for environmental affairs.
(7) General Directorate for Environmental Protection.
(8) Regional directorates for environmental protection.
(9) Bodies of the Inspectorate for Environmental Protection.

This concept does not, however, have any significance in assigning particular bodies to a group differentiated on the basis of the nature of tasks performed but rather stems from technical considerations in the composition of legislation.[37] For the same reason, a broader characterization of environmental protection administration is presented below.

II. Central Administration

A. *Supreme Authorities of Government Administration*

1. The Council of Ministers

75. The authority of the Council of Ministers in the area of environmental protection is not emphasized in the law in any specific manner. Within the borders of its constitutionally established authority, particularly under the general formula of conducting the Republic of Poland's internal and external policy and the presumption of competence in matters of state policy not reserved for other bodies of state and local authority, the Council of Ministers is responsible for developing the foundations of administrative policy and, to a large degree, the legal foundation for all protective measures.[38]

2. The Minister of the Environment and Other Ministers

76. The highest authority for environmental protection in Poland is the minister responsible for environmental affairs, presently bearing the title of Minister of the

37. Górski et al., *Prawo ochrony środowiska.*
38. Boć, Nowacki, Samborska-Boć, *Ochrona środowiska,* 200.

Environment. The legal foundations for a minister's activity are set forth in the Constitution, the Act on branches of governmental administration,[39] the Act on the Council of Ministers,[40] the so-called attribution regulation issued by the Prime Minister and rules of the work of the Council of Ministers (resolution of the Council of Ministers). Substantive law is responsible for defining particular tasks and competencies. The constitutional position of the Minister of the Environment is analogical to that of other ministers directing branches of governmental administration.

77. The Minister's tasks and competencies are exercised within the framework of the two types of functions performed by ministers:

– as a member of a collegial body – the Council of Ministers;
– as a one-person (monocratic) supreme authority of governmental administration.

78. The Minister of the Environment, as a member of the Council of Ministers, participates in conducting the internal and external policy of the Republic of Poland not reserved for other state institutions and local self-government bodies, in particular by ensuring the execution of statutes, issuing regulations and orders, coordinating and overseeing the work of governmental administration bodies, initiating and developing (within the scope of the branch of government under his/her control) the policy of the Government and presenting related initiatives and draft legislation during meetings of the Council of Ministers, and carrying out the policy adopted by the Council of Ministers.

79. As a supreme authority of governmental administration, the Minister of the Environment (as well as the remaining portfolio ministers whose authority extends to matters concerning environmental protection) undertakes the following types of activity:[41]

(1) normative (issuing regulations and orders);
(2) decisional (issuing administrative decisions, primarily ruling on appeals);
(3) oversight, supervision and coordination;
(4) programmatic;
(5) advisory;
(6) organizational;
(7) technical.

80. A more detailed scope of activity engaged in by the Minister of the Environment was laid out in the attribution regulation.[42] This act establishes that the Minister of the Environment is in charge of one branch of governmental administration: the environment. The environment branch includes such matters as protecting and developing the natural environment and rationalizing the use of its

39. Dz. U. 2018, item 762 with amendments.
40. Dz. U. 2012, item 392 with amendments.
41. Boć, Nowacki, Samborska-Boć, *Ochrona środowiska*, 202.
42. Dz. U. 2018, item 96.

resources, protecting nature, geology, management of natural resources, oversight of compliance with environmental protection regulations and performing research on the condition of the natural environment, forests, protection of forests and wooded lands, and genetically modified organisms (GMO).

81. The Minister of the Environment performs his/her tasks with the assistance of the Ministry of the Environment, which is comprised of secretaries and undersecretaries of state (vice-ministers), including the Chief Nature Conservator and Chief National Geologist, the director general, the political cabinet, departments and offices.

82. The department's structure also includes bodies, offices and organizational entities subordinated to or overseen by the Minister. These are listed in the Act on branches of governmental administration and the attribution regulation, and can be listed in such categories as: central bodies of government administration, i.e., the General Director for Environmental Protection, the President of the National Atomic Energy Agency and the Chief Inspector for Environmental Protection; and organizational bodies and research institutes, i.e., the Environmental Protection Institute, the National Fund for Environmental Protection and Water Management and the State Forests National Forest Holding (SFNFH).

83. Dozens of councils and committees work on behalf of the Minister of the Environment in an advisory capacity, founded on the basis of statutes or in accordance with the Minister's organizational competencies. These groups include the State Council on the Protection of Nature, the Commission on Genetically Modified Organisms, the Commission on Mineral Resources, and the Commission on Geological and Engineering Documentation. Special attention should be paid to the State Council on Environmental Protection. This Council's activities include drafting opinions in matters concerning environmental protection and also presenting proposals and conclusions aimed at fostering conditions for sustainable development and environmental protection, as well as to maintain and improve the condition of the natural environment. The Council is composed of a chairperson, two vice-chairpersons, a secretary and members (up to thirty) nominated by the minister responsible for environmental affairs for a five-year term and selected from the scientific community, professional organizations, ecological organizations and representatives of economic self-governmental bodies. The opinions and positions of the Council are formed on the basis of its members' expertise, and in the formation of an opinion or position on a given issue the Council is independent. The opinions and positions of the Council are not binding on the Minister.

84. The Minister of Maritime Economy and Inland Navigation is a competent body in maritime management, water management, fishing and inland navigation. Water management includes matters such as developing, protecting and rationalizing the use of water resources, flood prevention activities and the operations of both the state hydrological and meteorological service as well as the state hydrological service. The Minister's task is also protection of the marine environment.

85. A significant portion of matters related to environmental protection falls under the authority of the Minister of Agriculture and Rural Development, who oversees the following branches of governmental administration: (1) agriculture, (2) rural development, (3) agricultural markets. This minister is competent in matters of environmental protection that involve such aspects as the production of crops and protection of cultivated plants, seed production, animal production and husbandry, protection of animal health, veterinary protection of public health and protection of animals.

86. Other ministers also perform important functions, particularly the Minister of Health, the Minister of Infrastructure and the Minister of Energy.

B. Central Authorities of Governmental Administration

1. General Director for Environmental Protection

87. The Act of 2008 on the Sharing of Information on the Environment and its Protection, Public Participation in Environmental Protection and Environmental Impact Assessments established a central authority of governmental administration: the General Director for Environmental Protection. As in the case of nearly all such authorities, the Director is not a member of the government, and the legal status of the office is the result of statutory rather than constitutional regulation. As a central authority, the Director constitutes a singular organ whose reach and competencies extend across the entire country. The Director is subordinated to the minister responsible for environmental affairs and performs his/her tasks with the assistance of the General Directorate for Environmental Protection.

88. The General Director for Environmental Protection is appointed by the Prime Minister upon nomination by the minister responsible for environmental affairs, from among individuals selected by way of an open, competitive application process. The Prime Minister is also responsible for dismissing the General Director for Environmental Protection.

89. The functions of the General Director can be classified into the following groups:

(1) lawmaking (issuing orders and other acts constituting internal administrative law; central authorities of governmental administration are not empowered to enact universally binding law);
(2) decisional (issuing administrative decisions and rulings, as well as performing other tasks necessary for conducting administrative proceedings in the first or second instance);
(3) directing a quasi-ministry (competencies in the area of personal and official authority over subordinate employees and employees of organizationally subordinated entities, supervisory authority, and also organizational authority);

(4) additional functions proceeding from the special status of the General Director in the area of environmental protection policy. The General Director for Environmental Protection's tasks include:
   - cooperation in executing environmental protection policy in respect of nature protection and supervision of investment processes;
   - supervision of responsibility for preventing damage to the natural environment and for repairing damage to it;
   - collecting data and preparing information about the Natura 2000 network and other protected territories, as well as environmental impact assessments;
   - cooperation with the appropriate environmental protection authorities of other states, international organizations and the European Commission;
   - cooperation with the Chief Nature Conservator and the State Council on Nature Protection in matters of nature protection;
   - cooperation with local self-government bodies in matters of environmental impact assessments and nature protection;
   - participation in strategic environmental impact assessments;
   - participation in proceedings concerning trans-border environmental impacts;
   - performing tasks in respect of Natura 2000 as set forth in the Nature Protection Act;
   - performing tasks resulting from participation in the Eco-Management and Audit Scheme (EMAS) pursuant to the principles and scope set forth in the National Eco-Management and Audit Scheme Act of 15 July 2011;
   - cooperation with ecological organizations.

90. The General Director's advisory body in respect of environmental impact assessments is the National Commission on Environmental Impact Assessments. The Chairperson of the National Commission, deputy chairpersons, the secretary and members of the National Commission (between 40 and 60) are appointed and dismissed by the General Director for Environmental Protection from among members of the scientific community, practitioners and ecological organizations.

2. Chief Inspector for Environmental Protection

91. Another central authority is the Chief Inspector for Environmental Protection, who is responsible for directing the activities of the Inspectorate for Environmental Protection. The Chief Inspector is nominated by the minister responsible for environmental affairs, from among individuals selected by way of an open, competitive application process. The Prime Minister is also responsible for dismissing the Chief Inspector for Environmental Protection.

92. The primary tasks of the of the Inspectorate for Environmental Protection are oversight of compliance with environmental protection regulations, monitoring of the condition of the natural environment under the State Environmental Monitoring programme, and reacting to serious incidents. These tasks are laid out in detail in the Inspectorate for Environmental Protection Act of 20 July 1991, and can be classified as performance of the following functions:

(1) oversight;
(2) prevention;
(3) execution;
(4) conducting environmental monitoring;
(5) decisional;
(6) preventing serious incidents;
(7) cooperation with other bodies in environmental protection;
(8) developing and implementing analytical and research methods, as well as monitoring and measurement techniques.[43]

3. Other Authorities

93. When considering the administration of environmental protection from a broader perspective, other authorities of central administration should be mentioned whose specialized tasks and competencies encompass issues of environmental protection. These include the President of the National Atomic Energy Agency, the President of the State Mining Authority, the Chief Sanitary Inspector, the Inspector for Chemical Substances and the Chief Veterinary Officer.

III. Regional and Local Administration

94. The competencies of regional and local environmental protection authorities are divided between two segments of public administration: governmental and self-governmental. The fundamental constitutional principles of decentralization and ownership of a significant portion of public tasks are effected by assigning local self-government authorities tasks related to environmental protection (Article 16(1–2) of the Constitution).

95. The competencies of particular authorities are defined in a twofold manner in the Environmental Protection Act. Article 378, which contains the general concept of an 'environmental protection authority', introduces a detailed division of powers in particular matters among several bodies – county commissioner, provincial marshal, regional director for environmental protection, and prefect (mayor). The construction of this classification is rather complicated and is based on assigning given authorities powers by either indicating individual matters or by indicating categories while applying a variety of criteria – undertakings, events, locations, or entities. This enumeration is not a comprehensive indication of the competencies of a given authority. A second manner of defining powers consists of assigning particular tasks to the authorities expressly indicated in a particular provision (e.g., to

43. Jendrośka, Bar, *Prawo ochrony środowiska*, 552–555.

the county commissioner, provincial governor, etc.). In addition, other statutes (e.g., the Waste Act) assign particular tasks and powers to individual bodies of regional administration.

A. *Regional Authorities of Governmental Administration*

1. Voivode and Authorities of Unified Administration

96. The powers initially assigned to voivode in respect of environmental protection were transferred to provincial marshals (chairpersons of provincial self-administration) under the decentralization process, or to a specialized entity – the regional director for environmental protection. The Environmental Protection Act has left voivode with very few powers in respect of preventing serious negative events. At present it would seem rather inaccurate to assign voivode the label of 'environmental protection authorities', unless we take into account general functions associated with oversight and supervision of bodies of both central and local governmental administration, alongside functions related to performing the role of representative of the Council of Ministers in the territory of a given province. These general tasks naturally include tasks associated with environmental protection.[44]

97. The voivode is at the head of unified governmental administration. He performs his tasks with the assistance of directors of unified services, inspections and uniformed formations. A significant majority of these support entities possess powers either exclusively or largely associated with environmental protection tasks. These include the provincial environmental protection inspector, the provincial veterinary officer, the provincial sanitary inspector and the provincial inspector for plant health and seed inspection.

98. The most important of the structures within unified administration is the Inspectorate for Environmental Protection. The provincial inspector for environmental protection directs the activities of this body in a given province. The provincial inspector:

(1) performs tasks in accordance with the general policies, recommendations and guidelines of the Chief Inspector for Environmental Protection;
(2) works with the provincial governor to establish areas of activity and annual plans for the work of the Inspectorate for Environmental Protection in the province;
(3) develops and executes provincial environmental monitoring programmes;
(4) undertakes analyses and assessments in the province of:
   – adherence to the law;
   – the condition of the natural environment.

44. Górski et al., *Prawo ochrony środowiska.*

(5) presents to the Chief Inspector for Environmental Protection a report about the performance of the tasks of the Inspectorate for Environmental Protection within the province for a given year by 15 February of the following year, as well as at any other time on demand.

The inspector is assisted in the performance of his duties by the provincial inspectorate for environmental protection.

99. The Environmental Protection Act sets out tasks for the Inspectorate, performed by the provincial inspector for environmental protection, such as receiving information about the handover for use or completion of start-up of installations (new or modernized) classified as undertakings with a significant potential to have an impact on the environment and requiring obligatory reporting, as well as undertaking a wide range of activities related to preventing and ameliorating the effects of serious events, including issuing particular administrative decisions; conducting audits and imposing administrative financial penalties; issuing decisions suspending activity that is causing significant damage to the natural environment and/or threatening the life and/or health of people; issuing a decision ordering the suspension of operation of an installation; issuing a decision banning the production, import and sale of products which fail to meet environmental protection standards; and granting permission to resume suspended activities. The Act does not offer solutions to any issues concerning legal tools available to the Inspectorate in the performance of these tasks; such tools and modes of activity are to be found in the act establishing the Inspectorate.

2. Non-unified Administration

100. Bodies comprising non-unified governmental administration are regional governmental administration authorities subordinated to a minister or central governmental administration authority, as well as directors of state legal persons and directors of other state organizational entities performing the tasks of the central governmental administration in a province. They include the regional director for environmental protection, which is the authority responsible for performing tasks associated with environmental protection within the territory of an individual province. This authority is subordinated to the General Director for Environmental Protection.

101. The regional director for environmental protection performs his tasks with the assistance of the regional directorate for environmental protection and in cooperation with directors of landscape parks and landscape park complexes. His deputy is the regional nature conservator, with whose assistance he performs tasks concerning nature protection.

The regional director for environmental protection's tasks includes:

(1) participation in strategic environmental impact assessments;
(2) conducting or participating in environmental impact assessments;

(3) establishing and liquidating forms of nature protection on the basis of the Nature Protection Act;
(4) protection and management of Natura 2000 areas and other forms of nature protection pursuant to the provisions of the Nature Protection Act;
(5) issuing decisions on the basis of the Nature Protection Act;
(6) conducting proceedings and performing other tasks as set forth in the Environmental Damage Prevention and Amelioration Act;
(7) adding information to the database on environmental impact assessments and strategic environmental impact assessments, including information about documentation created under such proceedings;
(8) cooperation with local self-government authorities in matters concerning environmental impact assessments and nature protection;
(9) cooperation with ecological organizations;
(10) performing tasks including issuing decisions and ordering expert assessments in respect of waste management.

102. The Environmental Protection Act classifies the regional director as the environmental protection authority responsible in matters of all undertakings and events occurring in closed locations (Article 378(2)).

103. As at the central level, regional directors are assisted by commissions for environmental impact assessments, which are bodies able to provide opinions in matters related to environmental impact assessment procedures. The regional commissions' tasks include:

(1) providing opinions in matters presented by the regional director for environmental protection in conjunction with his statutory capacities;
(2) presenting opinions and conclusions concerning the development of instructional programmes in the area of environmental impact assessments;
(3) cooperating with the National Commission and other regional commissions.

104. Other authorities comprising non-unified governmental administration whose competencies include matters related to environmental protection are: directors of regional mining authorities and the president of the Specialist Mining Authority; directors of maritime affairs authorities, border region, and county veterinary officers; directors of inland maritime affairs authorities, regional sea fishing inspectors, and state border sanitary inspectors.

B. Self-government Authorities

105. While the Environmental Protection Act does not specifically designate all local self-government authorities as 'environmental protection authorities', it should be emphasized that they possess both tasks and powers in that area appropriate for both constitutive and oversight authorities as well as executive authorities. The powers of collective constitutive and oversight authorities are primarily associated with enacting general acts: local laws and programmes (strategies), while executive authorities (their heads in the case of monocratic offices) are vested with the power to issue decisions in individual cases, organizational activities, oversight and supervisory activities.

106. At the communal level, the communal (city) council enacts local laws of both an executive and public order nature associated with environmental protection. The executive authority (prefect/mayor), as an 'environmental protection authority', has been given regulatory powers to issue decisions in matters set forth in statute and has also been granted organizational, oversight and supervisory powers. Some examples of the powers granted to the commune's executive authority (in the Environmental Protection Act) are: receiving the results of emissions measurements, issuing decisions requiring additional emissions measurements to be conducted and receiving the results of such measurements, receiving notification of an installation that does not require an emissions permit, and issuing decisions determining environmental protection requirements for installations whose missions do not require a permit. The prefect (mayor) is only the competent authority in such matters when they concern normal use of the natural environment by a physical person.

107. The next level of local self-government – the county – performs its tasks through the county commissioner (*starosta*), who is assigned the title of 'environmental protection authority'. The county commissioner is the chair of the county commission and is in charge of unified county administration. The constitutive and oversight authority is the county council – a collegial body selected in direct elections. Its powers are linked with its function of enacting local law, adopting a county environmental protection programme and indicating areas of activity for the council and the commissioner. The commissioner's powers are typical of those held by a monocratic authority: regulatory and public order (issuing permits, decisions), oversight and audit, and organizational. At present the county commissioner is the responsible authority in cases such as issuing decisions on permissible noise emission levels, issuing decisions determining environmental protection requirements for installations whose emissions do not require a permit, issuing emissions permits, issuing decisions obliging the addressee to prepare and present an ecological review and issuing decisions establishing the obligation to limit negative environmental impact or to restore the environment to its previous condition.

108. At the provincial level, the relevant authorities are the provincial assembly, the provincial council and the marshal. A significant portion of the tasks set forth in the Environmental Protection Act are contracted tasks from the sphere of governmental administration. The provincial marshal, as an 'environmental protection authority', should undertake activities associated with facilities that have a particularly significant effect on the natural environment.

IV. State Holdings

109. The SFNFH (Lasy Państwowe) is an organizational unit without legal personhood. The legal basis for the holding is the Forest Act of 28 September 1991. It defines the principles of forest management of the State Forests and in the forests of other ownership types. The structure of the organization is defined by its statute, issued by Minister of the Environment (in 1994). Self-financing of the State Forests is possible due to the existence of the Forest Fund.

110. The State Forests management model is based on a three-tier structure: Director General of the State Forests appointed by the Minister of the Environment. He manages the organization by issuing ordinances and decisions. His office is the Directorate-General of the State Forests. The advisory body is the Council of the State Forests.

111. There are 17 regional directorates of the State Forests. Their task is to supervise the subordinate units and to coordinate their activities. Forest districts amount to 430. They conduct forest management on the basis of the forest management plan. The forest district manager is responsible for the condition of forest in the district area. The forest districts are divided into forest units.

112. Since 1 January 2018 the State Water Holding Polish Waters (Wody Polskie) has been operating. The legal basis is the Water Act of 20 July 2017. It is a state legal person whose main responsibility is management of national water. The structure of the Polish Waters consists of following organizational units: (1) National Water Management Directorate with headquarters in Warsaw; (2) regional water management directorates with offices in: Białystok, Bydgoszcz, Gdańsk, Gliwice, Kraków, Lublin, Poznań, Rzeszów, Szczecin, Warsaw and Wrocław; (3) directorates of the catchment; and (4) water supervision.

113. Polish Waters conducts activities in the field of protection against flood and drought and protection of water resources. The holding exercises ownership rights in relation to public waters that are owned by the State Treasury charges fees for water services and issues administrative decisions. The Polish Waters also acts as a regulatory body.

V. Funds

114. Institutions of environmental protection include the National Fund for Environmental Protection and Water Management and provincial funds for environmental protection and water management. These are juridical bodies whose task is to finance environmental protection and water management measures. They are responsible for conducting their own financial management, using both funds held and income received for the financing of tasks determined in statute and of operational costs. Particular objectives for which funding is allocated (areas of financial support) and activities undertaken are established in statute (Article 400a) in a casuistic and open catalogue (the cited provision lists over forty tasks). These tasks may be broadly categorized as tasks in the area of environmental protection, water management and water protection, protection of land surface and waste management, health protection but also the development, gathering and dissemination of knowledge, and finally other tasks.[45] Article 400a is also addressed to counties and communes, which are obliged to provide financing for some of the tasks listed (Article 403).

115. The funds' bodies are the Supervisory Board of the National Fund and the Management Board of the National Fund, and the supervisory boards of provincial funds and management boards of provincial funds. The funds function as decentralized entities. Oversight of the National Fund is exercised by the minister responsible for environmental affairs, while for provincial funds the relevant authority is the provincial governor. Resolutions of supervisory boards may be challenged by the oversight authority to an administrative court.

116. The Agricultural Land Protection Fund and the Forest Fund are special-purpose funds (which are different in character).

§5. Sources of Environmental Law

I. Introduction

117. As a unitary state with a positive legal system, Poland has a constitutionally determined catalogue of sources of law. The term 'source of law' should be understood to mean the form in which legal norms are expressed. A key concept is the 'normative act', which is 'an act of a state organ, more rarely of another authorized body, issued in a specific form on the basis of constitutionally or statutorily granted legislative authority, which imparts a binding force on norms establishing specific patterns of behaviour for specific addressees whenever the circumstances set forth in those norms arise'.[46] The dominant perspective in doctrine and in the jurisprudence of the Constitutional Tribunal is the material understanding of a normative act, which emphasizes the characteristics of the abstractness (repeatability) and generality of norms contained within it.

118. Of fundamental importance is the constitutional division of sources of law into universally binding provisions of law (regulating the status of individuals and other similar entities) and internal law (addressed to entities subordinated to the one issuing the act). The catalogue of universally binding law is closed, which means that such law is only enacted in forms (categories of normative acts) foreseen in the Constitution and only by bodies vested by the Constitution with the authority to enact particular types of regulations. Sources of internal law are given only a loose

45. *Ibid.*
46. W. Gromski, [in:] *Encyklopedia prawa* (ed. U. Kalina-Prasznic, Warszawa 2004).

constitutional framework and are not listed exhaustively, either in respect of the subject matter or the entities they address. Within the hierarchy of sources of law, internal law is subordinated to and dependent on universally binding law. It is emphasized in the relevant subject literature that the constitutional regulation addresses only positive (written) law. The limitation of the system of sources of law thus does not exclude customary law.[47] Also worthy of mention are the powers of the Constitutional Tribunal to assess the conformity of legal acts with those above them in rank (Article 188 of the Constitution). It is generally agreed that constitutive verdicts of the Constitutional Tribunal in which the non-conformity of a lower rank act with one of a superior rank (e.g., a statute with the Constitution) are law-making rulings, as they result in that act (the relevant provisions) losing its legal force. Administrative court rulings declaring the non-conformance of local legislation with the provisions of statute are similar in this respect.

119. Environmental protection law, as a separate branch of administrative law, itself a complex legal area, presents unique characteristics when considering sources of law. Of greatest significance is the large number of entities vested with the authority to enact law; indeed, organs of public administration are endowed with lawmaking powers. Also of note is the diversity of forms in which these regulations are formulated. In addition, sui generis sources of law stand out, with various names and legal characteristics. Awareness of the complexity of administrative legislation does not relieve us of the duty to place it within the framework of the more general constitutional system of sources of law, into which administrative lawmaking must fit.

120. Chapter III of the Constitution (Articles 87–94) is devoted to sources of law. General principles contained within the Constitution are also of importance:

(1) Article 2 – establishing Poland as a democratic state ruled by law, which implies *inter alia* the primacy of the law and respecting the hierarchy of norms.
(2) Article 7 – establishing the principle of legality as the foundation of the legal system.
(3) Article 8 – establishing the principle of the primacy and direct application of the Constitution.
(4) Article 9 – applying the international law principle of *pacta sunt servanda* to constitutional law.
(4) Article 10 – establishing the separation of powers.
(5) Article 16 – establishing the principle of territorial self-governance.

121. According to Article 87 of the Constitution, the sources of universally binding law are: the Constitution, statutes, ratified international agreements, regulations and enactments of local law. The Constitution also makes mention of regulations having the force of statute (Article 234) issued in specific circumstances during

47. *See* J. Boć (ed.), *Prawo administracyjne*, 121–124 (Kolonia Limited 2010).

periods of martial law. The Constitution does not expressly include legal acts of the EU in the catalogue of universally binding sources of law.

122. Internal law encompasses resolutions of the Council of Ministers and orders of the Prime Minister and other ministers. This is not, however, a closed catalogue considering that essentially every organ of public administration is authorized by statute to create such acts.

II. International and Supranational (EU) Law

123. Both international and EU law were implemented by the Constitution into the Polish legal regime as sources of law. The current Constitution is the first Polish constitutional legislation that directly regulates the relationship between Polish law and international law (including, indirectly, European law). Constitutional norms addressing international agreements establish the scope of their legal force and their place in the hierarchy of Polish sources of law. In this context, particularly important are Articles 9, 87, 89, 90, 91, 188 and 241 of the Constitution. It is also necessary to recall Article 8(1) of the Constitution, which declares that 'The Constitution shall be the supreme law of the Republic of Poland', especially in reference to the principle of primacy of EU law as expressed in the jurisprudence of the Court of Justice of the European Union (CJEU) and in the doctrine of EU law. The position of the Constitution was not altered by Poland's accession to the EU, neither by the obligation contained in Article 9 of the Constitution to respect international law binding on Poland.

124. International agreements are of primary importance in the system of sources of international law. Constitutional provisions in this respect are limited to establishing principles for the effectiveness of ratified international agreements and their place in the hierarchy of sources of law. Such agreements are counted among the sources of universally binding law in Poland. They are ratified either by the President of the Republic of Poland following the so-called minor ratification procedure or on the basis of the prior consent of the lower house (*Sejm*) of Parliament expressed in statute. Article 89(1) of the Constitution sets forth five categories of matters in which a statute is mandatory for ratification.

125. The primary method of incorporating international agreements into the domestic legal regime is detailed transformation, but other methods may also be applied: reference, repetition, etc. A ratified agreement becomes part of the domestic legal order following its promulgation in *Dziennik Ustaw* (Poland's official journal of legislation). It is imbued with the attribute of direct applicability unless its application is dependent on the passing of a statute. The rank of an agreement in the domestic legal system depends on the manner of its ratification. An agreement ratified upon the prior consent of the *Sejm* is given precedence over statutes (Article 91(1–2) Constitution). Article 241(1) of the Constitution assigns an analogical position and rank to international agreements ratified prior to the coming into force of the current Constitution if their connection with the categories of matters mentioned in Article 89(1) of the Constitution derives from the terms of an international agreement (general transformation).

126. When considering their effects in the domestic legal regime, non-ratified agreements can be compared to acts of internal law. They may not constitute the basis for a decision towards citizens or other 'external entities', and their direct application is limited to entities 'organizationally subordinated' to the authority concluding such an agreement: the Council of Ministers or a minister with portfolio. However, if the execution of a non-ratified agreement requires activity in the external environment, its contents must then be incorporated into a statute so as to render them universally binding law.

127. The Constitution does not use the terms 'European Union', 'European Law' or 'EU Law'. References in the Constitution to international organizations, international law, international agreements and laws enacted by international organizations are equally applicable to the EU, EU law, the founding treaties of the EU and to laws enacted by EU institutions.[48] However, because EU law has a certain autonomy in respect of international public law, and both the scope and strength of its influence on Polish law are far greater than that of international law (apart from EU law), it is necessary to formulate some appropriate distinctions.

128. When considering treaty law, the general principles concerning the position of international agreements in the domestic legal system apply. Thus, since the 'founding treaties' were adopted in the special mode set out in Article 90 of the Constitution, there can be no doubt that they constitute part of the domestic legal order, are to be applied directly and take precedence over statutes and all other acts below the rank of statute. The founding treaties also oblige Member States to comply in full with the remaining elements of the 'primary law' of the EU; an analogical conclusion can be drawn from Article 9 of the Constitution.

129. As concerns secondary law enacted by EU bodies, Article 91(3) of the Constitution provides a separate and clear foundation for its incorporation into the Polish legal order when read in conjunction with the appropriate provisions of the founding treaties. Law enacted within the EU '[is] applied directly and [has] precedence in the event of a conflict of laws.' EU law thus has the characteristics assigned to sources of universally binding law, as well as being above statute in rank. All EU legal norms that are suitable for direct application may constitute the basis for administrative decisions and other individual adjudications, and authorities responsible for the application of the law are obliged to give them precedence in the event of a conflict with a domestic statute.

48. R. Hauser, S. Biernat, M. Niedźwiedź, *Znaczenie prawa międzynarodowego i unijnego dla prawa administracyjnego i administracji publicznej w świetle Konstytucji RP*, [in:] *Konstytucyjne podstawy funkcjonowania administracji publicznej. System Prawa Administracyjnego. Tom 2*, 93–94 (R. Hauser, A. Wróbel, Z. Niewiadomski, CH Beck 2012).

III. Domestic Law

A. *Universally Binding Acts*

1. The Constitution of the Republic of Poland

130. The Constitution of the Republic of Poland, passed on 2 April 1997 and adopted in a nationwide referendum on 25 May 1997, establishes a general framework for environmental protection and sustainable development in Poland. It contains a significant number of provisions associated with the issue of protecting the natural environment as discussed in §2.II above. When considering sources of law and the Constitution's place in that system, of key importance is Article 8(1) of the Constitution, which declares that the Constitution is the supreme law of the Republic of Poland. Its position was not altered by Poland's accession to the EU, neither by the obligation to respect binding international law.[49] Also of importance is the fact that the Constitution's provisions apply directly unless the Constitution itself provides otherwise (Article 8(2)). The character of its norms, however, means that independent and direct application of the Constitution is rare. The prevailing, weaker version of direct application is that of constitutional norms applied in concert with statutory ones. This procedure facilitates the interpretation of a normative act of lower rank in a manner consistent with provisions of the Constitution (a pro-constitutional interpretation of law). Constitutional provisions are used as additional arguments giving weight to particular interpretations of provisions in statutes, or as clues for understanding concepts embedded in those provisions.

2. Statutes

131. The fundamental element of the legal system, including the regime for environmental protection law, is occupied by statutes, on which the heaviest burden of regulation rests. The supremacy of statute is expressed in the principles of autonomy, primacy and exclusivity of regulation. These characteristics have been subjected to a re-evaluation considering the expansion of judicial review of their constitutionality on the one hand, and limitation of the domestic legislature's independence owing to the growing subordination of states to international and EU law on the other.

132. The system of legal acts comprising the environmental protection regime, which is the product of several decades of development, encompasses dozens of statutes. Legal doctrine divides them into several groups based on their content, importance to the system as a whole, and their place in it.[50]

---

49. *See* verdict of the Constitutional Tribunal of 11 May 2005 (K 18/04).
50. Górski et al., *Prawo ochrony środowiska.*

133. The first group consists of acts of a general and horizontal character, which regulate legal institutions of significance to the entire system of environmental protection law. As acts designed to impose order on the system and play a leading role in it, they of are particular importance considering the perceivable tendency towards diversification of regulations and the creation of separate acts regulating increasingly smaller and individual issues. From among this group of statutes, the Environmental Protection Act is deserving of the most attention. It is an expansive legal act practically constituting a code. Its internal structure is complex, with several chapters: I. General provisions, II. Protection of natural resources, III. Counteracting pollution, IV. Serious accidents, V. Financial and legal measures, VI. Liability for protection of the environment, VII. Administrative bodies and institutions of environmental protection. These titles are then divided into sections and subsections.

134. The provisions contained in section II, title I 'Definitions and general principles' should play a significant role in standardizing the interpretation and application of all legislation addressing the protection of the environment. Of similar import for the entirety of regulation are provisions concerning constructions serving to protect environmental quality. Provisions of the Act addressing financial and legal instruments applied in environmental protection, as well as those regarding civil and administrative liability, are of a horizontal nature.

135. The horizontal dimension of the Environmental Protection Act has been significantly weakened by the appearance of two statues expanding particular provisions, or even 'extracting' them from the Act. This refers specifically to the Environmental Damage Prevention and Amelioration Act (of 13 April 2007)[51] and the Act of 3 October 2008 on the Sharing of Information on the Environment and its Protection, Public Participation in Environmental Protection and Environmental Impact Assessments.[52] Separating the spheres indicated above by regulating them in individual statutes which have not been the subject of an attempt to link them with the more general Act (nor even one to clearly delineate their mutual relationship) is assessed negatively in legal doctrine. The charge is raised that 'the Act is slowly becoming just another piece of legislation in a system in which the greatest importance is attached to particular regulations addressing the issue of guarding against pollution, such as emissions permits or the functioning of a system of fees and administrative financial penalties.'[53]

136. The second, more extensive group of regulations are statutes that have been labelled with the term 'sectoral' legislation; this results from the scope of the issues they regulate, encompassing particular sectors (elements) of the environment, or from specified types of activities influencing the environment. This group includes in particular acts providing relatively comprehensive regulation of the rules for using and protecting specific elements of the natural environment, such as the Water

51. Dz. U. 2018, item 954 with amendments.
52. Dz. U. 2017, item 1405 with amendments.
53. Górski et al., *Prawo ochrony środowiska.*

Act of 20 July 2017, the Nature Protection Act of 16 April 2004 and the Geological and Mining Act of 9 June 2011. Legislation regulating the economic exploitation of biosphere resources also belongs to this group (the Forest Act, Hunting Act, Fishing Act, legislation concerning ecological agriculture), as does law concerning the humanitarian protection of animals. Legislation addressing the protection of air quality, such as the Act of 15 June 2015 on Trade in Rights to Emissions of Greenhouse Gases, are also extensive. It is also worth mentioning legislation concerning the handling of dangerous substances (laws governing chemical substances and biocides).

137. The third group of acts includes those which do not directly address issues of environmental protection, but their construction and legal institutions constituted by them are applied in achieving related aims. In particular, these acts include the Spatial Planning and Management Act of 27 March 2003, and the Building Act of 7 July 1994, alongside regulations concerning quality standards and assurance.

138. Regulations contained in the Civil Code of 23 April 1964, the Criminal Code (CC) of 6 June 1997 and the Code of Petty Offences of 20 May 1971 are of importance regarding legal responsibility for environmental protection. The provisions of the Environmental Protection Act dealing with responsibility merely supplement the ones contained in the aforementioned acts.

3. Regulations

139. The issue of regulations addressing environmental protection enacted by the highest authorities of central administration does not differ from the basic determinations contained in the doctrine of these sources of administrative law.

140. A regulation is a secondary legislation linked to a particular statute. Among the acts of universally binding law it is the only one lower in rank than a statute which is issued at the central level. Regulations supplement statutes when a given statute either requires or permits them to do so. By issuing detailed regulations based on the initial foundation of a statute, regulations can make an impact upon the situation of external entities as well as the obligations of public authorities within the scope of statutory authorization. The content of regulations must be within the borders indicated by the relevant authorization; anything exceeding the established boundaries constitutes independent regulation, and as such is devoid of a legal foundation. The provisions of a regulation must be characterized by conformity with norms contained in statutes; thus, a regulation must not only comply with all of the provisions of the authorizing statute but must also not contain provisions running contrary to those of other statutes.

141. Regulations may only be issued by those organs explicitly indicated in the Constitution, which contains an exhaustive list of authorized bodies. In matters concerning environmental protection law these organs are generally the Minister of the

Environment and other ministers either in cooperation with the Minister of the Environment or independently exercising their own authority.

142. As secondary legislation, a regulation can only be issued in the event of an explicit authorizing provision contained in a statute. The content and objective of a regulation are defined by the objective of the statute containing this provision. Such authorization must be specific, meaning '[it] shall specify the organ appropriate to issue a regulation and the scope of matters to be regulated as well as guidelines concerning the provisions of such act' (Article 92(1) of the Constitution). Regulations concerning environmental protection are often possessed of extensive authorizations.

143. A large and particular category of regulations is composed of legal acts based on the Nature Protection Act of 2004 which established forms of legal protection, such as national parks. Borders of national park are determined and changed by way of a regulation of the Council of Ministers.

4. Local Law

144. All categories of regional and local organs of public administration, meaning organs of both government and self-government administration, are vested with the authority to enact local laws concerning environmental protection.

145. The Constitution establishes the contours of local law by delineating the borders which this law may not cross, but within them it allows the legislature to '[specify] the principles and procedures for enacting local legal enactments' (Article 94 of the Constitution).

146. The Constitution indicates five fundamental characteristics of local law:

(1) The local character (Article 87(2) of the Constitution), which limits the scope of application of local law to the territory in which the enacting organ operates.
(2) A limited range of bodies authorized to enact such law (Article 94 of the Constitution).
(3) A universally binding source of law (Article 87(2) of the Constitution) which provides for the capacity of local law to regulate the situation of external entities, thus leading to the requirement to promulgate such laws before they may take effect (Article 88(1) of the Constitution).
(4) Subordination to statute, which means that local law is lower in the hierarchy of normative acts and must be in compliance with statutory regulations (Article 184 of the Constitution).

(5) A secondary character, which means that local law may only be enacted 'on the basis of and within limits specified by statute,' (Article 94 of the Constitution).[54]

147. In determining the varieties of acts comprising the category of local law, of primary importance are the legal provisions contained in institutional statutes, which regulate the lawmaking powers of regional and local organs for every level of government and self-government administration individually.

148. Three primary types of acts enacting local law are identified in these statutes:

(1) acts issued on the basis of local self-government constitutional statutes, including those addressing the internal structure of local government, the organization of its offices and institutions, principles for managing assets and the use of public facilities;
(2) acts issued on the basis of particular authorizations contained in statutes; this is the most common type of local law, also in respect of environmental protection law;
(3) acts constituting public order regulations – in matters unregulated by other statutes – issued in the event of the necessity to protect particular states or values; this includes protection of the natural environment, which is explicitly listed among the values protected by public order regulations at the county level.

149. Acts of local law can be passed in the form of resolutions (when a collegial organ is authorized to enact them), as well as regulations and orders (in the event of monocratic organs).

B. Internal Law

150. Article 93 of the Constitution includes acts of internal law in the catalogue of sources of law. In establishing this category of sources of law, the legislator failed to provide a complete list of its types and authors. While Article 93 of the Constitution *expressis verbis* only addresses the authority of the Council of Ministers, the Prime Minister and ministers to issue such acts and only makes mention of 'resolutions' and 'orders', this does not constitute an enumeration. Practically every organ of public administration is authorized by statute to enact such acts. However, the scope of addressees is limited by introducing the criterion of their 'organizational subordination'. Acts of internal law may also not be cited as the basis for issuing 'decisions' to citizens and other outside entities. For example: pursuant to Article 111(2) of the Nature Protection Act, the Council of Ministers ratifies the

54. L. Garlicki, *Konstytucyjne źródła prawa administracyjnego,* [in:] *Konstytucyjne podstawy funkcjonowania administracji publicznej. System Prawa Administracyjnego. Tom 2*, 69 (R. Hauser, A. Wróbel, Z. Niewiadomski, CH Beck 2012).

national strategy for protection and sustainable exploitation of biodiversity and related activities by way of a resolution. Under Article 22(2) of that same Act, the Minister of the Environment sets forth, in an order, tasks for the protection of a national park, while the regional environmental protection director does the same for nature reserves.

C. Forms of Planning

151. Some sources of environmental protection law take the particular form of planning acts (plans, strategies, programmes and other planning documents). Their diverse character makes them difficult to qualify unequivocally. They may be informational, indicative or imperative. Their creation and application may be obligatory or may be the subject of discretionary authority. They are usually of an abstract and general character but, at times, can be individual and specific. They most often establish the obligations of administering entities but are not irrelevant to administered entities as they usually determine the latter group's legal situation, and at times their rights in public law. As a result, they can take the form of normative acts (constituting a source of law), or other general acts, individual acts, administrative operations, social and organizational activities and other types of operations and activities that cause difficulties in assigning them to the traditionally applied catalogue of legal forms of activity.[55]

55. J. Boć, *Przykład prawnych form działania w ochronie środowiska*, [in:] *Prawne formy działania administracji. System Prawa Administracyjnego. Tom 5*, 428–438 (R. Hauser, Z. Niewiadomski, A. Wróbel, CH Beck 2013).

Part I. Pollution Control

Chapter 1. General Law

152. The protection of environmental resources in Poland is implemented on the basis of the Environmental Protection Act and specific provisions. The protection of environmental resources is ensured, in particular, by defining the environmental quality standards, controlling their achievement and taking measures to prevent them from being exceeded or restored, along with reducing emissions.

153. The process of defining environmental quality standards shall be guided by the scale of emergence and type of substance or energy impact on the environment. Environmental quality standards may vary depending on the areas and are expressed as levels of substance or energy.

154. In order to achieve compliance with environmental quality standards in cases specified by the Environmental Protection Act or specific provisions, there are created programs, by way of a local law act. A program determines the area covered by its scope, the violated environmental quality standards and the scope of the violation, basic directions, and scope of activities necessary to restore environmental quality standards, material and financial schedule of the planned activities and entities to which the responsibilities set in the program are addressed. Programs are published in voivodeship official journals.

155. Exploitation of installations in Poland causing: a release of gases or dust into the air; release of sewage into waters or into the ground; waste generation – is permissible after obtaining a permit. The permit is issued, in principle, at the request of the operator of the installation. At the request of the operator of the installation, the environmental protection authority may issue one permit for all installations located in the area of its jurisdiction. The permit is issued by way of a decision by the environmental protection authority. The authority competent to issue a permit decides on the expiration, revocation, and limitation of the permit. The environmental protection authority immediately passes the final decisions to the provincial inspector for environmental protection.

156. The permit is issued for a fixed period, not longer than ten years, with the exception of the so called integrated permit, which is issued for an indefinite period. At the request of the operator, the integrated permit may be issued for a fixed period as well. The permit for the generation of waste for the operator of the ships recycling plant and the integrated permit for the operator of the ship recycling facilities are issued for a fixed period – not longer than five years. The authority competent to issue the permit shall, by way of a decision, terminate the permit if the circumstances specified in the Environmental Protection Act occur. The permit is subject to withdrawal or limitation with or without compensation.

157. If the installation is not properly operated, which poses a considerable threat to the deterioration of the environment or a threat to human life or health, the decision to withdraw or limit the permit is immediately enforceable.

158. The proceedings concerning the expiration, revocation or limitation of the permit are initiated ex officio or at the request of the operator of the installation. Compensation is awarded from the authority competent to withdraw or limit the permit, and determined by its decision, which is not actionable. A party dissatisfied with the awarded compensation may, within thirty days from the delivery of the decision, file an action at a common court.

159. An integrated permit is required to run an installation which operation, due to the type and scale of its activity, may cause significant pollution of particular elements of the environment or the environment as a whole, with exception to the installations or parts thereof used exclusively for research, development or testing of new products or technological processes.

160. The integrated permit defines the conditions of production and methods of managing waste on the terms specified in the provisions of the Waste Act, regardless of whether a permit to generate waste would be required for the installation.

161. The integrated permit also sets out, under the terms of the Water Act, the conditions for the abstraction of surface or groundwater, if these waters are collected only for the needs of an installation for which the integrated permit is issued.

162. Installations that require an integrated permit shall meet the requirements of environmental protection resulting from the best available techniques, and in particular, they must not cause an excess of the emission limit values. The fact that the emission level resulting from the application of the best available techniques does not exceed, does not exempt from the obligation to comply with environmental quality standards.

163. A condition for considering an application for issuing an integrated permit is to pay a registration fee. The registration fee cannot be higher than PLN 12,000. In an integrated permit, additional requirements related to the operation of the installation can be specified, if it is necessary to achieve a high level of protection of the environment as a whole. The register of applications for the issue of an integrated permit and issued integrated permits shall be kept by the minister responsible for environmental affairs.

Chapter 2. Air Pollution

164. Air Protection in Poland is oriented on ensuring its best quality. This objective is pursued, in particular, by maintaining the levels of the substances in the air below the levels acceptable for them or at least at these levels; reducing levels of substances in the air at least to acceptable levels when they are not met; reducing and maintaining levels of substances in the air below target levels or levels of long-term objectives or at least at these levels. The values of these levels are determined by way of regulation by the minister responsible for environmental affairs in consultation with the minister for health.

165. Air quality assessment is carried out in zones. The zones are classified into the following: an agglomeration with a population of more than 250,000 inhabitants; a city with a population of more than 100,000 inhabitants; and the remaining area of the voivodeship, which is neither part of a city, with more than 100,000 inhabitants, nor the agglomeration.

166. The minister responsible for environmental affairs, taking into account substances which level in the air is subject to assessment, determines by way of regulation, the zones including their names and codes. Air quality assessments and observation of changes are carried out within the framework of State Environmental Monitoring. For the purpose of determining the appropriate method of air quality assessment in particular zones, the provincial inspector for environmental protection performs, at least every five years,[56] classification of zones, separately in terms of the level of each substance.

167. The provincial inspector for environmental protection, every year by 30 April assesses the levels of substances in the air in a given zone for the previous year and classifies zones for each substance separately. The results of the evaluation and classification of zones shall be forwarded to the provincial board immediately.

168. The Chief Inspector for Environmental Protection supervises the determination by the provincial inspector for environmental protection of the method and performance of air quality assessment and classification of zones. Moreover, he coordinates activities in the area of ensuring the quality of measurements and air quality assessment by indicating quality procedures and supervises coordination, within the country, of participation in quality assurance programs organized by the European Commission.

169. For zones where the level exceeds the admissible level increased by the margin of tolerance, the provincial board within fifteen months from the date of receiving the results of the assessment of the levels of substances in the air and zone classification, prepare and submit to the competent prefects (mayors) and county

56. The classification for the level of a given substance shall be carried out within five years, if since the previous classification the total amount of this substance released into the air in the state will change by at least 20%.

commissioners, a draft resolution on the air protection program aimed at achieving admissible levels of substances in the air and the exposure concentration ceiling. The prefect (mayor) and county commissioner are obliged to give their opinion within one month from the day of receiving the draft resolution on the air protection program. Failure to deliver an opinion within this period constitutes acceptance of the draft resolution on the air protection program. The provincial assembly, within eighteen months from the date of receipt of the results of the evaluation of the levels of substances in the air and the classification of zones, determines, by way of a resolution, the air protection program. For zones in which the admissible levels of substances are exceeded, the provincial board develops a draft resolution on the air protection program or its update, which integral part is a short-term action plan.

170. For zones where the level is between the admissible level and the admissible level increased by the margin of tolerance, the provincial board determines the reasons for exceeding the levels of admissible substances in the air and informs the minister responsible for environmental affairs about measures taken to reduce emissions of substances causing these exceedances.

171. For zones where the level exceeds the target level, the provincial board, within fifteen months from the date of receiving the results of the evaluation of the levels of substances in the air and zone classification, elaborates and submits a draft resolution on the air protection program aimed at achieving the target levels of the substances in the air to the competent prefects (mayors) and county commissioners. The prefect (mayor) and county commissioner are obliged to give their opinion within one month from the day of receiving the draft resolution on the air protection program. Failure to deliver an opinion within this period constitutes acceptance of the draft resolution on the air protection program. For zones in which the admissible level or target level of more than one substance in the air has been exceeded, a common air protection program can be prepared.

172. Provincial boards cooperate in the preparation of air protection programs by the exchange of information on possible sources of exceedances of levels of substances in the air and exemplary activities aimed at reducing them and provide opportunities for public participation in proceedings related to the preparation of an air protection program. The draft air protection program prepared by the provincial board should comply with the objectives provided in other planning and strategic documents, including the national air protection program, provincial environmental protection programs, regional operational programs and the concept of spatial development of the country. In the case of zones for which air protection programs have been adopted, and air quality standards are exceeded, the provincial board is obliged to develop a program update project within three years from the date of entry into force of the provincial assembly resolution on the air protection program, defining protective measures in it for vulnerable population groups, including, in particular, older people and children.

173. In case where exceedance of the admissible levels or target substances in the air occurs in a considerable area of the country, and the measures taken by local self-government bodies do not cause the reduction of pollutants in the air, the minister responsible for environmental affairs may develop a national air protection program, which is a document of a strategic character that sets goals and directions of actions that should be included in air protection programs.

174. When there is a risk of exceeding the alarm, admissible or target level of substances in the air, the provincial board, within fifteen months from the date of receiving an information on the risk from the provincial inspector for environmental protection, prepares and presents to competent prefects (mayors) and county commissioners, draft resolution on the short-term action plan, which sets out activities aimed at reducing the risk of such exceedances and limiting the consequences and duration of the exceedances occurred. The prefect (mayor) and county commissioner are obliged to give their opinion within one month from the day of receiving the draft resolution on the short-term action plan. Failure to deliver an opinion within this period constitutes acceptance of the draft resolution on the short-term action plan.

175. The provincial assembly, within eighteen months from the date of receiving information from the provincial inspector for environmental protection, on the risk of occurrence of exceedance in the given zone of the alarm, admissible or target level of the substance in the air, determines, by way of a resolution, a short-term action plan.

176. In case of a risk of exceeding the alarm, admissible or target level of the substance in the air, the provincial crisis management team referred to in Crisis Management Act (2007)[57] informs the competent authorities about the need to take actions specified in the short-term action plan.

177. If, on the territory of the Republic of Poland, there is a risk of exceeding the admissible levels or exceedances of target or acceptable levels, increased by the margin of tolerance, or alarm levels and long-term objectives caused by transferring pollution from the territory of another country, the minister responsible for the environment affairs, after consulting The Chief Inspector for Environmental Protection, through the provincial board competent for the area where the risk of exceedances or exceedances were identified, conducts consultations with the competent authority of that country in order to analyse the possibility of eliminating or limiting the risk of exceedances along with their effects and duration.

178. When the information is received from another country, that there is a risk of either exceedance of admissible levels or exceedances of target or admissible levels, increased by the margin of tolerance, or alarm levels and long-term objectives, caused by transferring air pollutants from the territory of the Republic of Poland, consultations with the competent authority of another country are carried out by the

57. Dz. U. 2017, item 209 and 1566.

provincial board competent for the area where the transfer of air pollutants is suspected. The provincial board immediately informs the minister responsible for environmental affairs about the results of consultations. The minister responsible for environmental affairs may initiate cooperation with other EU Member States and the European Commission in terms of coordination of joint air protection programs or short-term action plans on the territory of the Republic of Poland. The minister responsible for environmental affairs shall establish cooperation, through the provincial board competent for the area where the risk of exceedance has been identified, with other EU Member States and the European Commission regarding coordination of joint air protection programs or short-term action plans in the territory of the Republic of Poland.

179. The Chief Inspector for Environmental Protection establishes cooperation, through the provincial inspector for environmental protection competent for the area where the risk of exceedance has been identified, with the authority competent in another EU Member State and the European Commission, in the assessment and ensuring air quality measurements. Information on the state of air quality, including the location of all zones in the territory of the Republic of Poland, where air quality is assessed and its state, are available on the website of the Chief Inspectorate for Environmental Protection.

180. The provincial crisis management team immediately informs the public and other entities using the environment who are obliged to limit or cease the release of gases or dust from the installation into the air, in a way customarily adopted in a given area, about the risk of exceeding the admissible levels.

181. The Chief Inspector for Environmental Protection, on the basis of the results and information obtained from the provincial inspector for environmental protection, prepares a collective assessment of air quality in the country. The Chief Inspector for Environmental Protection, by 31 October of each year, makes the annual reports on air quality assessment in the country for the previous year available on the website of the Chief Inspectorate for Environmental Protection.

182. In the area where admissible level of substances in the air is exceeded, in relation to plants where the installation is operated, is classified as a project likely to significantly affect the environment pursuant to the Act on the provision of access to information about the environment and its protection, the participation of society in environmental protection and on assessment of environmental impacts, the provincial marshal may, by decision, impose on the entity using the environment that conducts activities causing the release of substances into the air, the obligation to measure the levels of this substance in the air. The proceedings regarding the issue of the decision are commenced ex officio. The provincial assembly may, by way of a resolution, introduce restrictions or prohibitions on the operation of installations in which fuels are combusted in order to prevent a negative impact on human health or the environment.

183. The voivode, with the assistance of the provincial inspector for environmental protection, supervises the timely adoption of air protection programs and short-term action plans, a performance of tasks specified in air protection programs and short-term action plans prepared by the prefect (mayor), county commissioner and other entities.

Chapter 3. Water Pollution

184. Detailed principles of water protection are defined in the Water Act (2017). The Act regulates the administration of waters in accordance with the principle of sustainable development, in particular shaping and protection of water resources, use of waters and management of water resources. It also regulates the matters of ownership of water and land covered with waters, as well as the principles of managing these components as the property of the State Treasury. The provisions of the Act apply to inland waters and internal sea waters. Waters as an integral part of the environment and habitat for organisms are protected, regardless of the ownership. The protection objective is to achieve environmental objectives for uniform bodies of surface waters, uniform bodies of groundwater and protected areas as well as improvement of water quality and biological relations in the aquatic environment and in wetlands. Pursuing this objective, it should be ensured that water, depending on the needs, is suitable for supplying people with water intended for human consumption, sports, tourism or recreation, for bathing and for the existence of fish and other aquatic organisms under natural conditions, enabling their migration.

185. Protection of surface water against pollution includes joint reduction of emissions to water from sources of point pollution and from sources of area pollution. If the EU legislation on the protection of waters against pollution requires stricter emission limit values than specified in the Water Act, more stringent requirements should be applied. Temporary deterioration of the condition of uniform water bodies is permissible if it is the result of natural phenomena or the effect of force majeure, extraordinary or unpredictable, in particular, extreme flood events or long-term drought, incident of terrorist character, disruption of critical infrastructure within the meaning of the Crisis Management Act (2007), and unpredictable catastrophes.

186. To ensure the protection of waters, numerous prohibitions are introduced, including: release of sewage directly into groundwater and surface waters if it would be contrary to the conditions resulting from existing forms of nature protection, game animals' protection zones or refuges, along with protection zones for water intakes and protected areas of inland water reservoirs. It is prohibited to release sewage into surface waters within bathing areas, places occasionally used for bathing and public beaches over waters less than 1 km from their borders, to stagnant waters, lakes, if the time of sewage inflow to the lake would be shorter than twenty-four hours, natural watercourses natural and channels that are tributaries of lakes, if the time of sewage inflow to the lake would be shorter than twenty-four hours. It is also prohibited to release sewage to the ground if it contains substances particularly harmful to the aquatic environment if it would be contrary to the conditions resulting from existing forms of nature protection, game animals' protection zones or refuges, along with protection zones for water intakes and protection areas of inland water reservoirs.

187. Moreover, it is prohibited to release rainwater or snowmelt, from open or closed rainwater drainage systems used to discharge atmospheric precipitation, directly to groundwater and to water facilities, provided that these waters contain substances particularly harmful to the aquatic environment specified in separate regulations.

188. It is prohibited to release waste into the waters within the meaning of the Act of 14 December 2012 on Waste and Liquid Animal Manure. The prohibition includes floating of snow to the waters, exported from contaminated areas, in particular from city centres, industrial areas, storage areas, transport bases, high traffic roads with parking lots, along with storage of that snow in areas located between the embankment and the coastline, or at a distance of less than 50 m from the coastline. Washing of vehicles in surface waters and on the banks of these waters is prohibited as well.

189. Sewage released into waters or into the ground as part of the normal use of water or water services should be treated to the extent required by law.

190. Agricultural production, including special departments of agricultural production and activities in which animal waste or fertilizers are kept, is conducted in a way that prevents water pollution. In order to reduce the pollution of waters with nitrates from agricultural sources and to prevent further pollution, an action program is being developed and implemented throughout the whole country. The minister responsible for water management in agreement with the minister responsible for agriculture prepares a draft action program. The Council of Ministers adopts the action program by way of regulation. The action program is reviewed every four years and, if necessary, updated. The competent authority of the Inspectorate for Environmental Protection performs control over the application of the action program by entities obliged to use it. The minister responsible for water management evaluates the effectiveness of the action program. As part of the state monitoring of the environment, monitoring is carried out to assess the effectiveness of the action program. The competent authority of the Inspectorate for Environmental Protection shall provide the minister responsible for water management annually with the results of monitoring to assess the effectiveness of the action program for the previous year, including the results of nitrate concentrations, by 30 June.

191. To ensure the appropriate quality of waters stored as the water supply intended for human consumption and supplying plants requiring high-quality water, as well as water resources protection, there are established protection zones for water intakes and protected areas of inland water reservoirs. The voivode, at the request of the Polish Waters, establishes a protection area, by means of a local law, indicating restrictions or prohibitions regarding the use of land and the use of water in the protected area and the boundaries of this area.

192. In order to protect the marine environment, a marine strategy is developed and implemented. Environmental objectives for marine waters are achieved by taking actions defined in the marine water protection program. The government and self-government administration bodies perform their tasks in the field of environmental protection of marine waters. The draft program for the protection of marine waters is being developed by the Polish Waters in agreement with relevant ministries. The Polish Waters forward the draft program for the protection of sea waters to the minister competent for water management. The minister responsible for water management shall agree on a draft marine water protection program with members of the Council of Ministers. The minister responsible for water management submits a draft marine water protection program to the European Commission and interested EU Member States. The draft marine water protection program is submitted within three months from the day it is agreed with the members of the Council of Ministers.

193. The marine water protection program is accepted if, within six months from the date of submission, the European Commission will not reject the draft program in whole or in part. The Council of Ministers adopts, by regulation, a marine water protection program, taking into account the position of the European Commission and guided by the general nature of this program. If the European Commission rejects the draft marine water protection program in part, the minister responsible for water management develops a revised draft marine water protection program, regarding the position of the European Commission. If the European Commission rejects a draft marine water protection program as a whole, a new draft has to be developed. The minister responsible for water management submits to the European Commission a report on the progress in the implementation of the marine water protection program. The report shall be submitted within three years from the date of adoption of the marine water protection program, and subsequently after each update of the program. The marine water protection program is reviewed every six years and updated if necessary. The minister responsible for water management informs the European Commission, the Baltic Marine Environment Protection Commission and the interested EU Member States about the adoption of the marine water protection program and its updates. Information is provided within three months from the date of adoption of the marine water protection program or update of this program.

Chapter 4. Waste

194. The issue of waste in Poland is primarily regulated by the Waste Act (2012). However, it should be emphasized that there are also many detailed statutory regulations regarding this matter. These are, among others: the Act of 11 May 2001 on the obligations of entrepreneurs in regard to certain waste management and on the product fee,[58] the Act of 20 January 2005 on the recycling of end-of-life vehicles,[59] Act of 11 September 2015 on electrical and electronic waste, Act of 24 April 2009 on batteries and accumulators,[60] Act of 13 June 2013 on the packaging and packaging waste management,[61] or finally the Act of 13 September 1996 on maintaining cleanliness and order in communes.[62] The Waste Act specifies measures to protect the environment, life, and health of people, preventing and reducing the negative impact on the environment and human health resulting from the generation and management of waste and limiting the general effects of the use of resources and improving the efficiency of such use. The Act defines the basic concepts regarding waste, including waste administration, which shall be understood as the collection, transport, treatment of waste, including the supervision of such activities, as well as subsequent management of waste disposal sites and activities performed as a seller of waste or intermediary in waste trade. In turn, waste management includes both, waste generation and waste management.

195. Pursuant to the Waste Act, waste is any substance or object that the possessor discards or intends to discard or is required to discard. Bio-waste is the biodegradable waste from gardens and parks, food and kitchen waste from households, gastronomy, caterers, retail units, as well as comparable wastes from establishments producing or introducing food to the market. Municipal waste is waste generated in households, with the exception of end-of-life vehicles, and wastes that do not contain hazardous waste from other waste producers, which, due to their nature or composition, are similar to household waste. Medical waste was defined as waste generated in connection with the provision of health services and the conduct of research and scientific experiments in the field of medicine. Inert waste shall be understood as waste that does not undergo significant physical, chemical or biological transformations – it is insoluble, does not react physically or chemically, does not cause environmental pollution or danger to human life or health, is not biodegradable and it has no adverse effect on the matter it is contacting. The total content of impurities in these wastes is negligible.

196. Veterinary wastes are wastes generated in connection with the examination, treatment of animals or providing veterinary services, and in connection with conducting scientific research and experiments on animals. Green waste is municipal waste that which consists of parts of plants generated by keeping green areas,

58. Dz. U. 2018, item 650 with amendments.
59. Dz. U. 2018, item 578.
60. Dz. U. 2018, item 650.
61. Dz.U. 2018, item 150 with amendments.
62. Dz.U. 2018, item 1454 with amendments

gardens, parks, and cemeteries, as well as from marketplaces, with the exception of waste from cleaning streets and squares. The possessor of waste in accordance with the statutory definition is a waste producer or a natural person, a legal person and an organizational unit without legal personality in possession of waste. It is presumed that the owner of the land is the owner of the waste located on the property. Hazardous waste is considered to be waste that displays one or more of the hazardous properties. The properties that cause waste to be hazardous and the conditions for treating hazardous waste, except for waste recognition as infectious, are set out in Commission Regulation No. 1357/2014 of 18 December 2014 replacing Annex III to Directive 2008/98/EC of the European Parliament and of the Council on waste and repealing certain Directives[63] and Council Regulation 2017/997 of 8 June 2017 amending Annex III to Directive 2008/98/EC of the European Parliament and of the Council as regards the dangerous property of HP 14 'Ecotoxic'.[64]

197. Waste classification is made by classifying them into the appropriate group, subgroup, and type of waste, considering its origin, properties causing waste to be hazardous, components of waste for which exceeding the limit values of dangerous substances may cause that waste is hazardous waste. The minister responsible for environmental affairs by way of a regulation defines the waste catalogue divided into groups, subgroups, and types with an indication of hazardous waste, guided by the source of waste generation and waste properties.

198. An object or a substance generated in a production process whose primary purpose is not to produce them may be considered as a by-product which is not a waste. Recognition or refusal to recognize an object or substance as a by-product takes place by means of a decision issued by the provincial marshal after consulting the provincial inspector for environmental protection in charge of the area were object or substance is manufactured. The decision on recognizing an object or substance as a by-product is issued for a definite period, not longer than ten years.

199. Waste administration should be carried out in a manner ensuring protection of human life and health and the environment, in particular waste administration must not cause a hazard to water, air, soil, plants or animals and cause nuisance by noise or odour nor cause adverse effects on rural areas or places of special importance, including cultural and natural importance.

200. The legislator introduced a hierarchy of ways to deal with waste, indicating respectively: prevention of waste generation, preparation for reuse, recycling, other recovery processes, and disposal.

201. Anyone who takes action that causes or could cause the occurrence of waste, shall plan, design and conduct this activities using such production methods or forms of services and resources and materials, in order to first prevent waste generation or reduce the amount of waste and its negative impact on life and human

63. OJ L 365 of 19.12.2014, p. 89, as amended.
64. OJ L 150 of 14.6.2017, p. 1.

health and the environment, including the process of manufacturing products, and during and after their use. Waste which is inevitable, the possessor is first and foremost obliged to return to recovery.

202. The recovery, first of all, consists of the preparation of waste by the possessor for reuse or recycling, and if it is not possible due to technical reasons or is not justified for ecological or economic reasons – a waste becomes a subject to other recovery processes. The waste possessor is obliged to dispose of the waste which recovery is not possible. Only waste which disposal was otherwise impossible can be stored. Only wastes from which wastes suitable for recovery have been sorted out are disposed of.

203. Public administration bodies, within their scope of competence, undertake activities supporting the reuse and preparation for reuse of waste. Waste, considering the hierarchy of waste management methods, is primarily processed at the place of origin. Wastes that cannot be processed at the place of origin is transferred, considering the hierarchy of waste management methods and the best available technique and technology, to the nearest places where it can be processed.

204. It is prohibited to mix hazardous waste of different types, mixing hazardous waste with non-hazardous waste, and mixing hazardous waste with substances, materials or objects.

205. Waste management costs are covered by the original waste producer or by the current or previous possessor of the waste. In the cases specified in separate regulations, the costs of waste management are covered by the producer of the product or entity introducing the product in the territory of the country, specified in these regulations.

206. Shipments of waste are carried out in accordance with the requirements of environmental protection and safety of human life and health, in particular in a way that takes into account the chemical and physical properties of waste, including the state of aggregation, and the hazards that these wastes may cause. Shipment of hazardous waste which could be considered as dangerous goods within the meaning of Article 2(4) of the Act of 19 August 2011 on the transport of dangerous goods[65] is carried out in compliance with the provisions on the transport of dangerous goods.

207. Storage of waste is carried out in accordance with the requirements of environmental protection and safety of human life and health, in particular in a manner that takes into account the chemical and physical properties of waste, including the state of aggregation, and the hazards that these wastes may cause. Storage of waste is carried out only as part of the generation, collection or treatment of waste. Waste for storage may only be stored in order to collect the appropriate amount of this waste for transport to a landfill, but no longer than for a year. The waste possessor is obliged to immediately remove the waste from a place not intended for keeping

65. Dz. U. 2018, items 169 with amendments.

or storing. If the waste is not disposed of properly, the prefect (mayor), by way of a decision issued ex officio, orders the waste possessor to dispose of waste from a place not intended for keeping or storage, except when the obligation to remove the waste results from the decision to withdraw the decision related to the waste administration.

208. The waste producer is obliged to manage the waste he has produced. Waste is processed in installations or devices. Installations and devices for processing waste are used only if they meet the requirements of environmental protection, including that they do not exceed the emission standards referred to in the provisions on environmental protection, and if the residues resulting from waste treatment activities will be processed in compliance with the requirements set out in in the Act.

209. If it is impossible to incinerate waste in installations or devices intended for that purpose for safety reasons, the provincial marshal may authorize, by way of a decision, waste incineration outside installations or device. The permit for the incineration of waste outside installations and devices for enclosed areas is issued by the regional director for environmental protection. The competent authority for issuing a permit to incinerate waste outside installations and devices is the authority with territorial competent for the place of waste incineration.

210. The provincial inspector for environmental protection suspends, by way of a decision, the activity of the waste possessor, if the possessor collects or processes waste without the required permit for waste collection or permit for waste treatment.

211. If over a period of three years, counting from the end of the calendar year in which the decision to impose an administrative fine for violation consisting in a waste management contrary to the permission to collect waste or permit for waste treatment has become final, the waste possessor has been again charged with the fine for the violation consisting of waste management contrary to the permit for waste collection or permit for the waste treatment, the provincial inspector for environmental protection suspends, by way of a decision, the activity of this waste processor.

212. To achieve the objectives set in the environmental policy, to separate the trends in the growth of waste generated and their impact on the environment on the country's economic growth, to implement the hierarchy of waste management and the principles of self-sufficiency and proximity, and to establish and maintain an integrated and sufficient network of waste managing installations in the country that meet the requirements of environmental protection, waste administration plans are being developed. Plans are developed at the national and provincial level. The provincial waste administering plan should be in line with the national waste administration plan and serve the implementation of its objectives.

213. Public administration bodies develop waste administration plans that support activities aimed at the achievement of objectives and compliance with the requirements resulting from the provisions of the EU law. The Council of Ministers adopts the national waste administration plan prepared by the minister responsible for environmental affairs, in agreement with the minister competent for water management. The provincial assembly adopts the provincial waste administration plan prepared by the provincial board. The provincial board submits the provincial waste administration plan to the minister responsible for environmental affairs within one month from the date of adopting the plan. The project of the provincial waste administration plan is subject to the opinion of the executive bodies of communes from the area of the voivodeship that are not members of inter-municipal associations and executive bodies of inter-municipal associations, and in regard to water protection – by the competent director for the regional water management of the National Water Administration Polish Waters. Waste administration plans are updated at least every six years. The implementation of waste administration plans includes reports covering the period of three calendar years, as at 31 December of the year ending this period. Reports on the implementation of waste administration plans contain information on the implementation of the provisions of these plans, assessment of the state of waste administration, evaluation of the implementation of tasks and the achievement of objectives. The report on the implementation of the national waste administration plan is prepared and submitted to the Council of Ministers by the minister responsible for environmental affairs, eighteen months after the end of the reporting period, and the report on the implementation of the provincial waste administration plan – is prepared and submitted to the provincial assembly and the minister responsible for environmental affairs by provincial board, within twelve months after the end of the reporting period.

214. Waste collection and waste treatment require authorization. The permit is issued, by way of decision, by the authority competent for the area where the waste is collected or treated. The competent authority is the provincial marshal or county commissioner. The regional director for environmental protection is the competent authority to issue permits for waste collection and permits for waste treatment in closed areas. The issuing of a permit for the treatment of waste consisting of the disposal of infectious medical waste and infectious veterinary waste requires the consent of the Chief Sanitary Inspector.

215. The permit for waste collection and the permit for the waste treatment are issued for a fixed-term, not longer than ten years. If a waste holder who has obtained a permit for waste collection or permits for waste treatment violates the provisions of the Act within the scope of activities covered by the permit, significantly violates the requirements for fire protection or acts contrary to the issued permit, the competent authority calls on him to immediately cease violations, and designates deadline for removing irregularities. If the possessor of waste, despite the call still violates the provisions of the Act, acts in contrary to the issued permit, the competent authority withdraws by way of a decision the permit, without compensation, specifying the date of its implementation. Withdrawal of the permit results in the termination of the activity covered by this permit. The competent authority may impose this decision as immediately enforceable, considering the need for the environmentally safe end of operations. The possessor of waste, whose permit has been withdrawn, is obliged to remove waste and negative effects in the environment or environmental damage within the meaning of the Act of 13 April 2007 on the prevention and reparation of damage to the environment, within the activity covered by this permit, on his own cost, within the date specified in the decision. The proceedings regarding the issue of the decision are commenced ex officio.

216. The permit for waste collection and the permit for waste treatment expire after the expiry of the term for which it was issued and in a situation where the authorized entity ceased the activity covered by the permit or if for other reasons the permit became groundless and also when the licensed entity did not start activities covered by the permit within two years from the date on which the permit became final and if the authorized entity did not carry out the activity covered by the permit for two years.

217. The provincial marshal keeps a register of entities who introduce products, products in packaging and manage waste, making an entry in the register upon a request or ex officio. The provincial marshal makes an entry in the register upon request in cases regarding:

- the Act of 11 May 2001 on the obligations of entrepreneurs in regard to certain waste management and on the product fee;[66]
- the Act of 20 January 2005 on the recycling of end-of-life vehicles;[67]
- the Act of 11 September 2015 on electrical and electronic waste;
- the Act of 24 April 2009 on batteries and accumulators;[68]
- the Act of 13 June 2013 on the packaging and packaging waste management.

218. Ex officio, the provincial marshal makes an entry into the register of:

- a waste possessor who has obtained an integrated permit;
- a waste possessor who has obtained a permit to generate waste;
- a waste possessor who has obtained a permit for waste collection and for waste treatment;
- the entity that obtained the decision approving the mining waste management program or the permit to operate the mining waste disposal facility;
- the entity that obtained the concession for underground storage of waste under the Act of 9 June 2011 – Geological and Mining Law;
- an entity that has been entered in the register of regulated activities in the field of collecting municipal waste from property owners – pursuant to the Act of 13 September 1996 on maintaining cleanliness and order in communes.

66. Dz. U. 2018, item 650 with amendments.
67. Dz. U. 2018, item 578.
68. Dz. U. 2018, item 650.

219. Entry in the register is subject to a registration fee. The entity entered in the register has to pay a fee annually, by the end of February, for a given year. The registration fee shall not be paid by the entrepreneur entered in the register referred to in the Act of 15 July 2011 on the National Eco-Management and Audit Scheme (EMAS)[69] who submits the request for entry in the register, submits information confirming voluntary participation in the Eco-Management and Audit Scheme (EMAS). The amount of the registration fee and the amount of the annual fee is from PLN 50 to PLN 2,000. In case of the permanent cessation of activities requiring entry into the register, the entity is obliged, within fourteen days from the date of permanent cessation of this activity, to submit to the provincial marshal the application for deletion from the register. The provincial marshal refuses to enter and deletes the entity from the register, by way of a decision.

220. The waste possessor is obliged to keep current quantitative and qualitative records of waste in accordance with the waste catalogue. The obligation to keep waste records does not apply to, among others, producers of municipal waste, producers of waste in the form of end-of-life vehicles if these vehicles were handed over to the entrepreneur running the dismantling station or entrepreneur running the collection point. Reporting is also conducted in the field of products, packaging and waste administration.

221. If it is required to protect life, human health or the environment, the county commissioner, competent for the area where the waste from accidents was generated, by decision issued ex officio, may impose duties regarding accident waste management on the perpetrator of the accident, including the obligation to transfer them to the designated waste possessor. If the waste from accidents causes the pollution of the sea, the owner of the ship which caused the waste, if the ship is recognized, is considered to be the perpetrator of the accident.

222. The waste possessor who operates a metal waste collection point is obliged to fill in the metal waste acceptance form when accepting this waste from natural persons who are not entrepreneurs. A person transferring metal waste is obliged to present a document in order to confirm the identity.

223. The waste is stored in a landfill or in an underground waste disposal facility referred to in the Act of 9 June 2011 – Geological and Mining Law or in an Extraction Waste Treatment Facility referred to in the Act of 10 July 2008 on waste mining. There can be distinguished the following types of landfills: hazardous waste landfill; landfill for inert waste; landfill for non hazardous and inert waste. Waste storage at the landfill is prohibited.

224. The manager of the landfill may commence the activity of running a landfill after obtaining, respectively, an integrated permit or a permit for waste treatment; permission for the use of a landfill and decisions approving the instructions for operating a landfill. The decision approving the operating instructions for the

69. Dz. U. 2011, item 1060.

landfill is issued by the provincial marshal, at the request of the manager of the landfill, and in the case of projects and events in the closed areas – the regional director for environmental protection. The local authority's competence is determined by the location of the landfill.

225. Closure of a landfill or its separated part requires approval. Consent is issued by way of a decision. Before granting permission to close a landfill or its separated part, the provincial environmental protection inspector, at the request of a competent authority and with the participation of a representative of that authority, conducts a landfill inspection.

Chapter 5. Soil Pollution

226. The protection of the earth's surface should be considered in a twofold way. First, as all efforts to protect the qualitative composition of the earth's surface and, second, as protecting the earth's surface layer as such. against mechanical damage. The basic principles of protection of the earth's surface are set forth in the fourth chapter of the Environmental Protection Act and in the executive acts. Moreover, it should be noted that the issue of protection of the earth's surface is also regulated by the norms regarding the protection of arable and forest land, which is discussed in detail in Part II referring forests.

227. Protection of the earth's surface, pursuant to the Article 101 of the Environmental Protection Act, is based on rational management, maintenance of environmental, economic, social and cultural functions,[70] prevention of contamination with substances that cause risk and on remediation. On the level of mechanical protection of the earth's surface, there should be pointed out actions of maintaining the best soil condition by preventing water and wind erosion, minimizing the degree and mitigating the effects of soil scaling, preventing mass movements of the earth and their effects, and counteracting adverse changes in the natural shape of the earth's surface.[71]

228. According to Article 101a of the analysed Act, the pollution of the earth's surface is assessed on the basis of exceedance of the permissible level of substances causing harm to the soil or earth. With reference to the above-mentioned provision, the wording used by the legislator in Article 101a(4) may seem a quite unclear, as it excludes from this category substances of natural origin, which according to the legislator do not cause pollution. It is not always possible to unambiguously assess the origin of a given substance and its impact on the surface of the earth. In this respect, the minister responsible for the environmental affairs, specifies by way of a regulation the method of assessing the pollution of the earth's surface, indicating, among others, substances that cause risks particularly important for the protection of the earth's surface, their permissible contents in the earth, including analysis of its impact on human health and the environment, activities that are likely to cause historical pollution of the earth's surface, together with indicating examples of pollution for this activities, reference methods for conducting soil and earth pollution tests or specific requirements for assessing earth pollution at the site where an installation that requires obtaining an integrated permit is or has been in operation in the past, in order to ensure the identification of each pollutant before the installation is commissioned, during its operation and after its closure.

70. It should be understood here as the production of food and biomass, storage, filtering and transformation of nutrients, substances and water, the basis for development of life and biodiversity, sources of raw materials, reservoir of carbon, collection of geological, geomorphological and archaeological heritage.

71. This involves, *inter alia*, limiting the creation of, caused by the movements, or removal of earth and rock mass and mining waste, preventing and limiting the destruction of land cover with vegetation, ensuring the rational use of displaced or removed earth and rock masses, or reshaping the functions of areas where natural shape of the earth's surface is unfavourably transformed.

229. Substances that cause risks particularly relevant for the protection of the earth's surface, their permissible levels in the ground, stages of identification of contaminated sites, types of activities likely to cause historical pollution of the earth's surface, including examples of pollutants exemplified for these activities, reference methods for conducting earth pollution tests and specific requirements for assessing earth pollution at the site where an installation that requires obtaining an integrated permit is or has been in operation in the past, are defined in the Regulation of the Minister of the Environment of 1 September 2016 on the methods of assessing the pollution of the earth's surface.[72]

230. Substances that cause a risk of particular relevance for the protection of the earth's surface, their permissible content in the ground, in accordance with §3 of the Regulation are set out in Annex 1. Polluted areas are identified in five stages defined in §§6–10 of the Regulation, according to which the first stage includes determination of activities that may cause pollution in the given area, currently or in the past. The second stage of identification of a polluted area includes the establishment of a list of substances that cause the risk and that are expected to emerge in the earth in a given area. The third stage includes the collection and analysis of available and current sources of information relevant for the assessment of the risk of earth pollution in the given area and available and current earth pollution tests for substances that cause risk from the list established in the second stage. The fourth stage of identification of a polluted area includes the collection of information required for preliminary testing and conducting preliminary tests. The fifth stage is to carry out a detailed research.

231. The protection of the earth's surface also consists in keeping a register of historical pollution of the earth's surface, which pursuant to Article 101c is run by the General Director for Environmental Protection. The register collects information about, among others, potential historical pollution of earth's surface and historical pollution of the earth's surface, including its characteristics, location, time of emergence and the current status of the territory where it emerged. An important element of the register is the collection of information on carried remediation and the environmental effects achieved as a result. The register also contains information about the activities carried out in areas where potential historical pollution of the earth's surface or historical pollution of the earth's surface has emerged, currently and, if such information is available, in the past. The register also contains information on the name and surname or name of the landowner and the address of his residence or registered office, as well as the entity obliged to remediation and the address of his residence or registered office.

232. The entry on the potential historical pollution of the earth's surface is made by the regional director for environmental protection, by way of a decision addressed to the person administering the earth's surface, which contains an indication of the place where potential historical pollution of the earth's surface occurs.

72. Dz. U. 2016, item 1395.

Such an entry includes the indication of the current status of the territory as the territory with respectively potential historical pollution of the earth's surface, historical pollution of the earth's surface, historical pollution of the earth's surface during remediation or the territory where remediation was terminated.

233. The detailed scope of information collected in the register of historical pollution of the earth's surface is defined in the Regulation of the Minister of the Environment of 1 September 2016 regarding the register of historical pollution of the earth's surface.[73]

234. The county commissioner identifies potential historical pollution of the earth's surface, which pursuant to the Article 101d of Environmental Protection Act shall be determined by establishing activities that are likely to cause historical pollution of the earth's surface, establishing a list of substances causing a risk expected to emerge in the ground due to activity, analysis of available information on the risk of earth's pollution and, if necessary, the implementation of the first stage of research on soil and earths pollution by laboratory.

235. According to the Article 101e of the Environmental Protection Act, administrator of the earth's surface who stated historical pollution of the earth's surface, is obliged to immediately report this fact to the regional director for environmental protection, whereas the county commissioner may receive such a notification from any person who has identified potential historical pollution of the earth's surface. Subsequently, administrator of the earth's surface where historical pollution has emerged is obliged to carry out remediation.[74] Exceptionally, remediation is carried out by the regional director for environmental protection if it is not possible to initiate an enforcement proceeding regarding the obligation to carry out remediation against the administrator of the earth's surface or if the execution proved ineffective. Respectively, remediation is carried out by the regional director for environmental protection also in a situation when the administrator of the earth's surface proves that the pollution that emerged after the day when he became the administrator, has been caused by other responsible party, against whom enforcement procedure regarding the obligation to carry out remediation cannot be commenced, or if the execution proved ineffective and if due to risk to human health or the possibility of irreversible damage to the environment, it is necessary to carry it out immediately.

236. Pursuant to Article 101j, the regional director for environmental protection, sets the schedule of his tasks regarding the historical pollution of the earth's surface and updates it at least every five years it. Remediation of historical pollution of the earth's surface is carried out in accordance with the agreed remediation plan, and

73. Dz. U. 2016, item 1397.
74. The above does not apply if the administrator of the earth's surface proves that the historical pollution of the earth's surface that emerged after the day when he became the administrator, has been caused by other entity, hereinafter referred to as 'other responsible party'. In this situation, obligation to carry out remediation is transferred upon the other responsible party.

costs are covered by the administrator of the earth's surface unless the remediation is carried out by the regional director for environmental protection. In this case, regional director for environmental protection imposes, by way of a decision, obligation of reimbursement of remediation costs on the administrator, or the other responsible party will be obliged to reimburse remediation costs, if the administrator of the earth's surface proves that historical pollution of the land was caused by the indicated person.

237. The regional director for environmental protection assesses the carried remediation, which in accordance with Article 101n consists in confirming the compliance of remediation with the established remediation plan. If the remediation was found to be noncompliant with the established remediation plan, the provisions on administrative enforcement proceeding shall apply.

238. Remediation may consist in removing pollution, at least to an acceptable level of the substances causing risk in the earth, or other action, leading to the removal of a significant threat to human health and the environment, considering the current and, if possible, planned way of using the territory. There shall be indicated activities consisting in reducing the amount of pollutants or reducing the possibility of pollutants spreading and controlling pollution by periodically conducting earth's pollution tests at a given time or consisting in self-cleaning of the earth's surface.

239. The protection of the earth's surface also consists of appropriate principles related to the use of soil or earth for earthworks. In that regard, the basic principle formulated in Article 101r should be noted, which explicitly prohibits the use of soil or earth for earthworks, including sludge used for this work coming from the bottom of water bodies or running waters, if the permissible content of the substance causing the risk is exceeded for the ground where the soil or earth is used.

240. In regard to mechanical impacts on the earth's surface, there should be indicated the protective actions of the county commissioner, who, pursuant to Article 110a, conducts an observation of the territories threatened by mass movements of the earth and territories where these movements emerge, as well as he keeps a register containing information about these territories. The way of determining territories threatened by mass movements of the earth, methods, scope and frequency of observation of territories threatened by mass movements of the earth, information which on the register of territories threatened by mass movements the earth shall contain and the manner of conducting, form and layout of the register are specified in the Regulation of the Minister of the Environment of 20 June 2007 on information on mass movements of the earth. Pursuant to §3 of the Regulation, observations called 'monitoring' are carried out for territories where mass movements of the earth have emerged, and for areas threatened with mass movements of the earth either that either cause or may cause a direct threat to human life, technical or communication infrastructure. The register is kept in the form of electronic database, in a commonly available format, which should contain graphical data in the form of maps of territories where mass movements of the earth emerge (and areas threatened with the possibility of mass movements of the earth), registration cards, areas threatened by mass movements of the earth and landslides.

Chapter 6. Noise Pollution

241. The basic problems of environmental protection against noise are regulated in Part V of the Environmental Protection Act. Pursuant to Article 112, activities to ensure the best acoustic state in the environment, which are identified as noise protection, are carried out simultaneously in two aspects. First, it consists in keeping the noise level below or at least at the admissible level. Second, they indicate the obligation to take actions that reduce the noise level at least to the admissible level when it is not maintained.

242. Noise is defined in Article 3(5) of the Environmental Protection Act as sounds with frequencies from 16 Hz to 16,000 Hz. It should be emphasized, that noise is a type of energy that is released directly or indirectly, as a result of human activity, into the air, water, soil or land in the form of emissions. However, the provisions of the Act do not apply to the noise generated due to the common use of the environment.

243. The minister responsible for environmental affairs, by way of a regulation, defines a way of determining the value of the noise indicator, considering the need to conduct long-term policy in the area of noise protection, the need to apply noise indicators to determine and control the conditions of use of the environment and binding standardization documents in this area.[75]

244. The Regulation of the Minister of the Environment of 10 November 2010 specifies the method of establishing the value of the L_{DWN} noise index, indicating the appropriate formula with the reservation that the variability of noise sources throughout the year and variability of atmospheric conditions and the variety of factors affecting the propagation of noise in the environment should be included.

245. The minister responsible for the environmental affairs, pursuant to the Article 113 of the Environmental Protection Act, and in agreement with the minister for health, determines acceptable levels of noise in the environment guided by the need to ensure adequate protection of the environment against noise and taking into account the EU law relating to the assessment and management of noise in the environment. Pursuant to the Regulation of the Minister of the Environment of 14 June 2007 on admissible noise levels in the environment, the noise limits are different for areas for residential buildings, hospitals, and social welfare homes, buildings related to permanent or temporary stay of children and adolescents. Different admissible noise levels are set for territories designated for health resorts, recreation, and leisure purposes or for residential and service purposes. When determining the permissible noise level, the type of object or activity being the source of noise and the periods referred to by noise levels as reference time are also considered.

75. According to the Art. 112a noise indicator is understood as the noise parameters determined by sound level A expressed in decibels (dB).

246. The problem of combating noise is also provided for in the regulations related to the preparation of a local management plan, in which territories exposed to the exceedance of the admissible noise level should be included. According to the Article 114 Environmental Protection Act, if in closed areas and areas designated for production, keeping and storage activities there are residential buildings, hospitals, social welfare homes or buildings related to permanent or temporary stay of children and adolescents, protection against noise consists in applying technical solutions ensuring appropriate acoustic conditions in buildings. The territories designated for residential housing, hospitals, social welfare homes or buildings related to permanent or temporary stay of children and adolescents located on the border of the road lane are similarly treated. In the absence of a local spatial management plan, the competent authorities assess whether the area is exposed to the exceedance of the admissible noise, on the basis of the actual management and use of the given and neighbouring properties.

247. If the environmental protection authority determines, on the basis of its own measurements, measurements done by the provincial inspector for environmental protection or measurements of the obliged entity, that the admissible noise level is exceeded outside the establishment,[76] due to the activity of this establishment, the authority issues a decision on an acceptable noise level. The decision sets out noise levels outside the establishment with respect to the types of territories affected by the establishment. Such a decision may include the specification of requirements not to exceed the admissible noise levels outside the establishment.

248. Noise protection may also consist, in accordance with Article 116 of the Environmental Protection Act, on the introduction by the *poviat* council, by way of a resolution, restriction or prohibition of the use of water vessels or some of their types on specific surface water bodies and running waters, if it is necessary to ensure adequate acoustic conditions on areas designated for recreational and leisure purposes. Corresponding restrictions and prohibitions on inland waters are introduced in a way of regulation by the minister responsible for environmental affairs[77] in agreement with the minister for transport. Restrictions may not, however, apply to vessels that need to be used for public safety purposes or to maintain watercourses and reservoirs.

249. According to Article 117 assessment of the acoustic state of the environment and observation of changes are carried out within the framework of State Environmental Monitoring on the basis of the results of measurements of noise levels, including other data, in particular, demographic and data on the management and use of territory. Such activities are obligatory for agglomerations with more than 100,000 inhabitants.

---

76. This does not apply to situations where noise arises due to the operation of roads, railway lines, tram lines, cableways, ports, and airports or the activity of a natural person who is not an entrepreneur.
77. Such regulation establishes the name or other description of the watercourse or reservoir, or parts thereof, on which restrictions or prohibitions apply. The types of water vessels related to prohibitions or restrictions as well as prohibitions and restrictions regarding the use of vessels in the period of the year, days of the week or days, respectively, are specified.

250. For the purpose of assessing the acoustic condition of the environment, the county commissioner prepares, every five years, acoustic maps, which pursuant to the Article 118 of the Environmental Protection Act, in the descriptive part, should include, in particular, the characteristics of the area to be assessed, identification and characterization of noise sources, acoustic conditions resulting from the local spatial management plan, identification of areas threatened by noise or population at risk of noise. The graphical part usually includes information in the form of maps displaying noise emitted from individual sources and the acoustic status of the environment, with the indication of areas where the permissible noise levels are exceeded, with reference to the local spatial management plan. The acoustic map, developed on copies of maps included in the national geodetic and cartographic resources, is the basic source of data used to inform the public about noise hazards, to develop data for state environmental monitoring and to create and update programs for environmental protection against noise.

251. The detailed scope of data included in the acoustic maps and their layout and presentation for use in developing data for state environmental monitoring, creating and updating programs on environmental protection against noise and informing the public about noise hazards are set out in the Regulation of the Minister for the Environment of 1 October 2007 on the detailed scope of data included in acoustic maps and their layout and presentation.[78]

252. Another tool to decrease noise is the possibility of the *poviat* council to designate, by way of a resolution, a silent area in the agglomeration[79] or outside the agglomeration,[80] considering the specific noise protection needs of these areas and providing requirements to maintain noise levels at least at an existing level.

253. The amount of noise emission is determined and assessed on the basis of noise measurements in the environment. According to the Article 119 Environmental Protection Act, for areas where the noise level exceeds the admissible level, programs for the protection of the environment against noise are created, the aim of which is to adjust the noise level to the admissible level. The program should be specified within one year from the date of presentation of the acoustic map by the entity obliged to prepare it and updated at least once every five years, and in case of circumstances justifying a change in the plan or implementation schedule. The minister responsible for environmental affairs determines, by way of a regulation, the specific requirements to be met by the program for the protection of the environment against noise.

78. Dz. U. 2007, No. 187, item 1340 with amendments.
79. Pursuant to the Art. 3(10a) of the Environmental Protection Act, it is the area in which there are no exceedances of the admissible noise levels expressed in the noise indicator.
80. Pursuant to the Art. 3(10b) of the Environmental Protection Act, it is an area that is not exposed to the impact of traffic noise, industrial noise or noise from recreational and leisure activities.

254. In accordance with the Regulation of the Minister of the Environment of 14 October 2002 on detailed requirements to be met by the program for the protection of the environment against noise,[81] the program consists of three indispensable parts. The descriptive part contains a description of the area covered by the scope of the program, provides violation of admissible noise levels in the environment, specifies the basic directions and the scope of activities necessary to restore admissible noise levels in the environment, program implementation date, program implementation costs, sources of program financing, and an indication of the types of information and documents used to control and document the implementation of the program. The part specifying the limitations and obligations resulting from the implementation of the program includes the indication of competent authorities and entities using the environment together with their obligations. The last, third part concerning the justification of the scope of issues contains data and conclusions resulting from the acoustic maps, evaluation of the implementation of the previous program for the program being developed once again and analysis of materials, documents and publications used to develop the program.

255. According to the Article 120a of Environmental Protection Act, the provincial inspector for environmental protection keeps a register containing information on the acoustic state of the environment, based on measurements, tests and analyses performed as a part of State Environmental Monitoring. The provincial inspector for environmental protection submits to the Chief Inspector for Environmental Protection, by 31 March each year, information from the register for the previous year. The Regulation of the Minister of the Environment of 25 April 2008 on specific requirements regarding the register containing information on the acoustic state of the environment[82] specifies types of measurement results, tests and analyses subject to registration, a register system containing information on the acoustic state of the environment, and a form of recording measurement results, research, and analysis.

256. Relevant regulations related to noise reduction can also be found in special regulations, not directly related to the Environmental Protection Act. In that regard shall be indicated the provisions of Article 119 (5) of the Act of 3 July 2002 – Aviation Law, which is an exception to the principle of free access to Polish airspace. The Regulation of the Minister of Infrastructure of 19 May 2004 on flight bans for aircraft not meeting the environmental protection requirements in the scope of noise protection formulates in §3 a ban on performing air operations at an airport located on the territory of the Republic of Poland by aircraft which does not meet certain requirements.

257. The basis for noise restricting regulations is also provided by Article 11 (1) of the Act of 7 July 1994 – Construction Law,[83] which indicates that the minister competent for health shall determine, by regulation, admissible concentrations, and intensities of factors harmful to health emitted by construction materials, devices

81. Dz. U. 2002, No. 179, item 1498.
82. Dz. U. 2008, No. 82, item 500.
83. Dz. U. 2018, item 1202 with amendments.

and elements of equipment in premises intended for human residence.[84] Pursuant to §5 of the Order of the Minister of Health and Social Welfare of 12 March 1996 on admissible concentrations and intensities of harmful factors emitted by construction materials, devices and elements of equipment in premises intended for human residence, the admissible noise level emitted by devices and installations in the premises are defined by the Polish Norm PN-B-02151/02.

258. Furthermore, a reference to issues regarding noise restrictions can be found in the executive regulations. Regulation of the Minister of Labour and Social Policy of 26 September 1997 on general provisions regarding health and safety at work,[85] which in §15 specifies that in work premises, where there are factors harmful to health, including noise, technical solutions preventing the entry of these factors to other work and sanitary premises should be used. According to §45 of the Regulation, workplaces outside the premises should be located and organized so that employees are protected against hazards related in particular to noise that is harmful to health. The issue is addressed in particular in the fifth chapter of the Regulation – Protection against noise. Pursuant to §78, the employer is obliged to ensure protection of employees against hazards related to noise exposure, in particular to ensure the use of technological processes that do not cause excessive noise, machines and other technical devices that cause the smallest possible noise, and to implement solutions that lower the noise levels in work processes. In workplaces where, despite the application of possible technical and organizational solutions, the noise level exceeds acceptable standards, the employer is obliged to ensure in particular that employees receive their hearing protection, to limit the time of exposure to noise, or to mark noise zones.

259. The Regulation of the Minister of Transport, Construction and Marine Management of 7 August 2012 on the requirements to be met by aircraft due to environmental protection, in §2 specifies that aircraft should meet the requirements in regard to the protection of the environment against noise, relating to noise assessment measures, reference noise measurement points, admissible noise levels, tolerance limits for admissible noise levels and reference noise certification procedures.

260. Regulation of the Minister of Economy of 21 December 2005 on essential requirements for devices used outdoors in regard to noise emission to the environment, determines in particular the methods of measuring noise emitted by devices intended for outdoor use and types of devices intended for outdoor use subject to a noise emission limitation, for which a notified body's participation is necessary for the conformity assessment process.

261. Lastly, it should be noted a Regulation of the Council of Ministers of 29 September 2001 on the amount of unit punishment rates for exceeding the admissible noise level, which provides four compartments, for the lowest exceedance

84. M. P. 1996, No. 19, item 231.
85. Dz. U. 2003, No. 169, item 1650 with amendments.

from 1 to 5 dB in the daytime it sets PLN 11.37 per each dB exceeded. For the highest exceedance above 15 dB at night, it is PLN 51.26 per dB exceeded.

Chapter 7. Radiation and Vibrations

§1. Protection Against Electromagnetic Fields

262. Protection against electromagnetic fields is regulated in section VII of the Environmental Protection Act. Pursuant to the Article 121, it consists in ensuring the best possible state of the environment by maintaining levels of electromagnetic fields below admissible or at least at these levels and reducing the levels of electromagnetic fields, at least to admissible ones, when they are exceeded.

263. The Regulation of the Minister of the Environment of 30 October 2003 on the admissible levels of electromagnetic fields in the environment and methods of verifying compliance with these levels[86] determines acceptable levels of electromagnetic fields in the environment, differentiated for areas intended for residential building, places accessible to the public, frequency ranges of electromagnetic fields for which physical parameters characterizing the impact of electromagnetic fields on the environment are determined. It also defines methods for checking compliance with the admissible levels of electromagnetic fields, and methods for determining compliance with the admissible levels of electromagnetic fields.

264. The basic obligations of the installation operator and user of the device emitting electromagnetic fields are specified in Article 122a of the Environmental Protection Act. They are obliged to carry out measurements of electromagnetic field levels in the environment immediately after starting the use of the installation or device, as well as each time the operating conditions of the installation or device change.

265. The results of measurements are transferred to the provincial inspector for environmental protection and to the provincial sanitary inspector. The assessment of electromagnetic field levels in the environment and observation of changes is carried out within the framework of State Environmental Monitoring. The provincial inspector for environmental protection conducts periodic studies of the levels of electromagnetic fields in the environment.

266. Regulation of the Minister of the Environment of 12 November 2007 on the scope and way of conducting periodic studies of the levels of electromagnetic fields in the environment[87] defines the scope and way of conducting periodic studies of the levels of electromagnetic fields in the environment by provincial inspectors for environmental protection, including a way of selection of measurement points, the required frequency of measurements and ways of presenting measurement results. The scope of conducting studies of electromagnetic fields in the environment includes measurements of the intensity of the electrical component of the electromagnetic field in the frequency range of at least 3 MHz to 3,000 MHz at the measurement points.

---

86. Dz. U. 2003, No. 192, item 1883.
87. Dz. U. 2007, No. 221, item 1645.

267. As stipulated in the Article 124, the provincial inspector for environment protection keeps an annually updated register containing information on areas where the admissible levels of electromagnetic fields in the environment have been exceeded, specifying the exceedances for areas designated for residential buildings and places accessible to the public.

268. Regulation of the Minister of the Environment of 2 July 2010 on the notification of installations generating electromagnetic fields[88] specifies the standard form for the notification of installations generating electromagnetic fields and detailed requirements regarding the scope of data included in the notification of installations generating electromagnetic fields.

269. Regulation of the Minister of Family, Labour and Social Policy of 29 June 2016 on health and safety at work related to exposure to electromagnetic fields[89] sets out the requirements for recognizing technical facilities emitting electromagnetic field having an impact on health and safety at work. Subsequently, the requirements regarding the measurements and the assessment of exposure to electromagnetic fields, measures, and limits as well as the assessment of the direct impact of the electromagnetic field on the human body are determined. The Regulation also defines the conditions for protection against harmful, dangerous or arduous effects of direct or indirect electromagnetic field effects and protective measures used to prevent electromagnetic hazards.

270. Lastly, there should be noted specific regulations regarding protection against electromagnetic fields contained in the regulation of the Prime Minister of 9 December 2014 on the way of proceeding in the situation when the device generating the electromagnetic field causes harmful interference with the operation of another device.[90]

§2. Protection Against Ionizing Radiation

271. The Act of 29 November 2000 – Atomic Law[91] defines activities related to the peaceful use of nuclear energy associated with real and potential exposure to ionizing radiation from artificial radioactive sources, nuclear materials, devices producing ionizing radiation, radioactive waste and spent nuclear fuel. It also indicates the competent authorities in matters of nuclear safety and radiological protection. The Act also defines the rules for the monitoring of radioactive pollution and regulates the actions to be taken in the case of radiation events, as well as in the case of long-term exposure following a radiation event. There are also specified special rules for the protection of people against threats resulting from the use of ionizing radiation for medical purposes.

88. Dz. U. 2010, No. 130, item 879.
89. Dz. U. 2018, item 331.
90. Dz. U. 2014, item 1821.
91. Dz. U. 2018, item 792 with amendments.

272. Chapter 3 of the Act indicates nuclear safety and radiological protection and the health protection of employees. According to Article 7 of the Act, compliance with the requirements of nuclear safety and radiological protection is the responsibility of the head of the organizational unit performing activities related to exposure.

273. Chapter 3a of the Act regulates the use of ionizing radiation for medical purposes. According to Article 33a use of ionizing radiation for medical purposes includes patients' exposures resulting from medical examinations and treatment, including initial and periodic examinations of employees, persons subject to seeding tests with the use of ionizing radiation, healthy persons or patients participating in medical experiments or persons subjected to research with use of ionizing radiation for medical and legal purposes, when the undertaking of these tests does not result from health indications.

274. The sources of ionizing radiation are defined in Chapter 6 of the Act. According to Article 43 sources of ionizing radiation are controlled, and radioactive sources are also recorded.

275. The specification of regulations regarding protection against ionizing radiation can be found, *inter alia*, in the Regulation of the Council of Ministers of 27 April 2004 on protection against ionizing radiation of external workers exposed during work in controlled territory.[92] The Regulation defines specific obligations of the head of the organizational unit, external employer and external employee in the scope of radiological protection of external employees exposed during work in the controlled territory. It also defines the information placed by the head of the organizational unit, the external employer and the authorized physician in the dosimetric passport and determines the procedure of issuing and standard form of the dosimetric passport.

276. The legislator paid particular attention to issues related to the transport of nuclear materials, sources of ionizing radiation, radioactive waste and spent nuclear fuel. Articles 58–62 define respectively, the preparation of nuclear materials for transport and transport in a way preventing from the occurrence of a self-sustaining nuclear fission chain reaction and compliant with the principles of physical protection.

277. When preparing for transportation and transporting nuclear materials, sources of ionizing radiation, excluding devices producing ionizing radiation, radioactive waste and spent nuclear fuel, the hazards that their physical and chemical properties may pose have to be considered, as well the requirements and conditions for the transport of dangerous goods have to be met.

278. Exposure of persons participating in transport, including loading and unloading of transported nuclear materials, radioactive waste, spent nuclear fuel and

92. Dz. U. No. 102, item 1064.

sources of ionizing radiation, excluding devices generating ionizing radiation, is subject to control, and radiation doses received by these persons cannot exceed the limit doses.

279. The head of an organizational unit conducting activities involving the transport of nuclear materials, radioactive sources, radioactive waste or spent nuclear fuel, requiring a permit, shall submit a report on transported nuclear materials, radioactive sources, radioactive waste or spent nuclear fuel to the President the Agency. The President of the Agency shall specify requirements regarding the reports in the permit.

280. Import into the territory of the Republic of Poland and exports from this territory of nuclear materials, radioactive sources and devices containing such sources, as well as import and export of radioactive waste and spent nuclear fuel, are carried out on the basis of a permit or notification for performing these activities and within the scope of appropriate permit or notification.

281. Chapter 8a of the Act specifies the importation into the territory of the Republic of Poland, export from the territory of the Republic of Poland and transit through this territory of radioactive waste and spent nuclear fuel.

282. Supervision and control of compliance with nuclear safety and radiological protection, in accordance with the Article 63 of the Act, are performed by nuclear regulatory authorities – if the authority competent for issuing a permit or accepting a notification is the President of Agency or a provincial sanitary inspector, commander of a military preventive medicine centre or a state sanitary inspector of the Ministry of the Interior and Administration – within the scope of activities on which these authorities issue permits. Pursuant to Article 109, the President of the National Atomic Energy Agency is the central body of government administration competent in matters of nuclear safety and radiological protection within the scope defined by the Act.

§3. Protection Against Vibrations

283. Protection against vibration includes protection against mechanical vibrations, which according to the Regulation of the Minister of Economy and Labour of 5 August 2005 on health and safety at work related to noise exposure or mechanical vibrations,[93] are oscillations or tremors transmitted to the human body through parts of the body that are in direct contact with the vibrating oscillating; as a harmful factor in the work environment, it occurs in the form of local oscillations or general oscillations.

284. The sources of oscillations with general effects are, for example, floors, platforms, where workstations are located, seats and floors of means of transport,

93. Dz. U. No. 157, item 1318.

construction machines, metallurgical hammers. The sources of local vibrations are usually manual impact tools, manually operated machine and vehicle control levers. Oscillations cause changes in the human body depending on the place of entry into the body. Hence, we distinguish oscillations with general effects penetrating into the body through the legs, pelvis, and back as well as local ones acting through the upper limbs. Due to the prevalence of mechanical oscillations in the work environment, it is important to measure and test the level of hazards and assess the occupational risk of injury.[94]

285. Protection against vibrations consists primarily of technical measures and legal regulations that are to limit the penetration of vibrations with a level of negative impact especially on human health and the environment.[95]

286. The magnitude of the intensity of mechanical vibrations is determined by Polish Standards, among which can be indicated: PN-EN ISO 5349-1: 2004 – *Mechanical vibrations. Measurement and determination of human exposure to vibrations transmitted by upper limbs. Part 1* and *PN-EN ISO 5349-2: 2004 – Mechanical vibrations. Measurement and determination of human exposure to vibrations transmitted by upper limbs. Part 2.*

287. The most important regulations regarding protection against vibrations, besides the above-mentioned, are included in the provisions of the Act of 12 September 2002 on Standardization,[96] in all legal acts regulating health and safety at work, and norms of Construction Law with its executive acts.

94. H. Cwirko, Hałas i drgania mechaniczne, ABC nr 133295, Lex 2018.
95. Boć, Nowacki, Samborska-Boć, *Ochrona środowiska*, 324.
96. Dz. U. 2015, item 1483.

Chapter 8. Other Sectors

§1. Renewable Energy Sources

288. The Act of 20 February 2015 on renewable energy sources[97] defines the rules and conditions for conducting operations in the field of electricity generation, agricultural biogas, and bioliquids. It also regulates mechanisms and instruments supporting their production in renewable energy installations, rules for issuing guarantees of origin of electricity produced from renewable energy sources in renewable energy installations and principles of implementing the National Action Plan in regard to the energy from renewable sources. The subject of regulation of the Act are also the conditions and way of certification of installers of a renewable energy source installation as well as principles of international cooperation in the field of renewable energy sources and joint investment projects.

289. Article 2 of the Act defines the basic concepts related to renewable energy sources. The most important ones include:

- Biogas: gas obtained from biomass, in particular from installations for treating animal or vegetable waste, sewage treatment plants, and landfills.
- Agricultural biogas: gas obtained in the process of methane fermentation of agricultural raw materials, agricultural by-products, liquid or solid animal manure, by-products, waste or residues from the processing of agricultural products or forest biomass, or plant biomass.
- Biomass: a biodegradable portion of products, waste or residues of biological origin from agriculture, including plant and animal substances, forestry and related industries, including fisheries and aquaculture.
- Biomass of agricultural origin: biomass from energy crops, as well as waste or residues from agricultural production and industry processing its products.
- Bioliquids: liquid fuels for energy purposes other than in transport, including for generating electricity or heat, generated from biomass.
- Biochar: high-energy solid fuel with a calorific value of not less than 21 GJ/t produced in the process of thermal processing of solid substances of vegetable or animal origin, biodegradable and derived from products, waste, and residues from agricultural and forestry production.
- Energy wood: raw wood material, which due to its qualitative and dimensional characteristics has a reduced technical and functional value preventing its industrial use, as well as the wood material being biomass of agricultural origin.
- Aerothermal energy: non-ergogenic energy stored in the form of heat in the air in a given area.
- Geothermal energy: non-anthropogenic energy accumulated in the form of heat under the surface of the earth.
- Hydrothermal energy: non-ergogenic energy accumulated in the form of heat in surface waters.

97. Dz. U. 2018, item 1229 with amendments.

– Hydropower: the energy of inland surface water decline, excluding energy obtained from pumping work in pumped storage power plants or hydroelectric power stations with a pump element.

290. Pursuant to the Article 3 of the Act, the commencement and execution of the economic activity in the field of electricity production from renewable energy sources requires obtaining a concession under the terms and conditions specified in the Act of 10 April 1997 – Energy Law,[98] with exception to the generation of electricity in micro-installation, in a small installation, from agricultural biogas and exclusively from bioliquids.

291. As stipulated in Article 4 of the Act, the seller settles the amount of electricity entered by the prosumer[99] into the electricity network against the amount of electricity taken from this network in a quantity ratio of 1 to 0.7, except for micro-installations with a total installed electric power of not more than 10 kW, for which this ratio is 1 to 0.8.

292. The Act, in the following chapters, sets out in detail the rules and conditions for conducting operations in the field of electricity generation from renewable energy sources in micro-installation and small installations, excluding electricity generation from agricultural biogas or bioliquids (Chapter 2), rules and conditions for conducting activities in the field of generating electricity from agricultural biogas or bioliquids and production of agricultural biogas or bioliquids (Chapter 3), mechanisms and instruments supporting the production of electricity from renewable energy sources, agricultural biogas and heat, in renewable energy installations (Chapter 4), guarantees of origin of electricity generated from renewable energy sources in renewable energy installations (Chapter 5), national renewable energy action plan (Chapter 6), conditions and procedure for issuing certificates for installers of micro-installations, small installations and installations of a renewable energy source with a total thermal installed power of not more than 600 kW and accreditation of training providers (Chapter 7) and principles of international cooperation in the field of renewable energy sources and joint investment projects (Chapter 8).

293. The Act also provides the legal basis for issuing specific provisions included in the Regulations, which include the Regulation of the Minister of Energy of 7 August 2018 regarding the requirements for the calculation, measurement, and registration of the amount of electricity or heat produced in renewable energy installations,[100] Regulation of the Minister of Energy of 18 May 2017 on the detailed scope of the obligation and technical conditions for the purchase of heat from renewable energy sources and the conditions for connecting the installation to the

98. Dz. U. 2018, item 755 with amendments.
99. Prosumer is the final consumer purchasing electricity on the basis of a comprehensive contract, producing electricity only from renewable energy sources in micro-installations for its own consumption, not related to the economic activity regulated by the Act of 6 March 2018 – Entrepreneurs Law (Dz. U. item 646).
100. Dz. U. item 1596.

network,[101] Regulation of the Minister of Energy of 18 May 2017 on the amount and way of paying fees for the examination, issuing the certificate, extending its validity and on granting accreditation,[102] Regulation of Minister of Energy of 9 May 2017 on specific conditions of granting accreditation to training providers in the area of renewable energy sources and on training and examinations for persons applying for the issue or extension of the validity of the certificate[103] or, finally, the Regulation of the Minister of Energy of 9 December 2016 on the method of calculating the intensity ratio of electricity consumption by an industrial customer.[104]

§2. Protection Against Serious Accidents

294. Legal instruments for counteracting a serious industrial accident are formulated in section II of the Environmental Protection Act.

295. Pursuant to Article 3(23), by a serious accident shall be understood an event, in particular, emission, fire or explosion, emerged during an industrial process, storage or transport, in which there are one or more hazardous substances, leading to an immediate threat to human life or health or to the environment or leading to such threat with a delay. A serious industrial accident is defined in Article 3(24) as a serious accident in the plant.

296. According to the Article 248, a plant posing a threat of a serious industrial accident, depending on the type, category and quantity of a dangerous substance in the plant, is considered to be a plant with an increased risk of accident, or a plant with a high risk of the accident. The decisive in this respect is the regulation of the Minister of Development of 29 January 2016 on the types and quantities of dangerous substances in the plant, deciding about the plant being classified as a plant with an increased or high risk of a serious industrial accident.[105]

297. Chapter 2 of the Act specifies the obligations of an operator of the plant that poses a threat of an industrial accident, which includes, in particular, reporting the plant to the competent authority of the State Fire Service, preparing a program for the prevention of serious industrial accidents, developing and implementing a safety management system that guarantees an appropriate level of protection for people and environment, which is part of the overall plant management system, development of a safety report. The detailed rules for the preparation of the report are set out in the Regulation of the Minister of Development of 23 February 2016 on the safety report of a high-risk plant.[106] Furthermore, obligations of the plant operator include submission of the safety report to the provincial head of the State Fire Service and the provincial inspector for environmental protection and – at least every

101. Dz. U. item 1084.
102. Dz. U. item 1038.
103. Dz. U. item 1034.
104. Dz. U. item 2054.
105. Dz. U. item 138.
106. Dz. U. item 278.

five years – to analyse the safety report and introduce substantive changes or, for example to publicize the most important information related to the safety of the plant.

298. According to the Article 264, operator of the plant with an increased risk or high risk, in case of an industrial accident is obliged to immediately notify the competent State Fire Service and provincial environmental protection inspector, immediately inform the competent authorities about the circumstances of the industrial accident, hazardous substances related to the industrial accident and rescue actions taken, as well as activities aimed at limiting the effects of industrial accident and preventing its repetition.

299. Responsibilities of administrative bodies related to industrial accident are specified in Chapter 3 of the Act. These include, in particular, issuing opinions on programs to prevent accidents, approving safety reports, issuing opinions on internal emergency plans, establishing external emergency plans for the area exposed to the effects of an industrial accident outside a high-risk facility and in case of a threat of industrial accident or occurrence of industrial accident they immediately begin to implement the external emergency plan. According to the Article 268a, public administration bodies, and entities listed in the external emergency plan, in case of an industrial accident, are obliged to inform about its occurrence persons exposed to its effects.

300. Section III of the Act defines international cooperation in the field of preventing and combating an industrial accident of cross-border range. The provincial head of the State Fire Service is responsible for these actions, and the minister responsible for environmental affairs, after obtaining information about the emergence of an industrial accident on the territory of the Republic of Poland, immediately notifies the state on whose territory the effects of this accident may occur and provides all relevant information. In addition, the minister responsible for environmental affairs informs the European Commission.

301. Pursuant to the Article 271b of the Act, the Chief Inspector for Environmental Protection is the competent authority to carry out the tasks of the minister responsible for the environmental affairs in matters of preventing serious accidents, cross-border effects of industrial accidents and emergency pollution of border waters.

Part II. Natural Conservation and Management

Chapter 1. Introduction

§1. Legal Bases

302. The basic law in the Polish legal system of environmental protection, including the natural environment, is covered by the Environmental Protection Act.[107] Pursuant to Article 81 of the Environmental Protection Act, protection of the natural environment's resources is performed under the general framework of the Act, supplemented by other statutes addressing particular elements of the natural environment. Sectoral legislation includes:

(1) the Geological and Mining Act of 9 June 2011,[108] which establishes the principles of mineral resource management and extraction of deposits;
(2) the Nature Protection Act of 16 April 2004,[109] which establishes the principles for the protection of areas and objects of natural virtue, landscapes, animals and vegetation threatened with extinction, as well as trees, shrubs and greenery;
(3) the Water Act of 20 July 2017,[110] which establishes the principles for the water protection;
(4) the Forest Act of 28 September 1991,[111] establishing the principles for the protection of forests;
(5) the Inland Fishing Act of 18 April 1985,[112] the Nature Protection Act, the Hunting Act of 13 October 1995,[113] and the Fishing Act of 19 February 2014,[114] all of which address issues related to the protection of wild animals;

107. Dz. U. 2018, item 799 with amendments.
108. Dz. U. 2017, No. 2126 with amendments.
109. Dz. U. 2018, item 1614.
110. Dz. U. 2017, item 1566 with amendments.
111. Dz. U. 2017, item 788 with amendments.
112. Dz. U. 2018, item 1476 with amendments.
113. Dz. U. 2018, item 2033 with amendments.
114. Dz. U. 2014, item 1476 with amendments.

(6) the Animal Protection Act of 21 August 1997,[115] concerning the protection of farm and domestic animals;
(7) the Agricultural and Forest Land Protection Act of 3 February 1995,[116] establishing the principles for the protection of agricultural and forest lands.

§2. Protection of Nature: Definition

303. The Nature Protection Act declares that the protection of nature consists of the maintenance, sustainable exploitation and renewal of nature's resources, creations and constituent elements, including:

- wild plants, animals and fungi;
- plants, animals and fungi under species protection;
- migrating animals;
- natural habitats;
- habitats threatened with extinction, rare and protected species of plants, animals and fungi;
- animate and inanimate creations of nature as well as fossilized remains of plants and animals;
- landscapes;
- greenery in cities and rural areas;
- wooded areas.[117]

§3. Objective of Nature Protection

304. The legislator indicates that the objectives of nature protection are to preserve ecological processes and the stability of ecosystems, to preserve biodiversity, to preserve the country's geological and paleontological heritage; to ensure continuity in the existence of species of plants, animals and fungi along with their habitats through the maintenance or restoration to the proper state of protection; the protection of the virtues of landscapes, greenery in cities and rural areas, and wooded areas; the maintenance and restoration of natural habitats as well as other natural resources, creations and constituent elements, together with forming proper attitudes towards nature through education, information and the promotion of natural protection efforts.[118]

305. The objectives of nature protection thus established are to be realized by:

(1) considering the requirements of nature protection in strategies, programs and program documents, in environmental protection programmes adopted by local self-government bodies, in the national conception of spatial management, in provincial development strategies, in provincial spatial management

115. Dz. U. 2017, item 1840.
116. Dz. U. 2017, item 1167 with amendments.
117. Article 2(1) of the Nature Protection Act.
118. Article 2(2) of the Nature Protection Act.

plans, in communal development strategies, in municipal spatial management plans and spatial plans for internal waters, territorial waters and exclusive economic zones, and in commercial and investment activities;

(2) encompassing natural resources, creations and constituent elements with forms of nature protection;

(3) developing and carrying out the determinations of plans for the protection of areas under legal protection, as well as programmes for the protection of species, habitats and migration routes for protected species;

(4) carrying out a programme for the protection and sustainable exploitation of biodiversity, together with a plan of action;

(5) conducting educational, informational and promotional activities in respect of nature protection;

(6) conducting scientific research on issues associated with nature protection.

306. The legislator also emphasizes that it is the obligation of public administration bodies, legal persons and other entities, as well as of natural persons, to care for nature as a national heritage and treasure. Public administration authorities also bear the duty to ensure the legal, organizational and financial conditions necessary for the protection of nature, and the legislator additionally obliges public administration authorities, scientific and educational institutions and public mass media to conduct educational, informational and promotional undertakings in the area of nature protection.

§4. Forms of Nature Protection

307. Forms of nature protection are explicitly set out in Article 6 of the Nature Protection Act. Alongside species protection of plants, animals and fungi, the catalogue of these forms includes national parks, nature reserves, landscape parks, protected landscape areas, Natura 2000 sites, natural monuments, documentation sites, ecological sites and nature and landscape complexes. In addition, there is a possibility to establish a border area of natural value, by way of accord, in order to provide jointly for their protection.

Chapter 2. Monuments and Landscapes

§1. Individual Protection of Creations of Nature

308. Within particular forms of nature protection, we may distinguish the protection of individual creations of nature. This refers to specific creations of nature, in particular to natural monuments, documentation sites, ecological use areas and nature and landscape protected complexes. Individual forms of nature protection are established by way of a regulation of the voivode or resolution of the communal council in the event the voivode has not established such forms of nature protection.

§2. Natural Monuments

309. The phrase 'natural monument' was introduced by the German scientist Alexander Humboldt at the turn of the nineteenth century. The status of natural monuments as forms of nature protection is regulated by Article 40 of the Nature Protection Act.

310. In accordance with this provision, natural monuments are individual animate and inanimate creations of nature or collections of them possessing a particular natural, scientific, cultural, historical or landscape value. This category also encompasses creations of nature distinguished from other creations by their individual characteristics, such as trees of impressive dimensions, bushes of natural or foreign species, springs, waterfalls, karst springs, rocks, canyons, boulders and caves.

311. Natural monuments are classified as object forms, i.e., individual forms of nature protection. They are grouped into animate and inanimate natural monuments. Animate natural monuments include individual trees, groups of trees and tree avenues. Inanimate natural monuments are boulders, grottos and caves.

312. The designation of a natural monument is made by way of a resolution of the appropriate communal council. The resolution sets forth the name of the given object or area, its location, the authority responsible for supervision, the particular objectives of protection, and if necessary determinations concerning its active protection and restrictions applicable to the monument. Draft resolutions require consultation with the appropriate regional director for environmental protection.

313. Revocation of the status of natural monument as a form of nature protection takes place by way of a resolution of the communal council in the event of loss of the natural values for which it was established or in the event of the need to realize an investment with a public objective, or as necessary to ensure public safety.

314. For a tree to be designated as a natural monument, its circumference at a height of 1.3 m should be greater than the guideline values established for a given species. Guideline minimum circumferences of native tree species for monumental trees are set on the basis of the instructions for organizing forests in national parks and nature reserves issued by the Ministry of Forestry and Timber Industry.

315. Specimens of particular tree species at the border or outside the border of their natural distribution may also be designated natural monuments while being of smaller sizes. The second essential criterion for assigning monument protection to a given tree is its health. The criterion for recognizing boulders as nature monuments is their circumference as measured at the broadest point, and the minimum circumference is set at 300 cm.

316. A natural monument may be reported by anyone, either in person or by correspondence. Information necessary for identifying the object should be provided, in particular, the object of protection (whether it is a boulder, tree, bush or another object; its estimated circumference and location); if it is located in a city, the address and type of real property should be given, whereas in the case of a forest the name of the forest inspectorate, division and subdivision should be provided. The notification should be accompanied by a sketch or map of the area with the object clearly marked.

317. The minister responsible for environmental affairs may establish, by way of regulation, the criteria for designating animate and inanimate creations of nature as natural monuments, taking into consideration the need to protect trees and bushes due to their size, age, type and historical significance.

318. The criteria for designating inanimate creations of nature as natural monuments are their scientific, aesthetic and landscape significance. Trees constituting natural monuments which are located in undeveloped areas are protected up until the moment of their natural and total disintegration, on condition that they do not constitute a danger to people or property.

319. It is possible with respect to natural monuments to introduce restrictions on the destruction, damage or alteration of the object, the performance of earthworks causing permanent changes in the landform with the exception of those associated with storm or flood protection or with the construction, reconstruction, maintenance or repair of water infrastructure. It is forbidden to damage and pollute soil and to alter hydrographic conditions if such changes do not serve to protect nature or rational agricultural, forest, water or fishery management. It is also forbidden to liquidate, fill up and transform natural water reservoirs, oxbow lakes and wetlands, as well as to empty slurry pits with the exception of fertilizing agricultural lands in use. It is forbidden to change the designation and manner of use of land, as well as to collect stones, including peat and petrification, such as the buried fossils of plant and animal remains, minerals, and amber for commercial purposes. It is equally forbidden to wilfully kill wild animals, destroy their lairs, dens, other shelter and breeding grounds, as well as spawning grounds and laid eggs, with the exception of amateur fishing and activities performed in the framework of rational agricultural, forest, fishery and game management. Restrictions also encompass the gathering, destruction or damaging of plants and fungi in ecological use areas established for the purposes of protecting stations, communities and groupings of protected plants and fungi, and it is forbidden to erect billboards and other similar advertising equipment.

320. The aforementioned restrictions do not apply to work performed in relation to meeting the needs of nature protection upon prior consultation with the authority responsible for establishing a given form of nature protection, as well as to the realization of public purpose investments upon prior consultation with the authority responsible for establishing a given form of nature protection. They also do not apply to tasks resulting from threats to national security nor to eliminating immediate threats to public safety or rescue missions.

321. Data from 2018 shows that the number of natural monuments in Poland is 31,111, of which the most number of natural monuments are present in the voivodeship of Masovia, whilst the least number are in the voivodeship of Opolskie. The oldest tree in Poland is a common yew located in Henryków Lubiański (voivodeship of Lower Silesia), which is over 1,200 years old, over 13 m in height and has a trunk circumference of 5.12 m.[119]

§3. Documentation Sites

322. Under the legal definition, documentation sites are locations of scientific and didactic importance, both indistinguishable on the surface or possible to distinguish, where there are occurrences of geological formations, groupings of petrification or mineral outgrowths, caves, rock outcroppings and silts, as well as closed surface and underground excavations. Additionally, documentation sites may be places in which mineralized fossils of plants and animals are present. Documentation sites are classified as object forms, i.e., individual forms of nature protection.

323. Documentation sites are established by way of a resolution of the communal council. The resolution sets forth the name of the given area, its location, the authority responsible for supervision, the particular objectives of protection, and if necessary determinations concerning its active protection and restrictions applicable to the area or portions of it.

324. The revocation of established nature protection takes place by way of a resolution of the communal council. Draft resolutions require consultation with the appropriate regional director for environmental protection. The revocation of this form of nature protection takes place in the event of loss of the natural values for which it was established or in the event of the need to realize an investment with a public objective, or as necessary to ensure public safety.

119. Central Statistical Office. Environmental Protection 2013, 310 (Warszawa 2013).

325. Documentation sites are often areas which are completely indistinguishable on the surface of the land, but they must be marked by appropriate signage. Any destruction or alteration of a protected site is subject to punishment. It is also forbidden to interfere in any way with the soil and to extract minerals, peat or petrification. All of the flora and fauna found in documentation sites are subject to protection.

326. It is possible with respect to a documentation site to introduce restrictions on the destruction, damage or alteration of the area, and on the performance of earthworks causing permanent changes in the landform with the exception of those associated with storm or flood protection or with the construction, reconstruction, maintenance or repair of water infrastructure. It is forbidden to damage and pollute soil or to alter hydrographic conditions if such changes do not serve to protect nature or rational agricultural, forest, water or fishery management. It is also forbidden to liquidate, fill up and transform natural water reservoirs, oxbow lakes and wetlands, as well as to empty slurry pits with the exception of fertilizing agricultural lands in use. It is forbidden to change the designation and manner of use of land, as well as to collect stones, including peat and petrification such as the buried fossils of plant and animal remains, minerals, and amber for commercial purposes. It is equally forbidden to wilfully kill wild animals, destroy their lairs, dens, other shelter and breeding grounds, as well as spawning grounds and laid eggs, with the exception of amateur fishing and activities performed in the framework of rational agricultural, forest, fishery and game management. Restrictions also encompass the gathering, destruction or damaging of plants and fungi in ecological use areas established for the purposes of protecting stations, communities and groupings of protected plants and fungi, and it is forbidden to erect billboards and other similar advertising equipment.

327. The aforementioned restrictions do not apply to work performed in relation to meeting the needs of nature protection upon prior consultation with the authority responsible for establishing a given form of nature protection, as well as to the realization of public purpose investments upon prior consultation with the authority responsible for establishing a given form of nature protection. They also do not apply to tasks resulting from threats to national security nor to eliminating immediate threats to public safety or rescue missions.

328. As of 2018, Poland has 177 documentation sites. The largest number of documentation sites can be found in the voivodeship of Małopolska, whilst the smallest numbers of them are in the voivodeships of Lower Silesia, Lubuskie and Warmia-Mazury.[120]

---

120. *Ibid.*, 310.

§4. Ecological Sites

329. As stipulated in Article 42, ecological sites are protection worthy ecosystem residues of importance for the preservation of biodiversity – natural water reservoirs, mid-field and mid-forest ponds, clumps of trees and shrubs, swamps, peat bogs, dunes, patches of unused vegetation, oxbow lakes, rock outcrops, escarpments, stones, natural habitats and sites of rare or protected species of plants, animals and fungi, their refuges and places of reproduction or seasonal residence.

330. Establishment of the ecological site takes place by way of a resolution of the competent municipal council. This resolution specifies the name of a given object or area, its location, a person in charge of supervision, specific security objectives, and if necessary, arrangements for its active protection and prohibitions applicable to that object. Draft resolutions need to be agreed with the appropriate regional director for environmental protection. The revocation of the status of the ecological site as a form of nature protection takes place in case of loss of natural values, due to which it was established, or if it is necessary to implement a public purpose investment and to ensure common safety. The municipal council revokes the form of nature protection by means of a resolution.

331. In relation to ecological sites, prohibitions may be introduced to destroy, damage or transform the object, perform earthworks permanently distorting the relief, with the exception of work related to preventing storm water or flood protection, or construction, reconstruction, maintenance, renovation or repair of water equipment. One shall not damage or pollute soils, change water conditions if these changes do not protect nature or are not needed for rational farming, forestry, water or fisheries management. It is prohibited to liquidate, cover and transform natural water reservoirs, oxbow lakes, and wetlands as well as pouring slurry, except for fertilization of used arable land. Changes in use of land, mining for economic purposes of rock, including peat, and fossils, including fossil remains of plants and animals, as well as minerals and amber, are prohibited. Moreover, deliberate killing of wild animals, destruction of burrows, animal beds and spawning grounds and complex eggs is prohibited, with the exception of amateur fishing, and activities related to rational farming, forestry, fishing and hunting. The prohibition also includes the collection, destruction, and damage to plants and fungi in the areas of the ecological sites created to protect the sites, habitats or refuges of protected plants and mushrooms and placing advertising boards.

332. Prohibitions do not apply to works carried out for the purposes of nature protection after consultation with the body establishing a given form of nature protection and implementation of public purpose investment after agreement with the body establishing a given form of nature protection. Prohibitions do not refer to tasks in the field of national defence in the event of a threat to the security of the state, or the elimination of sudden threats to public security and conducting rescue operations

333. In Poland, in 2018, there were 7,626 ecological sites.

§5. NATURE AND LANDSCAPE PROTECTED COMPLEXES

334. Nature and landscape protected complexes are fragments of the natural and cultural landscapes deserving of protection due to their scenic or aesthetic virtues.

335. Nature and landscape protected complexes are established by way of a resolution of the communal council. The resolution sets forth the name of the given object or area, its location, the authority responsible for its supervision, the particular objectives of protection, and if necessary determinations concerning its active protection and any applicable restrictions. Revocation of protection for a 'nature and landscape protected complex' takes place by way of a resolution of the communal council. Draft resolutions require consultation with the appropriate regional director for environmental protection.

336. Revocation of this form of nature protection takes place in the event of loss of the natural values for which it was established or in the event of the need to realize an investment with a public objective, or as necessary to ensure public safety.

337. With respect to the area of a nature and landscape protected complex, the same restrictions as in the case of natural monuments and documentation sites may be imposed.

338. In 2018, Poland has 260 nature and landscape protected complexes.

§6. PROTECTED LANDSCAPE AREAS

339. A protected landscape area is one of the forms of nature protection under discussion that encompasses areas protected due to their distinguishing landscape with diverse ecosystems, valued for their capacity to satisfy needs related to tourism and recreation or due to the performance of the function of ecological corridors.

340. Demarcation of a protected landscape area takes place by way of a resolution of the provincial assembly, which sets forth the name, location, area, supervisory authority, determinations as to the active protection of ecosystems and restrictions applicable to a given protected landscape area or its parts resulting from the need to protect it.

341. Liquidation or adjustment of the borders of a protected landscape area takes place by way of a resolution of the provincial assembly following consultation with the appropriate communal councils and is associated with the irreversible loss of a distinguishing landscape with diverse ecosystems with the capacity to satisfy needs related to tourism and recreation. Draft resolutions of the provincial assembly require consultation with the appropriate regional director for environmental protection. Draft studies of communal land use conditions and directions for spatial management, local spatial management plans, spatial management plans for voivodeships, inland sea waters, territorial sea waters and exclusive economic zones in portions intersecting with a protected landscape area require consultation with the appropriate regional director for environmental protection in respect of provisions of those plans that may have a negative impact on nature protection in the protected landscape area.

342. Restrictions may be introduced in a protected landscape area banning the killing of wild animals, the destruction of their dens, lairs, other forms of shelter and breeding grounds as well as spawning grounds and deposited eggs, with the exception of amateur fishing and the performance of activities associated with rational agricultural, forest, fishery and hunting management.

343. Restrictions apply to undertakings with a potentially significant environmental impact as understood by the provisions of the Act of 3 October 2008 on providing information on the environment and environmental protection, public participation in environmental protection and on environmental impact assessments. This restriction does not apply to undertakings with a potentially significant environmental impact for which an environmental impact study has demonstrated no significant negative impact on nature protection in the protected landscape area.

344. It is forbidden to destroy and remove inland, roadside and waterfront woods unless necessary for flood protection purposes or for ensuring the safety of road or water traffic, or for the construction, reconstruction, maintenance or repair of water infrastructure. It is also forbidden to collect stones, including peat and petrification, such as the buried fossils of plant and animal remains, minerals, and amber for commercial purposes.

345. It is forbidden to perform earthworks causing permanent changes to the landform in a protected landscape area, with the exception of works associated with storm, flood or drought amelioration efforts, or with the construction, reconstruction, repair or renovation of water infrastructure.

346. In areas encompassed by protection it is forbidden to alter hydrographic conditions for purposes other than nature protection, sustainable use of agricultural and forest lands or water and fishery management, as well as to liquidate natural water reservoirs, oxbow lakes and wetlands.

347. In addition, it is forbidden to locate structures within a 200 m-wide belt from the edge of cliffy shores and in the technical belt of the seashore. The aforementioned restrictions do not apply to the performance of tasks associated with national defence and national security, nor with the execution of investments realizing a public objective.

348. In 2018, Poland has 404 protected landscape areas. This condition may change as a result of the establishment of new protected areas by communal self-government authorities, or by their redesignation as other forms of nature protection such as landscape parks.

349. The greatest number of protected landscape areas can be found in the voivodeships of Masovia and Warmia-Masuria. Protected landscape areas are a form of nature protection under less rigorous protection, primarily serving recreational purposes. In comparison to the restrictions in place in national parks or nature reserves, commercial activity in protected landscape areas is subject to only a small amount of regulation.

§7. NATURA 2000 SITES

350. Of those listed in Article 6 of the Nature Protection Act, the Natura 2000 site is one of the forms of nature protection. According to Article 5(2b), the Natura 2000 site is a site of special bird protection, a special habitat protection site or a site of Community importance, created to protect populations of wild birds or natural habitats or species of Community importance. In Article 5(1b), the integrity of the Natura 2000 site is defined as the coherence of structural and functional factors determining the sustainable life of populations of species and natural habitats, for the protection of which the Natura 2000 site was designed or designated.

351. As stipulated in Article 25, the network Natura 2000 covers special bird protection sites, special habitat protection sites and sites of Community importance. The Natura 2000 site may cover some or all of the sites and objects covered by forms of nature conservation.

352. According to the Article 26, the minister responsible for environmental affairs shall determine, by way of a regulation, types of natural habitats and species of Community importance, including natural habitats and priority species, and requiring protection in the form of Natura 2000 sites. It also defines the criteria for selecting sites eligible for recognition as sites of Community importance and for designation as special sites of conservation for habitats and sites eligible to designate as special bird protection sites, with regard to preserving individual valuable or endangered components of biodiversity on the basis of which the Natura 2000 network is designated.

353. Regulation of the Minister of Environment of 13 April 2010 on natural habitats and species of Community importance, and the criteria for the selection of sites eligible for recognition or designation as Natura 2000 sites,[121] specifies criteria for the selection of sites eligible for recognition as sites of Community importance and designation as special habitats conservation sites Natura 2000 and as special bird conservation sites Natura 2000.

354. The General Director for Environmental Protection prepares a draft list of Natura 2000 sites, in accordance with the provisions of EU law. The designation of the Natura 2000 site, change of its borders or liquidation takes place in agreement with the minister for responsible agricultural affairs, the minister responsible for

121. Dz. U. 2014, item 1713.

rural development, the minister responsible for fisheries and the minister responsible for water management, by way of a regulation of the minister responsible for environmental affairs. Such regulation specifies the name, administrative location, site and map of the site, purpose and subject of protection. The minister responsible for the environmental affairs, issuing the regulation, is guided by the state of natural habitats and plant and animal species as well as by the necessity to preserve particularly valuable or endangered components of biodiversity. Supervision of the Natura 2000 site is carried out by the competent regional director for environmental protection or in sea areas – director for the maritime office.

355. Change of borders or liquidation of the special habitats conservation sites and special bird conservation sites happen if it is justified by natural changes detected as a result of monitoring and supervision, and after obtaining the consent of the European Commission.

356. Special habitats conservation sites are set by the minister responsible for the environmental affairs after consultation with the European Commission within six years from the date of approval of this site by the European Commission as an area of Community importance.

357. For the Natura 2000 sites, the supervisor of the site establishes a draft plan of protective tasks for a period of ten years. The protection plan established for the national park, nature reserve or landscape park located within the Natura 2000 site becomes a protection plan for this part of the Natura 2000 site. The person supervising the Natura 2000 site prepares and submits to the General Director for Environmental Protection an assessment of the protection implementation of this site. The General Director for Environmental Protection supervises the functioning of Natura 2000 sites, keeping records of data necessary to undertake actions in regard to their protection.

358. In Article 33 of the Act, bans concerning the Natura 2000 site are defined, where it is prohibited to take actions that may, individually or in combination with other activities, significantly adversely affect the conservation objectives of the Natura 2000 site. In particular, it is necessary to indicate the ban on deterioration of natural habitats or habitats of plant species and animals for which conservation the Natura 2000 site has been designated, the ban on adverse impacts on species for which the Natura 2000 site has been designated, or a ban on worsening the integrity of the Natura 2000 site or its connection with other sited. If the necessary requirements of overriding public interest are in favour of this, and due to the lack of alternative solutions, the competent regional director for environmental protection, and in the maritime areas – the director of the relevant maritime office, may authorize the implementation of a plan or actions that may significantly affect the conservation objectives of the Natura 2000 site ensuring the implementation of environmental compensation[122] necessary to ensure the coherence and proper functioning of the Natura 2000 network of sites.

359. The General Director for Environmental Protection submits to the European Commission reports and notifications concerning Natura 2000 sites and applies for opinions on these areas. The costs related to the implementation and functioning of the Natura 2000 network in the part not covered by the Community financing are financed from the state budget and from the budgets of local self-government units and from the funds of the National Fund for Environmental Protection and Water Management and voivodeship funds for environmental protection and water management.

360. In 2018, in Poland, only in the Lower Silesian Voivodeship, there are eighty-nine special habitat conservation sites and ten special bird conservation sites. Most of the special conservation sites are established in the Lubelskie Voivodeship. There are ninety-eight special habitat conservation sites and twenty special bird conservation sites.

122. According to the Art. 3(8) of Environmental Protection Act, that is a set of activities including, in particular, construction works, earthworks, soil remediation, afforestation, or creation of vegetation clusters leading to the restoration of natural balance or creation of vegetation clusters leading to the restoration of natural balance in a given area, compensation of damage done to the environment by the implementation of the project and preservation of landscape values.

Chapter 3. Parks and Reserves

§1. National Parks

361. The establishment of national parks is one of the earliest forms of state activity intended to protect natural resources in the broadly-understood public interest. National parks are established in order to preserve biodiversity, inanimate elements of nature and landscape virtues, to restore the proper condition of resources and constituent elements of nature, and to reconstitute deformed habitats.

362. Pursuant to Article 8 of the Nature Protection Act, a natural park is an area distinguished by particularly significant natural, scientific, social, cultural and educational virtues, with a total area of not less than 1,000 ha within which protection is extended to the entirety of nature and all landscape virtues contained therein.

363. Within the area of a natural park we may distinguish areas of enhanced, active and landscape protection, differentiated by the character and methods of protection. National park border areas are a buffer zone for the park, in which a protective zone for game animals may be established for the protection of animals inside the national park.

364. The minister responsible for environmental affairs establishes by way of regulation a protective zone for game animals, defining the areas comprising it, as well as the criteria and means of maintaining the appropriate numbers and population structure of particular game animal species. The protection of game animal species is one of the tasks assigned to the director of a national park. As was mentioned previously, the creation or expansion of a national park is a public objective as understood by the Real Property Administration Act of 21 August 1997, which is why the provisions of that Act concerning expropriation apply in the event of the establishment of a national park on lands not owned by the State Treasury.[123]

365. The natural resources of national parks are counted among Poland's strategic natural resources pursuant to Article 1 of the Act of 6 July 2001 on maintaining the national character of the country's strategic natural resources.[124] In order to undertake tasks aimed at protecting a national park's ecosystems, providing access to a national park and conducting nature education activities, national parks are vested with legal personhood.

366. As juridical persons, national parks may conduct commercial activities under the provisions of the Act of 6 March 2018 – Entrepreneurs Law.[125] National parks conduct independent financial administration on the basis of an annual financial plan, financing the performance of their statutory tasks and operational costs out of their own resources and income generated by their activities.

---

123. Dz. U. 2018, item 121 with amendments.
124. Dz. U. 2018, item 1235 with amendments.
125. Dz. U. item. 646.

367. The supervision of national parks is performed by the minister responsible for environmental affairs and involves the endorsement of yearly substantive and protective tasks resulting from the protection plan, as well as audits. Audits encompass the functioning of a park, the conducting of commercial activity, performance of tasks and financial plans, and the activities of the director of the national park performed as a nature protection authority. The supervising minister confers a charter on a national park setting forth its internal organization and mode in which the authority operates, with a view to ensuring the park's efficient operation and proper performance of its tasks. It is the obligation of the minister responsible for environmental affairs to draw up an annual summary report on the activity of national parks, prepared using information provided by individual park directors.

368. A national park director is the authority which oversees the operations of a national park and represents the national park before third parties. Park directors are appointed by the minister responsible for environmental affairs from among individuals selected by way of an open and competitive recruitment process, and they are dismissed by the same minister as well. In the event of dismissal of a national park director, the minister responsible for environmental affairs may entrust the duties of the park director to the deputy national park director from the day of the dismissal until the day on which a new park director is appointed, but for a period not longer than six months. Recruitment for the position is a competitive process during which the knowledge and traits necessary for performing the tasks of a director are examined, as are management skills. A national park director is appointed in order to implement the provisions of the protection plan, as well as to issue orders concerning the functioning of the national park. A national park director has the right to conduct proceedings in matters of petty offences against nature protection, as well as to participate in court proceedings as a public prosecutor and to submit appeals against decisions and verdicts of courts in matters concerning petty offences against nature protection. A national park director may authorize an officer of the Park Ranger Service to exercise those competences.

369. Establishing and changing the borders of a national park is achieved by way of a regulation issued by the Council of Ministers in which its area and borders are defined. The order is issued on the basis of an assessment of the actual state of the area's natural virtues. The liquidation or reduction of the area of a national park only occurs in the event of the irreversible loss of the park area's natural and cultural virtues. Determining and changing borders may take place following consultation with the appropriate local self-government constitutive authorities, and after the submission of opinions by interested non-governmental organizations within thirty days of release of the proposed changes. Failure to provide an opinion within the statutory period is considered equivalent to the absence of remarks.

370. With the day of entry into force of a statute establishing a national park or of a regulation concerning the changing of its borders, the national park acquires *ex lege* perpetual usufruct rights to the real property owned by the State Treasury located within its borders and serving the attainment of its objectives, as well as the ownership of buildings and other facilities located on such property. The acquisition of the aforementioned rights may not infringe the rights of third parties. The voivode confirms the acquisition of those rights by way of an administrative decision issued within twelve months of the day on which the act establishing the national park or regulation adjusting its borders enters into force. Appeals against the decision of the voivode are heard by the minister responsible for environmental affairs. The national park director is obliged to submit an application for entry of the national park's perpetual usufruct rights into the land and mortgage register within six months of the day on which the final decision is duly served. A national park has the right of pre-emption to real property located within the borders of the national park to the benefit of the State Treasury.

371. Contracts concerning the disposition of real property are, as a rule, concluded by way of a tender process organized and conducted by the director of the national park concerned.

372. The area of a national park may be made accessible in a manner that does not cause a negative impact on nature to be found inside the national park. A national park protection plan includes an indication of its areas that may be made accessible and the maximum number of people permitted in them at any given time.

373. Fees may be collected for entry to a national park or for access to some parts of it. The amount of such fees is determined by the national park director, but they may not be in excess of the valorized amount of PLN 6 for a single-entry into the park. Fees are paid in the form of a single-entry ticket or multiple-entry ticket purchased either at fee collection locations or by means of bank transfer to the bank account of the national park. Fees for access to a national park or to portions of it may not be collected from children up to seven years old, neither from individuals in possession of a permit from the director of the national park for conducting scientific research on nature protection. This exemption also extends to pupils and students receiving instruction in a national park within a scope agreed upon with the national park director. In addition, residents of communes located within the borders of a national park and those adjacent to a national park, as well as individuals travelling to designated beaches or places of religious significance within a national park, are exempt from entrance fees. A discount of 50% on the entrance fee to a national park is provided to pupils and students, pensioners and individuals collecting disability benefits, disabled persons and soldiers on active duty.

374. The minister responsible for environmental affairs is responsible for establishing, by way of regulation, the national parks and/or areas of them for which entrance fees are collected, taking into account such factors as the diversity of natural and landscape virtues, volume of tourist traffic and its impact on the natural beauty of national parks.

375. Within the borders of national parks it is forbidden to erect or rebuild buildings and technical infrastructure with the exception of those serving the objectives of the national park or a nature reserve.

376. Individuals on the territory of a national park are forbidden from capturing or killing wild animals, gathering or destroying eggs and young or developmental forms of animals, intentionally startling vertebrate animals, gathering antlers, destroying dens, nests, lairs and other forms of animal shelter and breeding grounds. With the exception of areas where such activities are expressly permitted, it is forbidden to hunt or to gather, destroy or intentionally damage plants and fungi. This restriction also applies to the destruction, pollution and alteration of natural objects, areas and resources, formations and constituent elements of nature.

377. It is equally forbidden to alter hydrographic conditions and the regulation of rivers and streams if such changes do not serve the protection of nature, to collect stones, including peat and petrification such as the buried fossils of plant and animal remains, minerals and amber. The destruction of soil and changes to the designation and use of land is also forbidden. Restrictions also apply to bonfires, smoking tobacco and using open flames as a source of light, with the exception of places designated by the national park director.

378. Liability is set forth in statute for the application of chemical and biological means of plant protection and fertilizers, harvesting wild plants and fungi or portions of them, fishing and capturing other marine life, foot and bicycle traffic, skiing, horse riding and bringing dogs into areas encompassed by enhanced and active protection, with the exception of designated areas.

379. Climbing, as well as the exploration of caves and water reservoirs, is forbidden, as is the operation of motor vehicles outside of public roads and roads indicated by the national park director. The restriction set forth in Article 15 of the Act also applies to placing signs, writing, commercial advertisements and other symbols not associated with nature protection, except for road signs and other signs necessary for ensuring security and public order. It is impermissible to violate the peace, to perform earthworks causing permanent changes to the landform, or to camp in places other than those specially designated by the national park director.

380. It is forbidden in a national park to conduct scientific research without the permission of the park director, as well as to introduce species of plants, animals and fungi without the permission of the minister responsible for environmental affairs, and to introduce GMO. These restrictions do not apply to the performance of tasks resulting from the protection plan nor other protection tasks, nor to rescue missions. They also do not apply to activities relating to public safety and the performance of tasks associated with national security in the event of a threat to the security of the State.

381. Upon the opinion of the national park director, the minister responsible for environmental affairs may allow for exceptions to restrictions if justified by the needs of nature protection, the performance of scientific research, as well as for educational, cultural, tourism, recreational, sporting or religious purposes under the condition that such activity does not produce a negative impact on the nature of the national park. The opinion is issued as a written statement of the relevant authority assessing the planned activities in respect of their influence on the nature contained in the national park. A permit may be issued with regard to the need to undertake line investments for public purposes, and in the event of there being no alternative solutions, upon the guarantee of nature compensation. A permit for an exemption from restrictions is issued by way of administrative decision for a fixed period of time, not to exceed five years.

382. In national parks, tasks associated with the protection of property and with combating crimes and petty offences are performed by the Park Ranger Service, constituting part of the National Park Service. During the performance of their duties, officials of the Park Ranger Service have the right to demand identification from individuals suspected of committing a crime or petty offence, as well as from witnesses to such events, in order to establish their identity. They verify payment of fees, and they may detain individuals and hand them over to the police or other authorities in the event of suspicion of commission of a crime or petty offence.

383. A Park Ranger has the right to detain and inspect means of transport to determine their cargo and to inspect the contents of personal effects in the event of justified suspicion of the commission of a crime or petty offence. A Park Ranger may also search premises and other locations. In the course of performing their duties, Park Rangers secure objects that may constitute material evidence, verify and retain documents attesting to the right to possess elements of nature originating from the area of the national park, and scrutinize entities conducting commercial activity within the borders of the national park in respect of adherence to legal regulations.

384. Park Rangers are authorized to perform their duties within the borders of a national park as well as outside them in the event of a justified suspicion that a crime or petty offence has been committed to the detriment of a national park. The provisions of the Code of Criminal Proceedings (CPP) and the Code of Proceedings in Respect of Petty Offences apply.

385. To date, twenty-three national parks have been established in Poland, encompassing an area of 316,748 ha. This constitutes approximately 1% of the country's total area. The largest concentrations of national parks are located in the Carpathians and in north-eastern Poland. National parks in Poland are primarily forested and wooded areas.

386. Poland implemented nature protection in the form of national parks in 1932, establishing the Pieniński National Park. At present, the largest national park in Poland is Biebrzański National Park (59,233 ha), while the smallest is Ojcowski National Park (2,146 ha). The title of World Biosphere Reserve, given to areas afforded protection under the UNESCO Man and the Biosphere programme due to their significant natural virtues, has been awarded to eight Polish national parks: Babiogórski National Park, Białowieski National Park, Bieszczadzki National Park, Kampinoski National Park, Karkonoski National Park, Poleski National Park, Słowiński National Park and Tatrzański National Park, while seven parks are protected under the Ramsar Convention on Wetlands, which protects waterfowl habitat: Biebrzański National Park, Narwiański National Park, Karkonoski National Park, Poleski National Park, National Park 'Ujście Warty', Słowiński National Park and Wigierski National Park. All of Poland's national parks are part of the Natura 2000 European Ecological Network.

§2. Nature Reserves

387. Pursuant to Article 13(2) of the Nature Protection Act, a nature reserve is an area maintained in its natural state or altered insignificantly, containing ecosystems, natural dwellings and refuges, and also habitats of plants, animals and fungi, as well as inanimate creations and constituent elements of nature. Nature reserves are elements distinguished by particular natural, scientific and cultural values, as well as landscape virtues.

388. Recognition of an area as a nature reserve is made by way of an act of local law, consisting of an order of the regional director for environmental protection. The order sets forth the name of the reserve, the location and course of its borders and buffer zone if one has been established, the purposes of the protection extended and the class, category and subcategory of the nature reserve as well as the authority responsible for oversight.

389. Upon seeking the opinion of the regional nature protection council, the regional director for environmental protection may issue an order expanding the area of a nature reserve, revise the purposes of the protection extended, or liquidate a nature reserve in the event of the irreversible loss of the natural values for which the reserve was established.

390. Draft plans for spatial management in respect of those portions affecting a nature reserve and its buffer zone must be consulted with the regional director for environmental protection with regard to determinations that may have a negative impact on the purposes of protection of the nature reserve.

391. In order to perform similar tasks in respect of nature reserves located in coastal areas, the consent of the director of the relevant maritime office is required with regard to their impact on the exercise of that authority's competences. These arrangements are to be completed within thirty days of the day on which an application for arrangements is duly served. If the director of the relevant maritime office declines to express a position by the expiration of that deadline, it is considered that all matters raised have been duly coordinated. Territorial jurisdiction of the regional director for environmental protection in respect of coastal areas extends along the coastline of a given voivodeship.

392. The regional director for environmental protection may issue an order establishing a fee for entering the territory of a nature reserve if justified by the needs of nature protection. The maximum fee for a single-entry to a nature reserve may not exceed the valorized amount of PLN 6. Income from fees are to be used for purposes related to nature protection.

393. With a view to ensuring protection for areas presenting valuable and diverse natural virtues, as well as to designating an appropriate number of nature reserves based on the dominant object of protection and leading type of ecosystem, the minister responsible for environmental affairs defines the classes, categories and subcategories of nature reserves. This was accomplished in the Regulation of 30 March 2005 on the matter of classes, categories and subcategories of nature reserves.[126]

394. The Regulation defines nine types of reserves: forest, water, grassland, halophyte, faunistic, floristic, peatland, inanimate nature and landscape.

395. The objects of protection of a forest reserve (L) are the remnants and fragments of old-growth forests, types of forest communities and tree stands at the edges of distributions.

396. Water nature reserves (W) protect the waters of lakes, rivers, streams and the sea together with plant communities and species of animals.

397. A grassland reserve (St), primarily on a calciferous substrate.

398. A halophyte reserve protects coastal and inland halophytes. The objects of protection on a faunistic reserve (Fn) are populations and habitats of mammals, fowl, reptiles, amphibians, fish and invertebrates. Similar to a faunistic reserve, a floristic reserve (Fl) secures the populations and habitats of species of spore-producing plants and flowers, as well as cap mushrooms and lichens.

399. A peatland reservation (T) protects communities and species of fen, poor fen and raised bog.

400. An inanimate nature reserve (N) protects geological outcrops, karst topography, soils, rock formations, caves, cave deposits, petrified objects, examples of erosion and other processes shaping the landform, geological formations and dunes.

401. A landscape nature reserve (K) protects natural landscapes characteristic of particular geographical regions, often with landmarks present in those areas.

402. Nature reserves may be differentiated on the basis of the dominant object of protection, including the categories of floristic, phytocenotic, fungi, biocenotic and physiocenotic, faunistic, geological and soil, landscape, plantings and crops, and cultural. Further subcategories of nature reserves are contained within this framework. Floristic nature reserve subtypes are reserves of spore-producing plants,

126. Dz. U. No. 60, item 533.

herbaceous plants and shrubs, bushes and trees, and plants at the edge of a distribution. Subcategories of phytosenotic reserves are reserves of forest and non-forest communities, and subcategories of fungi reserves are cap mushroom reserves and lichens.

403. The Regulation lists biocenotic nature reserve subcategories as natural and semi-natural biocoenosis reserves and anthropogenic biocoenosis reserves. Faunistic reserve subcategories are given as reserves of mammals, fowl, reptiles, amphibians, fish and invertebrates. Geological and soil reserve subcategories include geological formation reserves, tectonic and erosion formation reserves, as well as rock, mineral, deposit, soil and dune reserves.

404. Landscape reserve subcategories include natural and anthropogenic landscape reserves, while planting and crop reserves encompass old-growth trees and phytocenoses.

405. Cultural reserves come in the form of landmark reserves, places of worship and places of national memory. Nature reserves may also be differentiated by the primary type of ecosystem found in a given reserve, such as forest and woodland, meadow, pasture, grass and brush, water, peatland, halophyte, dune, underground, rock, crop and other ecosystems.

406. As in the case of the previous classification, there is a further breakdown into subcategories within the framework of the reservation types differentiated. Forest and woodlands reserves occur in the form of lowland, highland, mountain and submontane, mixed lowland, mixed mountain and submontane forest and woodlands reserves. Meadow reserves include such forms of reserves as hydrophilic meadow, mesophilic meadow, pastures, high mountain meadows, and xerothermic pitch and growth.

407. A water reserve may take the form of a seawater reserve, oligotrophic lake reserve, mesotrophic lake reserve and eutrophic lake reserve, as well as ponds, dystrophic lake reserve, as well as rivers and their valleys, streams and springs.

408. A peatland reserve may be classified as a reserve for lowland, highland or transitional peatland.

409. Halophyte reserves include inland halophyte as well as coastal halophyte types. Dune reserve subcategories are inland dunes and coastal dunes.

410. An underground nature reserve is a general term encompassing both natural and man-made reserves.

411. Particular forms of rock reserves include magma rock reserves, sedimentary rock reserves and other rocks.

412. Agricultural reserves encompass two subcategories – field and garden – as well as parks and other greenery.

413. Regulations related to reserves of various ecosystems include the subcategories of forest and water reserve, forest and meadow, forest and peatland, non-forest land ecosystems, water ecosystems and mosaics of various ecosystems.

414. The fundamental difference between the organizational character of a national park and that of a nature reserve lies in the scope of the purposes of protection. National parks have complex protection objectives, which differs from a reserve established for particular protection aims. Certain legal provisions concerning national parks are also applicable to nature reserves. Reserves are subject to the same restrictions set forth in Article 15 of the Nature Protection Act concerning the erection of structures and technical infrastructure, capturing or killing wild animals, hunting, altering hydrographic conditions, applying chemical and biological substances for protecting plants or fertilizers, gathering wild plants and fungi, climbing, exploring caves and water reservoirs, as well as motor vehicle traffic outside of public roads and roads designated by the responsible authority. The same set of exemptions from those restrictions also applies.

415. As of 31 December 2012, Poland contained 1,483 nature reserves. The oldest nature reserve in Poland, and also the second oldest in Europe, is the Cisy Staropolskie Reserve, while the world's first forest nature reserve is the Wierzchlas Yew Reserve, founded in 1826 in Bory Tucholskie.

§3. Landscape Parks

416. Under the definition set forth in Article 16(1) of the Nature Protection Act, landscape parks are established in protected areas valued for their natural, historical and cultural virtues as well as their landscape virtues, and for the popularization of these values in a sustainable development framework.

417. A landscape park is established or expanded by way of a resolution of the provincial assembly. Such a resolution sets forth its name, area, borders and buffer zone if necessary, particular protection objectives and restrictions appropriate for the given landscape park resulting from the need for protection leading to its establishment.

418. Liquidation and reduction of the area of a landscape park are also accomplished by way of a provincial assembly resolution. A draft resolution of the provincial assembly concerning the establishment, adjustment of borders or liquidation of a landscape park must be prepared in consultation with the relevant communal council and regional director for environmental protection. Agricultural and forest land as well as other real property located inside the borders of a landscape park continue to serve those functions.

419. The provincial council enacts by way of resolution the charter of a landscape park or complex of landscape parks, setting forth their organizational structure.

420. The director of a landscape park is appointed by provincial self-administration after seeking the opinion of the regional nature protection council. A decision appointing a landscape park director for a park located on the territory of more than one voivodeship is taken by provincial self-administration appropriate to the seat of the park, in cooperation with their counterparts in the other voivodeships. Under Article 105 of the Nature Protection Act, the competencies of a landscape park director include the protection of nature and landscape values as well as of the park's historical and cultural values. The director is tasked with organizing educational, tourist and recreational activity, as well as cooperating with the relevant organizational entities, juridical persons and natural persons in respect of nature protection. The park director is the relevant authority for submitting proposals to local spatial management plans concerning the spatial management of areas encompassed by the landscape park.

421. Draft studies of communal land-use conditions and directions for spatial management, as well as of spatial management plans in respect of portions concerning the nature park and related buffer zones, must be prepared in consultation with the relevant regional director for environmental protection concerning their provisions that may have a negative impact on nature protection within the borders of the landscape park.

422. In order to facilitate the management of landscape parks, landscape park complexes may be established as a public sector entity as defined by provisions of public finances law.

423. The area comprising a nature park is, as a rule, far more freely accessible over a greater space for tourists than national parks, yet they are also subject to individual restrictions and conditions of access to portions of the park for purposes related to tourism.

424. Pursuant to Article 17 of the Nature Protection Act, it is permissible in a landscape park to introduce restrictions on undertakings with the potential to have a significant environmental impact as defined by the provisions of the Act of 3 October 2008 on providing information on the environment and environmental protection, public participation in environmental protection and on environmental impact assessments.[127]

425. These restrictions do not apply to undertakings for which there is no obligation to compose an environmental impact assessment report, and the environmental impact assessment procedure has not demonstrated a negative impact on the nature of the landscape park. It is equally forbidden to wilfully kill wild animals,

127. Dz. U. 2017, item 1405 with amendments.

destroy their lairs, dens, other shelter and breeding grounds, as well as spawning grounds and laid eggs, with the exception of amateur fishing and activities performed in the framework of rational agricultural, forest, fishery and game management. It is forbidden to destroy and remove inland, roadside and waterfront woods except for purposes related to the needs of flood amelioration, of ensuring the safety of road and maritime traffic or of the construction, reconstruction, maintenance, repair or renovation of water infrastructure. It is also not permitted to gather rocks and peat for commercial purposes, as well as petrification, including buried plant and animal fossils, and also minerals and amber. Additionally, restrictions apply on the performing of earthworks causing permanent changes to the landform, with the exception of those associated with storm and flood protection, or with the construction, reconstruction and maintenance of water infrastructure. The introduction of changes to hydrographic conditions is also forbidden if such changes do not serve the protection of nature or rational agricultural, forest, water or fishery management, as well as the construction of new structures within a 100 m-wide belt. Exceptions apply to the placement of structures within a 200 m-wide belt from the edge of a cliffy shore and in the service strip of a coastline, as well as the liquidation, filling and conversion of water reservoirs, oxbow lakes and wetlands. It is forbidden to empty slurry pits (with the exception of fertilizing one's own agricultural land), to raise animals using free-range methods, to maintain open sewage ditches and septic pits, to organize automobile races, and to use motorized watercraft and other motorized equipment on open water reservoirs.

426. The restrictions set forth in Article 17 do not apply to the performance of tasks resulting from a protection plan, tasks associated with national defence and national security, rescue missions and activities associated with public safety. It is also permissible to undertake investments with a public objective as understood in Article 2(5) of the Spatial Planning and Management Act of 27 March 2003.[128] The restriction on using motorized watercraft and other motorized equipment on open water reservoirs does not apply to the entities listed in Article 17(4), which include the watercraft of rescue services, those of the waters' owners for organizational purposes and water infrastructure located on waters, those of inland waterway inspectors, of the State and Volunteer Fishing Service, ferries operating within public rights-of-way, watercraft used in the conducting of rational fishery management, and for the performance of duties in respect of nature protection by the Landscape Park Ranger Service.

427. Tasks regarding the protection of nature, landscape and cultural virtues and educational activities are carried out within a landscape park by the Landscape Park Ranger Service. Its tasks include taking an inventory of natural habitats, communities of plants, animals and fungi encompassed by species protection and their habitats, and also inanimate creations and constituent elements of nature worthy of protection. The Service identifies and assesses existing and potential threats from both internal and external sources to the landscape park and applies for the initiation of activities intended to eliminate such threats and their effects, as well as other

128. Dz. U. 2018, item 1945 with amendments.

activities supporting improvement in the functioning of the landscape park and protection afforded it. The Landscape Park Ranger Service collects documentation concerning nature and historical, cultural and ethnographic virtues. It performs tasks associated with the protection of other forms of nature within the borders of the landscape park and provides information about the principles of nature protection to individuals present in areas encompassed by protection and in places where creations and constituent elements of nature given protection are located. The Park Ranger Service's duties also include conducting nature education in schools and among the local community, and also promoting the values of the landscape park, cooperating with local self-government bodies, managers of areas of landscape parks, ecological organizations and other entities involved in the protection of the landscape park. During the performance of their tasks, employees of the Landscape Park Ranger Service are authorized to confirm the identification of an individual violating regulations on nature protection, and if such a person refuses to present a document allowing for the determination of his/her identity, the Landscape Park Ranger Service may request that the police or other authorities establish that individual's identity.

428. An institution common to landscape parks, national parks and nature reserves is the protection plan. It is established within five years of the founding of a national park, the designation of an area as a nature reserve, or the establishment of a landscape park. A draft protection plan for a national park is prepared by the national park director. Nature reserve protection plans are drafted by the regional director for environmental protection, or by the reservation's managing authority or supervisory authority, in consultation with the reserve's director. In respect of a landscape park, the responsible authority is the director of the park or of a park complex. The authority responsible for preparing the draft protection plan is obliged to ensure the possibility of the public's involvement in its creation, pursuant to the principles and mode set forth in the Act on providing information on the environment and environmental protection, public participation in environmental protection and on environmental impact assessments, in proceedings having as their object the drawing up of a draft. The draft plan must be submitted for review by the relevant communal councils. These regulations are also applicable in the case of amending a protection plan.

429. The minister responsible for environmental affairs enacts a protection plan for a national park by way of a regulation within six months of the day on which the draft plan is received, or refuses to implement the plan if its draft is not compliant with the objectives of nature protection, taking into account the necessity of adapting protection practices to the protection objectives of a national park.

430. In the case of a nature reserve, the regional director for environmental protection enacts a protection plan in the form of an order, within six months of the day of receipt of its draft. The provincial assembly enacts a landscape park's protection plan by way of a resolution within six months of the day of receipt of its draft; it may refuse to do so if the draft plan is inconsistent with the objectives of nature protection. They may be revised if the needs of nature protection so require.

The draft resolution of the provincial assembly in that matter must be consulted with the appropriate regional director for environmental protection.

431. A protection plan for a nature reserve located on the territory of more than one voivodeship is enacted by way of an order constituting an act of local law jointly by the regional directors for environmental protection in whose areas of jurisdiction a portion of that reserve is located.

432. Protection plans for a landscape park located on the territory of several voivodeships are enacted by the provincial assembly of the voivodeship in which the park's directorate has its seat, in cooperation with the remaining provincial assemblies.

433. The protection plan of a national park, nature reserve and landscape park is prepared for a twenty-year period, and it takes account of a profile and assessment of the state of nature, identification and assessment of existing and potential threats from both internal and external sources, profile and assessment of social and economic conditions, analysis of the effectiveness of previously applied protection means, and a profile and assessment of the condition of spatial management.

434. Work on drafting a protection plan consists of assessing the condition of resources, creations and constituent elements of nature, landscape virtues, cultural values, and existing and potential threats from both internal and external sources; this assessment may be undertaken in the form of detailed descriptions. Planning consists of developing a conception for the protection of resources, creations and constituent elements of nature and of cultural values, as well as in the elimination or limitation of existing and potential threats from both internal and external sources coupled with an indication of protection tasks, their type, scope and location. A protection plan for a national park and nature reserve sets forth the objectives of nature protection and indicates the natural and social conditions necessary for their achievement. It identifies and defines manners of eliminating or limiting existing and potential threats from both internal and external sources along with their effects, and indicates areas of enhanced, active and landscape protection.

435. The plan contains defined protective activities in areas of enhanced, active and landscape protection with the type, scope and location of such activities as well as areas and locations accessible for scientific, educational, tourist, recreational, sporting and amateur fishing purposes, along with an indication of the manners in which they are to be made accessible.

436. Park protection plans indicate places where manufacturing, trade and agricultural activity may be conducted, and also contains determinations concerning studies of communal land-use conditions and directions for spatial management, local spatial management plans, spatial management plans for voivodeships, inland sea waters, territorial sea waters and exclusive economic zones in respect of eliminating or limiting internal and external threats.

437. A protection plan for a landscape park sets forth the purposes of nature protection, as well as the natural, social and economic conditions of their achievement. It identifies and defines the manner of eliminating or limiting existing and potential threats from both internal and external sources along with their effects. It indicates areas for the performance of protective activities, defines the scope of activities associated with nature protection and landscape formation, and it sets forth areas accessible for scientific, educational, tourist, recreational and amateur fishing purposes as well as for other forms of management, along with indications of the manner in which these areas may be used. Moreover, the plan contains determinations as to studies of communal land-use conditions and directions for spatial management, local spatial management plans, spatial management plans for voivodeships, inland sea waters, territorial sea waters and exclusive economic zones in respect of eliminating or limiting internal and external threats.

438. Protection plans for a national park, nature reserve or landscape park intersecting with a Natura 2000 area should include the scope of the plan for protective activities applicable in that area. For national parks, nature reserves and landscape parks the minister responsible for environmental affairs establishes by way of a regulation the manner of drafting a protection plan, the scope of work necessary for the purposes of drafting the plan, the manner in which it may be amended, and the scope and manner of the protection of resources, creations and constituent elements of nature. This is to be performed taking account of the need to protect the resources, creations and constituent elements of both animate and inanimate nature in national parks, nature reserves and landscape parks, with allowances for their technical, organizational and financial capacities and the state of knowledge and science in the area of nature protection. Until a protection plan for a national park or nature reserve is enacted, the authority responsible for its oversight prepares a draft list of protection tasks.

439. Protection tasks are established for a national park by way of an order of the minister responsible for environmental affairs, while the regional director for environmental protection does this for a nature reserve. Protection tasks include the identification and assessment of existing and potential threats from both internal and external sources, as well as the manner of eliminating or limiting those threats and their effects. They additionally contain descriptions of means for the active protection of ecosystems, with the type, scale and location of particular tasks and a description of the protection envisioned for species of plants, animals and fungi. Protection tasks also indicate areas encompassed by enhanced, active and landscape protection. Protection tasks may be established for a period of one year or several years, up to a maximum period of five years.

440. In 2018, in Poland was home to 123 landscape parks, constituting 8.3% of the country's total landmass. The largest concentration of landscape parks is in the voivodeship of Lubelski, while Opolskie contains the fewest. The oldest of them is the Suwalski Landscape Park, established in 1976. The largest landscape park in terms of area is the Dolina Baryczy Landscape Park, with 84,040 ha spanning the voivodeships of Lower Silesia and Wielkopolskie. Other landscape parks of significant size are Puszcza Knyszyńska, Pogórze Przemyski, Popradzki and Mazurski Landscape Parks.

Chapter 4. Species Protection of Plants and Fungi

441. The protection of selected species of plants is present in nearly every country. It is generally held to have begun in Poland with regulations protecting yews which were introduced in the Middle Ages. Species protection of plants in the modern sense began in Europe at the end of the nineteenth century in Switzerland, followed by regulations in Austria concerning the protection of edelweiss. The first six species to be encompassed by enhanced protection in Poland were appointed in 1919, and in 1946 the first regulation was enacted on species protection, which extended protection to 110 species of plant life.[129] This act was replaced by a new regulation in 1957.[130] Later on, the list of protected plants was amended on multiple occasions, with changes made to both the list of protected species and the legal bases of species protection (in 1983,[131] 1995,[132] 2001,[133] 2004,[134] 2012[135] and 2014[136]).

442. The legal acts presently determining the subjective and objective scope of species protection of plants and fungi are the Environmental Protection Act, the Nature Protection Act and provisions constituting *lex specialis* contained in the Regulation of the Minister of the Environment of 9 September 2014 on plant species protection[137] and the Regulation of the Minister of the Environment of 9 September 2014 on the matter of species of wild fungi afforded protection.[138]

443. There is no legal definition of plants and fungi, which means that none of the aforementioned legal regulations contains a direct definition of those concepts. Both plants and fungi are defined indirectly by reference to a catalogue of protected species of plants or fungi and the manner of their protection.

---

129. Regulation of the Minister of Education of 29 August 1946 issued in cooperation with the Minister of Agriculture and Agricultural Reform and the Minister of Forestry on the introduction of species protection of plants (Dz. U. 1946, No. 70, item 384).
130. Regulation of the Minister of Forestry and Timber Industry of 28 February 1957 on introducing species protection of plants (Dz. U. 1957, No. 15, item 78).
131. Regulation of the Minister of Forestry and Timber Industry of 30 April 1983 on introducing species protection of plants (Dz. U. 1983, No. 27, item 134).
132. Regulation of the Minster of the Environment, Natural Resources and Forestry of 6 April 1995 on introducing species protection of plants (Dz. U. 1995, No. 41, item 214).
133. Regulation of the Minister of the Environment of 11 September 2001 on lists of native plant species encompassed by enhanced partial species protection and restrictions for those species and exceptions from those restrictions (Dz. U. 2001, No. 106, item 1167).
134. Regulation of the Minister of the Environment of 9 July 2004 on protected wild plant species (Dz. U. 2004, No. 168, item 1764).
135. Regulation of the Minister of the Environment of 5 January 2012 on plant species protection (Dz. U. 2012, No. 47, item 81).
136. Regulation of the Minister of the Environment of 5 September 2014 on plant species protection (Dz. U. item 1409).
137. Dz. U. 2014, item 1409.
138. Dz. U. 2004, No. 168, item 1765.

444. The protection of both plant life and of animals falls under the scope of protection of the natural environment, which means that the Environmental Protection Act contains consolidated regulations addressing related issues in section 8.

445. Under Article 127 of that Act, the protection of plant life consists of preserving valuable ecosystems, biodiversity and the equilibrium of the natural environment. Protection is also understood as creating conditions that ensure the proper development of plants and optimal fulfilment of their biological functions in the natural environment. Protective activities facilitate the prevention or limitation of negative environmental impact factors that may have an undesirable influence on plant conditions and resources, as well as the amelioration of threats to complexes and creations of nature.

446. The aforementioned provision also contains an open catalogue of activities through which the protection of plants takes place. These activities include encompassing areas of natural value with protection, establishing protection for species of plant life and restricting the possibility of harvesting wild plants while ensuring conditions for their reproduction.

447. Environmental protection in its broad sense also encompasses the protection of forests and wooded areas against pollution and fire, restricting the possibility of cutting trees and bushes and of liquidating green areas, as well as afforestation and the creation of communities of plant life as an element of plant species protection. The supervision of the introduction of GMO constitutes another component in the protection of plant life. Another provision regulates the special situation of plant protection in proving grounds of the Armed Forces of the Republic of Poland. Protection is to be ensured by locating proving grounds in areas of insignificant natural value, clearly marking areas of natural value such as protected plant communities, implementing appropriate limitations on training activities, and applying organizational and technical solutions limiting damage coupled with the successive removal of damage. The rules of plant protection in proving grounds are taken into account in training instructions.

448. The Nature Protection Act indicates species protection of plants as one of the forms of nature protection. The preservation of sustainable exploitation and renewal of resources, creations of nature and constituent elements of wild plants and fungi, as well as of plants and fungi encompassed by protection, natural habitats and habitats of threatened rare and protected species all constitute nature protection activities. One of the objectives of nature protection is to ensure the continuity of the existence of species of plants and fungi together with their habitats through preservation and restoration of the proper state of protection.

449. Article 46 of the Act provides direct regulation of the issue of species protection of plants, establishing its objectives and subjective scope. This protection encompasses specimens of species as well as habitats and refuges of plants and fungi. Its objective is to secure wild plants and their habitats, particularly rarely-occurring species, endemic species, those species vulnerable to threats and threatened by extinction, and also those protected under international agreements. A further objective is the preservation of the diversity of species and genetic diversity. Special protection zones can also be established to more fully realize the idea of species protection of plants and fungi. These are areas considered exceptional with a view to the protection of refugees and communities of plants and fungi encompassed by species protection.

450. Pursuant to the provisions of Article 51 of the Nature Protection Act, the protection of wild plants and fungi encompassed by species protection serves as grounds for introducing restrictions on their wilful destruction, removal or damage, the destruction of their habitats and refuges, introducing changes to hydrographic conditions, the application of chemical substances and the destruction of forest cover or soil in refuges. Additional restrictions may be imposed on the breeding, harvesting, gathering, holding or possession of specimens of species of plants and fungi, as well as on their sale or offering for sale, exchange, presenting as a gift and transport. It may also be forbidden to introduce specimens of species of plants and fungi from other countries as well as to transport them outside the country's borders, and to wilfully relocate or introduce them in the natural environment.

451. Exemptions may be granted to the aforementioned restrictions on the condition that no alternative solutions exist and that there is no threat to maintaining the proper conditions of the protection of wild populations of protected plants and fungi.

452. An exception to the restrictions listed above is the performance of activities associated with conducting rational agricultural, forest or fishery management in the event the technology applied in such work makes it impossible to observe applicable restrictions. This does not, however, apply to species encompassed by enhanced protection listed in Annex IV to Council Directive 92/43/EEC of 21 May 1992 on the conservation of natural habitats and of wild fauna and flora (OJ L 206, 22.7.1992, pp. 7–50 with amendments; OJ L EU special Polish edition, Ch. 15, vol. 2, p. 102). This Directive lists such species as *Adenophora liliifolia*, *Agrimonia pilosa*, *Apium repens*, *Artemisia eriantha*, *Artemisia campestris*, *Bromus grossus*, *Campanula bohemica*, *Dianthus arenarius*, *Cochlearia tatrae*, *Galanthus nivalis*, *Gladiolus palustris* and *Pulsatilla vulgaris*. Failure to observe restrictions may be justified in the event plants and fungi are destructive to building materials or structures.

453. Another exception may be granted with the issuance of a permit by the regional director for environmental protection or the General Director for Environmental Protection allowing the harvesting of defined species of plants and fungi, as well as the holding, possession, disposal, offering for sale, exchange or gifting, and the removal from the country of specimens of species of plants and fungi harvested on the basis of such a permit. A permit may also be issued in the event that non-compliance with restrictions would be in the interest of the protection of wild species of plants and fungi or protection of natural habitats, or results from the necessity to limit significant damage to crops, livestock, forests, fish populations, water or other forms of property.

454. It may be allowed to engage in restricted activities if they are in the interest of public health or safety, or are vital to the performance of scientific experiments, educational activities or for purposes associated with the reconstitution of populations, the reintroduction of species of plants and fungi or objectives associated with the reproduction of plants, including by artificial methods.

Additionally, such activities are allowed if they facilitate, under tightly-controlled conditions and to a limited extent, the acquisition, harvesting or holding of specimens of protected plants and animals in such quantities as specified by the authority issuing the permit. Even in the case of species encompassed by enhanced protection as listed in Annex IV to Directive 92/43/EEC of 21 May 1992 on the conservation of natural habitats and of wild fauna and flora, such activities may be allowed if they result from the necessary imperative reasons of overriding public interest, including those of a social or economic nature, or requirements associated with beneficial effects of fundamental significance for the environment.

455. Particular regulations apply to species of plants and fungi under the threat of extinction, regulated under Article 47 of the Nature Protection Act. These species are subject to protection *ex situ* in zoological and botanical gardens, as well as in gene banks. The Act defines protection *ex situ* as the protection of species of plants and fungi outside their natural habitat. It should have as its objective the restoration of these species to the natural environment.

456. In order to preserve biodiversity, resources, creations and constituent elements of inanimate nature and landscape virtues, and also to restore the proper condition of natural reserves and constituent elements of nature, and primarily to reconstitute distorted natural habitats, plant habitats and fungi habitats, national parks are established.

457. Within the borders of national parks a large number of restrictions for the purposes of protecting plants and fungi are in place. They include a ban on the gathering, destruction or wilful damaging of plants and fungi, the use of chemical and biological means of plant protection and fertilizers, and also harvesting wild plants and animals or their parts with the exception of locations designated by the national park director; such places may be designated in nature reserves by the regional director for environmental protection. Restrictions are also in place on the introduction of species of plants and fungi without permission from the minister responsible for environmental affairs.

458. Alongside zoological and botanical gardens, an area in which particular protection is extended to plants and fungi is the landscape park; within its borders, tasks concerning the protection of nature, landscape virtues, cultural and historical values, and educational activities are carried out by the Landscape Park Ranger Service. One of this body's significant tasks is the conducting of surveys of natural habitats, communities of plants and fungi under species protection and their habitats, and also inanimate creations and constituent elements of nature deserving of protection.

459. With a view to ensuring the effective protection of species of plants and fungi threatened with extinction, the General Director for Environmental Protection is responsible for developing a protection programme. Under Article 57(2) of the Nature Protection Act, such programmes contain a description of the manners in which protection-related activities are conducted having as their objective the reconstitution of populations of species threatened by extinction, specification of the time and place of performance of such activities, indication of the responsible authority and information about the associated costs and sources of financing.

460. Authorities responsible for nature protection are obliged to initiate and support scientific research in respect of the protection of natural habitats, protection of habitats of plants encompassed by species protection, determination of changes in the population numbers of species of plants and animals, and also determining the impact of negative effects of chemical pollution on the population numbers of species of plants and animals under species protection.

461. These authorities are also assigned with particular tasks under Article 60(1) of the Nature Protection Act, to be performed with a view to rescuing species of plants and fungi under species protection from extinction; this consists of transporting these species to other places, eliminating the sources of threats to them, initiating protection *ex situ*, and creating conditions that facilitate their reproduction. If any stated or foreseen changes to the natural environment pose or may pose a threat to plants or fungi under species protection, the regional director for environmental protection or, in coastal areas, the General Director for Environmental Protection is, upon obtaining the opinion of the appropriate regional nature protection council and of the owner or manager of the terrain in question, to undertake activities in order to ensure the survival of the species and their habitat or refuge, to eliminate the sources of the threat, and to improve the condition of protection of their habitat or refuge. The regional director for environmental protection may, by way of an administrative decision, establish and liquidate zones of protection for refugees and communities of plants encompassed by species protection, as well as zones of protection for refugees and communities of fungi encompassed by species protection. Zones of protection are clearly marked by borders with appropriate signage containing the inscription 'plant refuge' or 'fungi refuge' and forbidding the entry of unauthorized persons.

462. Furthermore, apart from the indicated zones of particular care for the protection of plants and fungi, under Article 53 of the Nature Protection Act the regional director for environmental protection has the right to establish within the territory of a given voivodeship the protection of species of plants and fungi not encompassed by species protection under particular provisions of statute by way of an order constituting an act of local law. This order is effective for a defined period of time. Apart from indicating specific additional species of plants and fungi, it may also establish appropriate restrictions and exemptions from them.

463. The regional director for environmental protection also enacts a plan of protection tasks for a Natura 2000 area, taking into account the necessity to preserve and restore the proper condition of protection for natural habitats and species of plants or animals for whose protection the Natura 2000 area has been established. This plan contains a precise description of the borders and a map of the area, as well as the identification of existing and potential threats to the preservation of the appropriate condition of protection for natural habitats and species of plants and their habitats encompassed by protection.

464. A particularly important aspect of the protection of plants and fungi is the management of resources and constituent elements of nature. This issue is regulated by section 9 of the Nature Protection Act. The management of resources of wild plants and fungi, as well as of their genetic resources exploited by humans, should ensure their durability, optimal population numbers, and protection of genetic diversity. Protection is ensured in particular by facilitating the conditions for the reproduction and propagation of plants and fungi threatened with extinction, as well as the protection and restoration of their habitats and refuges.

465. The Nature Protection Act penalizes activities undertaken which are incompatible with nature protection. As a rule, the removal of trees gives rise to the obligation to pay a fee. An exception is set forth under Article 86, according to which fees are not collected for the removal of trees if such removal results from the need to protect plants and fungi encompassed by species protection or the protection of natural habitats. An administrative fine, assessed by the prefect (mayor), is imposed for the destruction of green areas, trees and bushes resulting from the improper performance of earthworks or from the use of mechanical equipment or technical equipment, as well as from the application of chemical substances in a manner harmful to plant life. A penalty is also imposed for the destruction of plant life resulting from the failure to apply or misapplication of substances for cultivation resulting in permanent damage to plants. A penalty for the destruction of green areas is waived in its entirety if the holder of the property reconstitutes the destroyed green area in the nearest vegetation season.

466. A departure from the forms of protection defined in the Nature Protection Act is to be found in the situation regulated under Article 125. This provision indicates that plants and fungi, as well as their habitats, that are not encompassed by forms of nature protection may only be damaged or destroyed in conjunction with the performance of tasks justified by the needs of nature protection, the conducting of scientific experiments or educational activity, rational management, or harvesting for one's own needs. The destruction of plants and fungi may also be justified by the conducting of rescue missions, public safety, sanitary and veterinary safety, the protection of human health and life, and prevention or removal of the effects of natural disasters.

467. Article 48 of the Nature Protection Act constitutes a reference to secondary legislation, and indicates that the minister responsible for environmental affairs, in consultation with the minister responsible for agriculture, shall issue a regulation listing the species of plants under enhanced protection, active protection, and partial protection which can be collected along with the manner of their collection, as well as those requiring the establishment of protection zones for their communities and refuges.

468. Additionally, this regulation sets forth the restrictions and relevant exemptions applicable to particular species and groups of species, as well as the manners of species protection, including the size of protection zones. The minister responsible for environmental affairs shall issue the regulation with a view to the need for protecting wild plants, their habitats, refuges and communities, as well as to ecological, scientific and cultural demands, and also taking account of the relevant provisions of EU law.

469. Currently binding Regulation of the Minister of the Environment on species protection of plants is the relevant secondary legislation in effect. Its objective is to eliminate discrepancies in the transposition of Directive 92/43/EEC of 21 May 1992 on the conservation of natural habitats and of wild fauna and flora, known as the 'Habitats Directive', as well as to adapt the contents of the legal act in question to the provisions of the Nature Protection Act, as amended by the Act amending the Nature Protection Act and other legislation.

470. The Regulation, first, establishes the species of wild plants encompassed by enhanced protection, with the designation of those species requiring active protection. This category includes the *Taxus baccata*, *Pinus* cembra, *Pinus mugo*, *Betula nana*, *Polypodium*, *Viola epipsila*, *Dianthus armeria*, *Anemone alpina*, *Anemone narcissiflora*, *Linum flavum*, *Primula* and *Daphne mezereum*. The second category defined in the Regulation are plants encompassed by partial protection, including *Pleurozium schreberi*, *Abies alba*, *Primula veris*, *Ribes nigrum* and *Convallaria majalis*. The third group of plants is composed of plants under partial protection but which can be harvested, and permitted manners of their gathering are also defined. The Regulation also lists plants requiring the establishment of protection zones for their refuges and communities, as well as the size of such zones. Furthermore, the Regulation sets forth the restrictions applicable to individual species or groups of species and exemptions from those restrictions. These restrictions are largely the same as those enumerated in Article 51 of the Nature Protection Act. In respect of plants representing species occurring in the wild, it is forbidden to pick, destroy or damage them and to destroy or damage their habitats and refuges, as well as to alter hydrographic conditions, to apply chemical substances, and to destroy forest cover and soil in refuges. In addition, it is forbidden to harvest, gather, hold, possess, prepare and process specimens of species, as well as to dispose of, acquire, offer for sale, exchange or gift, and to remove from the country specimens of those species.

471. The Regulation sets forth the manners of species protection of plants in great detail. This protection consists of securing the refuges and communities of plants against external threats. Additionally, it consists of the undertaking of protective measures for preserving the proper condition of plant habitats, in particular the preservation or restoration of proper lighting conditions for a given species, the preservation or restoration of proper soil and water conditions for a given species, the preservation or restoration of appropriate hydrographic conditions for a given species, the mowing of habitats in a manner appropriate for a given species, and the grazing of animals in the area of a habitat in a manner appropriate the protected species; the Regulation also addresses the numbers of plants, fungi and animals exerting their influence on protected species. Other protective activities include supporting the reproduction of a species in natural communities, the observation and monitoring of sites, refuges and populations of species and securing a representative portion of a population through protection *ex situ.* Reinforcing natural populations through introducing specimens bred *ex situ*, the restoration of plants from such facilities to the natural environment and removing threatened plants to new communities all have an impact on species protection of wild plants. Other means of protection are described in the literature as socioeconomic methods, which include education in recognizing protected species and ways of protecting them, rational cultivation of protected plant species used for commercial purposes, and promoting technology associated with rational agricultural, forest and fishery management that facilitate the preservation of refugees and communities of protected species.

472. If changes in the natural environment caused by human activity generate threats to plants under enhanced protection, the voivode is obliged to undertake appropriate action in order to ensure the preservation of the given species and its communities or to prevent or limit damage. Such actions may concern the maintenance of traditional forms of land-use of an area in which a threatened plant species is present, the development of a biotype for the protection of a threatened plant, and activities associated with plant reproduction.[139]

473. Issues involving species protection of fungi are regulated in a manner analogous to species protection of plants. Under Article 50 of the Nature Protection Act, the minister responsible for environmental affairs, in consultation with the minister responsible for agriculture, shall issue a regulation determining the species of fungi under enhanced protection, active protection, and partial protection which can be collected along with the manner of their collection, as well as those requiring the establishment of protection zones for their communities and refuges. Furthermore, this Regulation sets forth the restrictions applicable to individual species or groups of fungi species and exemptions from those restrictions. With a view to the need to protect wild fungi, their habitats, refuges and communities, as well as ecological, scientific and cultural demands, and the relevant EU law, specific manners of species protection for fungi have been established, including provisions taking into account the size of protection zones.

139. Boć, Nowacki, Samborska-Boć *Ochrona środowiska*, 260.

474. The current legal act in force governing issues of species protection of fungi is the Regulation of the Minister of the Environment of 9 September 2014 on the protection of species of fungi.[140] As in the case of regulation on plant protection, it is forbidden to pick, destroy or damage protected fungi and to destroy their habitats, influence their development in any way, and to prepare and process specimens of species, as well as to dispose, acquire, offer for sale, exchange or gift, or to remove them from the country. The Minister of the Environment may give consent to exceptions to restrictions in the case of fungi under enhanced protection, while the voivode may do so for partially protected species. The *Inonotus obliquus* and *Cetraria islandic lichen* may, with the permission of the voivode, be harvested in limited quantities for use by herbalists. The destruction of fungi and lichen in the process of farming, forest and fisheries management is generally not considered a violation of species protection regulations, but these exceptions do not apply to *Fomitopsis officinalis*. In the event of any threat at all to communities of protected species (including natural ones) the voivode is obliged to undertake appropriate action in order to protect the community. Means of protection of wild fungi species include securing refuges and fungi communities from external threats, as well as ensuring the presence and protection of the various types of undergrowth on which protected fungi species develop, including trees of a certain age and species, disintegrating trees, rocks and gases.

475. The Regulation specifies protection activities for preserving the appropriate condition of fungi habitats, which include the preservation or restoration of appropriate light conditions for a given species, as well as of soil quality, hydrographic conditions, mowing of a habitat in a manner appropriate for a given species, and grazing by farm animals in the area of a habitat. Protection activities also consist of securing a representative portion of a population through protection *ex situ,* reinforcing natural populations through introducing specimens bred *ex situ*, the restoration of fungi from such facilities to the natural environment and removing threatened fungi to new communities. The preservation of refugees and communities of protected species is also furthered by education in recognizing protected species and ways of protecting them, as well as promoting technology associated with rational agricultural, forest and fishery management that facilitate the preservation of refugees and communities of protected species.

476. The Regulation names four groups of wild fungi species. The first of them are those under enhanced (total) protection. Among them are *Boletus radicans*, *Boletus regius*, *Boletus parasiticus*, *Strobilomyces strobilaceus* and *Microstoma protractum*. The second group of protected wild fungi species are those afforded partial protection. The third category consists of fungi given partial protection that may be harvested using defined means. Partial protection does not rule out reducing population volumes. If necessary, protective actions may be taken in order to restore the natural condition of ecosystems and constituent elements of nature, as well as to preserve natural habitats and those of plants and fungi. The fourth category,

140. Dz. U. 2014, item 1408.

however, includes the four rarest species of lichen, for which an additional 50 m or 100 m protection zone around their communities is also designated.

Chapter 5. Protection of Animals

§1. Legal Foundations for the Protection of Animals

I. Animal Protection and Constitutional Provisions

477. Regulations concerning the protection of animals in Poland have been introduced in legal acts of various rank. This legislation extends a greater amount of consideration to animal life than is usual when contrasted to other regulations addressing the natural environment. The mere fact that this element is a part of nature is not a sufficiently important value in qualifying it as a good that is inherently owed protection. The civilization in which we live takes the ultimate decision as to whether a particular constituent element of reality will be given protection. 'We will thus protect what is protected by civilization, and we will not protect what people decide is not intended for protection but rather intended for elimination through consumption or in the name of protecting other resources'.[141] The scope of protection of animals can also be applied to types of human behaviour that are manifestations of culture which simultaneously aim at ensuring sustenance for people that is natural, polluted to the smallest degree possible and raised in appropriate conditions consistent with broadly-accepted standards.

II. The Catalogue of Legislation Regulating the Protection of Animals

478. The catalogue of legislation regulating the protection of animals is grounded in generally applicable normative acts. The Constitution of the Republic of Poland of 2 April 1997,[142] as the highest-ranking legal act in the system, contains no direct mention of issues associated with the protection of animals. It does, however, contain provisions regulating the protection of the natural environment reflecting the concept of caring for all elements created by nature. Mention should be made here of Article 5, which places a clear emphasis on the need to ensure the protection of the natural environment, following the principle of sustainable development.

The placement of the requirement to protect the natural environment in the fundamental section of the Constitution allows for the conclusion that the Republic considers issues surrounding the protection of the environment to be among those of the greatest importance, equal to safeguarding the independence and the integrity of its territory. The issue of protection of the natural environment is further explored in Chapter II, 'The Freedoms, Rights and Obligations of Persons and Citizens'. Worthy of mention here are the provisions of Articles 74, 68(4), 86 and 31(3). They regulate the obligation of public authorities to pursue policies ensuring the ecological security of current and future generations, to protect the natural environment, providing information about the condition of the natural environment and its protection, to provide support for initiatives undertaken by citizens to protect and

141. Boć, Nowacki, Samborska Boć, *Ochrona środowiska*, 263.
142. Dz. U. No. 78, item 483 with amendments.

improve the environment, and to prevent the negative health consequences of degradation of the environment. Additionally, public authorities oblige every citizen and all other entities to care for the natural environment, while allowing for the potential of them to bear liability for activities resulting in damage to it. A guarantee of protection of the aforementioned rights is to be found in Article 31(3), which sets forth that any limitation upon the exercise of constitutional freedoms and rights may be imposed only by statute, and only when necessary in a democratic state for the protection of its security or public order, or to protect the natural environment, health or public morals, or the freedoms and rights of other persons. Such limitations shall not violate the essence of freedoms and rights.

Such constitutional regulations are, however, very general; they establish a starting point for further regulation, providing a basis for norms of a lower rank to extend and clarify legislation addressing the issue of animal protection. This is realized in statutes and regulations. The most important acts regulating the issue of the protection of animals are the Environmental Protection Act of 27 April 2001[143] the Nature Protection Act of 16 April 2004,[144] and the Animal Protection Act of 21 August 1997.[145] Other legal acts regulate more specific areas of protection. Some examples of this type of regulation are the Hunting Act of 13 October 1995[146] and Act of 22 June 2001 on microorganisms and GMO.[147] This detailed legislation can serve as the basis for distinguishing a classification of specific cases of animal protection. This classification includes the humanitarian and functional protection of animal species and protection regulations concerning GMO.

§2. The Evolution of Animal Protection Regulation

I. Subjective Scope of Animal Protection

479. The Environmental Protection Act determines the subjective scope of the protection of animals by specifying that it consists of preserving valuable ecosystems, biodiversity and maintenance of natural equilibrium, fostering conditions for proper development, preventing or limiting negative environmental impact factors that could have a detrimental effect on animal resources and welfare, and preventing threats to natural complexes and formations. This is achieved through extending protection to spaces and objects of natural value, establishing the protection of animal species, limiting the possibility of capturing wild animals, recreating populations (including ensuring the reproduction of wild animals) and overseeing the introduction of GMO into the natural environment. This is also achieved through protecting forests and forested areas from pollution and fire, limiting the cutting of

143. Dz. U. 2018, item 799 with amendments.
144. Dz. U. 2018, item 1641 with amendments.
145. Dz. U. 2017, item 1840 with amendments.
146. Dz. U. 2018, item 2033.
147. Dz. U. 2017, 2134 with amendments.

trees and brush, and eliminating greenery by afforestation or by introducing concentrations of vegetation, particularly when this is necessary for protecting soil and animals, influencing the climate.

II. The Development of Animal Protection in Poland

480. Humanitarian protection of animals is a type of protection of animals from humans and human activity that generates animal suffering. It is grounded in human ethics, which forbids inflicting unnecessary suffering on animals.[148] The first Polish legal regulations intended to ensure legal protection for animals were enacted in the twentieth century. These regulations included the Regulation of the President of the Republic of Poland on the protection of animals[149] and the Regulation of the Ministry of Higher Education on determining the conditions and manner of conducting animal experimentation and procedures for issuing related permits of 16 November 1959.[150] This protection encompasses all categories of animals (household, cultivated, wild and domesticated) and also guarantees such protection to animals not belonging to any of those categories, such as fish, birds and amphibians. The substance of this protection consisted of a ban on all forms of abuse and suffering inflicted on those beings without an appropriately important and justified cause, as well as the obligation to ensure appropriate living conditions. Scientific experiments and associated necessary activities involving the use of animals were not considered as abuse, insofar as they were performed by persons holding special permits from oversight bodies. These experiments could only be conducted in scientific research centres of institutions of higher education and of the Polish Academy of Science, as well as research institutes, medical treatment facilities and pharmacological research facilities. In later years there was a resurgence of discussion in international public opinion concerning the humanitarian treatment of animals. This led to changes in the relevant legislation in 1972 with the entry into force of the Code of Petty Offences of 20 May 1971.[151] At the time, regulation on petty offences concerning animal abuse was included in section VII, 'Offences against public order and peace'. The punishment of temporary jailing was foreseen, categories of individuals that could be held responsible for animal abuse were expanded, and it was decided to penalize both the acts of incitement and aiding and abetting. The legal situation of animals, and by the same token the scope of protection afforded them, was affected by the entry into force of the Animal Protection Act of 1997. This Act definitively declared that an animal is not considered an object, using a legislative technique termed as the normative 'dereification' of animals. This brought Polish legislation into line with that of other European legal orders. The application of dereification in Polish legislation was doubtlessly encouraged by processes taking place on a global scale, finding their reflection in the expansion of humanitarian protection of animals, in a range of spheres in relations between humans and animals.

148. L. Jastrzębski, *Prawo ochrony środowiska w Polsce*, 124 (Warszawa 1990).
149. Dz. U. No. 36, item 332.
150. Dz. U. No. 71, item 452.
151. Dz. U. 2013, item 482 with amendments.

This significant legislative undertaking was representative of a reassessment of the human-animal relationship. It served as an expression of the new conception of the animal as a subject of legal relationships. Additionally, in this regulation emphasis was placed on the criteria that decided upon the legal nature of animals and the necessity to protect them. Animals were acknowledged as belonging to the world of living beings, recognition was given to their capacity to experience suffering (which allows for differentiation of animals from other living organisms, particularly vegetation), and ultimately they were contrasted with things as the expression of inanimate material.

481. The regulation in the aforementioned Act encompasses all animals, declaring that every one of them was entitled to humanitarian treatment.[152] In this Act we may differentiate regulation concerning humanitarian treatment, transport, sacrifice, and cases involving scientific experimentation, itself regulated in separate, specific legislation. The killing of animals is generally banned, while there is a catalogue of circumstances justifying deviations from that principle. Such exceptions are foreseen in Article 6(1), which lists circumstances involving the slaughter and putting to death of cultivated animals, wild birds and mammals raised for the purposes of meat production and harvesting of hides, the necessity of immediate sacrifice, actions vital to removing a serious threat to sanitation, the removal of specimens constituting a direct threat to humans and/or other animals if there are no other means of doing so, hunting, culls and limiting the population of wild game and the killing of animals from species presenting a threat to native species and/or natural habitats and nesting places. A similar, radical approach by the legislator to situations involving the abuse of animals is expressed in Article 6(1a), which introduces a legal definition of abuse that the statute gives as inflicting or consciously allowing the infliction of pain and/or suffering. Following that, a catalogue of example situations that should be determined as abuse is given. Abuse here is considered to be the deliberate infliction of injury or mutilation on an animal, the conducting of all operations intended to change the appearance of an animal for any reason other than rescuing its health or life, the use of animals that are too old, too young or sick for labour or for purposes of sport and recreation, as well as forcing animals to perform activities that could cause pain, beating animals in order to cause pain, treatment of animals in a manner that causes needless suffering and stress, forcing animals to be assume unnatural positions that cause needless pain, corporeal damage or death, cruel frightening and/or excitement of animals, keeping animals in improper living conditions, discarding animals, applying cruel methods in the housing and/or husbandry of animals, and organizing fights between animals. The Act includes provisions protecting an animal that has been treated cruelly, by allowing for the seizure of the animal from its owner or caretaker upon a decision by the prefect (mayor) with authority in the animal's place of residence and handing it over to a shelter, another household or zoological garden. Such a decision is taken by the appropriate authority after receiving information from the police, local law enforcement authorities, a veterinarian or authorized representative of a civic organization whose statutory activity comprises the protection of animals, and this decision is subject to

152. M. Goettel, *Sytuacja zwierzęcia w prawie cywilnym* (Lex 2013).

immediate enforcement. In cases of immediate concern, when remaining with its owner would constitute a threat to the health or life of the animal, the police or their authorized representative shall seize the animal, then immediately inform the prefect (mayor) of such. Anyone keeping domesticated or cultivated animals is obliged to ensure them shelter from cold, heat and atmospheric precipitation with access to sunlight and allowing them freedom of movement, and to provide them with appropriate sustenance and constant access to water. It is forbidden to give animals in stalls feed containing growth hormones, as well as to fatten geese and ducks to the extent of bruising their liver. It is also forbidden to import animals and animal products raised or kept in conditions violating the Act's provisions. An individual who comes across a discarded animal, particularly one that is tethered, is obliged to inform the nearest animal shelter, local law enforcement body or the police. Securing and providing care to homeless animals is the task of commune authorities. The commune council is obliged to perform this duty by passing a resolution not later than 31 March of every year containing a programme outlining care for homeless animals and preventing animal homelessness.

§3. Particular Regulations Concerning the Protection of Animals

I. The Use of Animals for Recreational Purposes

482. The fourth section distinguishes situations in which animals are used for such purposes as recreation, entertainment and film production. It specifies that the prevailing conditions in performances, rehearsals and training, as well as handling methods applied to these animals, may neither pose a threat to their health and life nor cause suffering. The conditions in which animals perform must be reviewed and approved by the Chief Veterinary Officer or a duly appointed individual. It is forbidden to subject such animals to pharmacological and mechanized methods, as well as to drugging. These animals should be provided with appropriate living conditions similar to those of domesticated and cultivated animals, and they should be given continual veterinary care. The use of animals in performances and sports characterized by cruelty, particularly fights involving the participation of bulls, dogs and roosters, is banned. Dressage and pageantry and entertainment displays may only feature animals born and raised in captivity, and only such animals for which conditions of existence appropriate for the given species can be provided. Training may not be conducted with the sole intent of inducing greater aggressiveness. The detention, breeding and presentation of free-range animals are permissible only in stables, circuses and circus bases, as well as in locations designed for such animals, under the supervision of the Veterinary Inspectorate in a manner ensuring the safety of people and animals. Animals living in the wild are a public good, and conditions for their development and free existence are to be ensured. The obtaining of wild animals for taxonomy or collection requires a permit from the Marshal of the province.

II. Transport of Animals

483. Section 7 of the Act also regulates matters concerning animal transport, assuming that it is performed using means adapted for such purposes and in appropriate conditions, ensuring the animals' proper positioning, temperature and rest. Inspections, licences, permits and registers are the tools employed for compliance purposes, with the county veterinary officer acting as the relevant authority. Veterinary and medical treatments may be performed to save the lives and health of animals, as well as for population control; they may only be undertaken by authorized individuals, with due care, and in a manner limiting the suffering and stress experienced by the animal.

III. The Killing of Animals

484. The killing of animals (tenth section) may only take place in a humanitarian manner, understood as one involving the lowest possible levels of physical and psychological suffering. In the event it is deemed necessary to immediately put an animal down in order to relieve its suffering, this necessity is to be declared by a veterinarian or other authorized entity. In the event animals constitute an extraordinary threat to human life and health or to wildlife management, it is permissible to take measures aimed at limiting the populations of such animals. This is carried out by the provincial assembly, which passes a resolution to that effect. Vertebrate animals can only be slaughtered in abattoirs after being rendered unconscious by individuals holding the proper qualifications. The Veterinary Inspectorate is responsible for supervision over the compliance with animal protection regulations. Social organizations whose statutory purpose is to engage in animal protection are authorized to cooperate with the Veterinary Inspection in carrying out such oversight. Section 11 of the Animal Protection Act contains regulations that provide for the criminal liability of those who do not adhere to its orders.

IV. Animal Testing

485. Animals used for experiments constitute a separate category in respect of protection, and while they are relatively few in number, their situation is regulated in the Animal Experimentation Act.

486. The Act regulates the rules and conditions for the protection of animals used for scientific or educational purposes, specifying the rules of performing procedures and conducting experiments, conducting activities by breeders, suppliers and users and conducting inspections of breeders, suppliers and users. The conditions for keeping animals used for scientific or educational purposes and the way of dealing with these animals as well as the tasks and competences of ethics committees for animal experimentation are also specified. The procedures shall be carried out only for the purpose of carrying out research, ensuring animal welfare or improving the conditions of husbandry or breeding of a livestock, development and production of medicinal products, foodstuffs, protection of the environment in the interests of health or human and animal welfare and higher education or training in to acquire or improve professional competences. The implementation of procedures is permissible only if the research method ensuring the achievement of research objective without animal testing (substitution principle) cannot be applied, or the number of animals used for that purpose is limited to the level necessary to achieve the objectives (the principle of limitation). The permissibility of procedures is also determined by the indication of the animals used, which are to be maintained in conditions appropriate for their species, and the test methods used in the procedures shall be chosen to minimize or eliminate pain, suffering, distress or the possibility of permanent damage to the animals' organism (principle of improvement). It is unacceptable to perform the procedure if it is associated with severe pain, suffering or distress, which can be long-lasting and cannot be relieved. Procedures are not carried out with the use of *Hominoidea*, wild animals and homeless animals (Article 8).

487. Chapter 3 specifies the requirements for conducting activities in regard to the use of animals for scientific or educational purposes, whereas in accordance with Article 26, the activity of husbandry, delivering animals or performing procedures requires obtaining an entry in the register of breeders, suppliers and users, hereinafter referred to as the 'register'. Competent authorities on granting and changing the permit for animal experimentation are the National Ethical Committee for Animal Experimentation and local ethics committees for animal experimentation. According to the Article 42 experiments are carried out after obtaining the permit of the local commission issued at the user's request. The *poviat* veterinary officer competent for the location of the centre exercises control over the of breeders, suppliers and users in the scope of their activity covered by the entry in the register (Article 54).

V. Farm and Domestic Animals

488. Preservation of animal use value encompasses farm and domestic animals, animals used for recreational and special purposes, and wild game. Protection of farm animals is regulated by the Farm Animal Husbandry Act of 29 June 2007.[153] This regulates the manner in which the husbandry of farm animals is conducted, and it provides a definition of farm animals by listing animals which qualify as such. Article 2(1–3) lists farm animals as horses and horse-like animals, cattle, cervids, poultry, hogs, sheep, goats, honeybees and fur-bearing animals maintained for the purpose of producing raw material for the fur, meat or textile industries. The Act regulates matters related to husbandry and the maintenance of genetic resources, the assessment of their use and husbandry value, the maintenance of husbandry records and registers, and also the oversight of husbandry and facilities for farm animals. In other words, it contains provisions aimed primarily at improving the genetic stock (genotype) of farm animals and, as a result, their value in use and husbandry. The

153. Dz. U. 2017, item 2132.

aforementioned Animal Protection Act provides explicit protection to farm animals. The protection of farm animals consists of ensuring care and appropriate living conditions for them. Thus, conditions of rearing and husbandry may not cause injuries, bodily harm or other suffering to animals. Forbidden practices include fattening geese and ducks to induce bruised livers, housing calves over 8 weeks of age in individual pens or tethers (except during feeding periods for not longer than one hour), and holding animals in spaces not compliant with norms established for a given species, age and physiological condition. The manner and conditions of using animals for labour may not constitute an unjustified threat to their life and health, nor cause suffering. This includes bans on overworking animals; using ill or undernourished animals for labour; using harnesses, bits, saddles, packsaddles, horseshoes, vehicles or other tools whose poor condition or improper construction may cause bodily harm or death to animals; using objects or instruments for driving animals that may cause injury; forcing animals bearing and/or towing loads to a trot or gallop leading to exhaustion; and using horses under 5 years of age in logrolling. In addition, an individual using an animal for labour is required to ensure proper periods of rest during every twenty-four-hour period necessary for a given breed to recover its strength. Additionally, entities maintaining farm animals are required by the legislator to store veterinary documentation recording courses of treatment and other veterinary operations, as well as to keep records of dead animals, for a three-year period. The introduction of rearing technologies previously not applied within the borders of the Republic of Poland requires the receipt of a special permit verifying that the given technology fulfils statutorily-defined requirements.

489. Another group of animals provided with protection is that of domestic animals kept by people for the satisfaction of their emotional needs. They are to be provided with appropriate care and proper treatment. Domestic animals are legally defined in Article 4(17) of the Animal Protection Act as those traditionally accompanying humans in their home or other appropriate space, kept as company. This issue and related matters concerning the protection of animals used for recreational purposes have been extensively discussed in reference to the humanitarian treatment of animals. However, it is necessary to add some remarks concerning the husbandry of dog breeds recognized as aggressive, in respect of which the legislator sets forth certain restrictions. Pursuant to Article 10(1), breeding or keeping a dog of a breed recognized as aggressive requires a licence from the relevant commune authority for the planned location of the kennel, issued upon application of the individual intending to operate the kennel or house such a dog. This decision is issued in the first instance by the prefect (mayor). A schedule of dog breeds regarded as aggressive is contained in the regulation of the Minister of the Interior and Administration of 28 April 2003 concerning a schedule of dog breeds regarded as aggressive, which contains eleven particular breeds[154] and lists breeds such as the American Pit Bull Terrier, Dogo Argentino, Tosa Inu and Caucasian Shepherd.

154. Dz. U. No. 77, item 687.

VI. Wild Game Animals

490. Protection of wild game animals is governed by the Hunting Act of 13 October 1995.[155] It defines hunting as 'an element of protection of the natural environment that denotes protection of wild game animals and management of their resources in accordance with the principles of ecology and of rational farm, forestry and game management.' Underlying the organization of protection and exploitation of game is the fact that animals living freely in the wild are the property of the State Treasury. Under the current legal regime, the concept of game is specified in a Regulation of the Minister of the Environment of 11 March 2005 on establishing a schedule of game animal species.[156] It lists seven species of big game animals (moose, red deer, sika deer, fallow deer, roe deer, boar, mouflon) and twenty-four species of small game (fox, raccoon, badger, pine marten, marten, American mink, polecat, raccoon, muskrat, hare, wild rabbit, grouse, pheasant, partridge, greylag goose, bean goose, white-fronted goose, mallard, teal, pochard, tufted duck, pigeon, woodcock, coot, golden jackal). In respect of environmental protection, the Act places emphasis on reconciling hunting with the scientific principles describing the bonds and reciprocal influences shared between plant and animal life and their environment. Further reconciliation places emphasis on compliance with rational agricultural, forest and fishery management, while indicating the unique nature of the concept and understanding of hunting's social and economic significance. The primary objectives of hunting as listed in the Act include maintaining diversity and managing the populations of game animals, protecting and influencing the natural environment so as to improve the living conditions of game animals, achieving the best possible individual condition and quality of game trophies and the appropriate population levels of particular species, while simultaneously maintaining the equilibrium of the natural environment and satisfying the social needs of those who wish to practice hunting, cultivate its traditions and develop its ethos and culture. The protection of game animals consists of creating conditions for their safe existence, particularly by fighting against poaching and all instances of hunting sabotage, and banning such activities as the startling, catching, detention, injuring and killing of animals outside of hunting and fishing activities; the gathering and possession of eggs and chicks; the manufacture and possession of eggshells; and the destruction of lairs, burrows and birds' nests. Planned game animal management, as indicated by J. Boć and E. Samborska-Boć,[157] is conducted on the basis of annual hunting plans drawn up by the leaseholders of game districts after receiving the opinion of the prefect (mayor), then confirmed by an authorized forester from the SFNFH in cooperation with the Polish Hunting Union. In districts without leaseholders, plans are drawn up by the managers of those districts and confirmed by the head of the local directorate for the SFNFH. Multiannual game husbandry plans are also prepared by heads of regional directorates of the SFNFH in cooperation with provincial governments and the Polish Hunting Union. Game animal population management requires such activities as the establishment of fixed and temporary

155. Dz. U. 2018, item 2033 with amendments.
156. Dz. U. No. 45, item 433.
157. Boć, Nowacki, Samborska-Boć,*Ochrona środowiska*, 286.

shelter for game animals (forests, woods, sheds, shelter for breeding grounds); the enrichment of natural food stocks for game animals in forests; the maintenance of natural water reserves alongside the reconstruction and development of new ones; a rational application of chemicals in agriculture and forestry; the application of agrotechnology that will not pose a threat to the living conditions of game animals in a given territory; the maintenance of wildlife corridors for game animals; maintaining an age and gender structure as well as an abundance of the game animal population appropriate for ensuring ecosystem balance and for accomplishing fundamental economic objectives in agriculture, forestry and fishing; and protecting game animals from the dangers posed by automobiles on national and provincial roads. Hunting, as a permissible form of animal acquisition, may only be undertaken in forest or field hunting districts created by the provincial governor and leased to hunting associations. Use of such districts is dependent on the conclusion of a contract of lease. Domestic and foreign trade in live game (excluding trade performed by leaseholders), game animal carcasses and body parts, as well as the sale of tour packages including hunting, require a permit from the Minister of Environment.

VII. Species Protection of Animals

491. Another form of protection provided for in Polish legislation is the species protection of animals, broadly regulated by the provisions of the Nature Protection Act of 16. Pursuant to Article 52(1) of that Act, in relation to wild animals covered by species protection, bans can be imposed on their wilful killing, injury and capture as well as transport, acquisition, keeping, rearing and husbandry; the possession of live animals; collecting, keeping and possessing specimens of species; the wilful destruction of their eggs and other youth and developmental forms; the destruction of their habitats and refuges; the destruction of nests, hives, burrows, lairs, lodges, dams, spawning grounds, winter habitats and other forms of shelter; the gathering, possession and storing of eggs; the gathering, possession and storing of eggshells; preparing specimens of species; the disposal, acquisition or offering of specimens of species for sale, exchange or as gifts; and importing and exporting specimens of species. In addition, there is a strict requirement to limit wilful startling and upsetting, photography, filming and observation that may cause disquiet and disturbance. Also, it is forbidden to relocate such animals from places they regularly occupy to other locations, as well as to relocate animals born and reared in captivity to wild habitats. A catalogue of wild animals placed under full and partial species protection is set forth in the regulation of the Minister of the Environment of 16 December 2016 on species protection of animals.[158] Pursuant to Article 52(2), when there are no alternatives then it is permissible to introduce exceptions to the aforementioned prohibitions insofar as they do not cause a threat to wild animals encompassed by species protection. The legislator also allows for exemptions from the prohibitions and restrictions set forth in a legal act that introduces species protection on the bases of individual legislative acts. Authorities charged with protecting the natural environment are also under the obligation to initiate and support

158. Dz. U. 2016, item 2183.

scientific research; such research in respect of animals includes the protection of the habitats of animals under species protection and of migrating animals and habitats along migration routes, along with the protection of places where they hibernate or nest, as well as research determining population fluctuations of animal species. The import and export of protected species are also subject to certain restrictions. It is forbidden to introduce animals into the environment that are foreign to native flora and fauna.

VIII. Species Protection of Fishes

492. Animal protection is also regulated under the Inland Fishing Act of 18 April 1985.[159] It defines the manner in which rational fishing management is to be conducted as well as the introduction and transport of foreign species in bodies of water, detailed conditions for fishing and protection, and the subject of permit issuance.

493. Maritime resources are also regulated in the Marine Fishing Act of 19 December 2014,[160] which establishes protection for the sensible engagement of fishing, including protection for animate maritime resources through oversight and supervision of those engaged in fishing and trade in its products.

IX. Genetically Modified Organisms and Trans-genetic Animals

494. In an age of rapid technological advances in the field of genetic engineering, the legislator could not leave issues surrounding GMO and transgenic animals unregulated. In order to achieve characteristics desirable in breeding, such as quicker growth, greater resistance to disease and high milk production levels, breeders conduct selective breeding of animals to shape the genetic characteristics of future farm animals. In spite of the fact that animal modification is not nearly equal in prevalence to plant modification, its development serves as a basis for experiments on human illnesses. The most important areas of scientific work are related to the production of antibiotics and vaccines, human proteins and antibodies, and the use of animals as producers of organs used in human transplants. There are a large number of ethical objections to these practices, however. It is difficult to call into question the potential benefits from the use of GMOs, but their mere presence gives rise to serious doubts as to ecological security. Regulation addressing GMOs, as indicated by J. Jendrośka and M. Bar, is presently one of the most dynamically developing branches of environmental protection law. In Polish law, the issue of using and handling GMO is regulated in the Microorganisms Genetically Modified Organisms Act of 22 June 2001.[161] A genetically modified organism is defined by Article 3(13) as an organism other than a human in which the genetic material has

159. Dz. U. 2018, item 1476 with amendments.
160. Dz. U. 2018, item 514 with amendments.
161. Dz. U. 2017, item 2134.

been altered in a manner that does not occur naturally, as a result of cross-breeding or natural recombination, including by, but not limited to, the use of detailed techniques. The legislator presently lists five types of activities associated with GMOs and microorganisms requiring that certain standards are met, including the requirement to be issued with an administrative decision. These activities comprise the use of GMOs and microorganisms in closed systems, the intended introduction of GMOs and microorganisms into the environment, bringing GMOs to market. These regulations are not, however, applicable to genetically modified human genomes, food products and pharmaceutical products. The user of a GMO is required to obtain a valid decision from the minister competent in matters concerning the environment allowing the introduction of a GMO product to market. Such permits are issued for a fixed time, not longer than for ten years. The governmental administration body authorized to deal with matters concerning GMOs is the minister competent in matters concerning the environment. This minister's activities include giving approval to an intended introduction of a GMO into the environment or the use of a GMO in a closed system, issuing permits for introducing GMO products to market. Permits and approvals are granted by the minister competent in matters of the environment, who issues an administrative decision. Additionally, the minister responsible for environmental affairs is tasked with developing a draft of the National Biological Safety Strategy and associated programme of activities accompanying it, which are then confirmed by a resolution of the Council of Ministers. Transparency and the requirement to keep the public informed of proceedings concerning the genetic modification of organisms are to ensure that society has the possibility to participate in any decision-making process addressing the use of GMO in a closed system, activities involving the planned release of a GMO into the environment, and also the introduction of GMO into trade. The competent advisory body is the commission on GMO matters, which issues its opinion on permit applications submitted to the appropriate minister, verifies such applications involving a review of the assessment of threats to human health and the environment, and offers opinions on state GMO policy. Administrative, civil and criminal liability can all be incurred as a result of either damage proceeding from the use of GMOs or the violation of criminal provisions contained in the statute.

§4. Summary

495. By focusing on the issue of animal protection in domestic legislation, it has also been possible to demonstrate the practical dimension of the protection afforded to animals in Poland. It would seem appropriate here to refer to the words of M. Gabriel-Węglowski, who feels that 'the positive law in force at a given moment and in a given place is, in every area of life, a highly valuable contribution that says a great deal about the current level of development of the civilization served by that law. This development can be reflected as in a mirror, or it can also be stimulated.'[162] One such reflection can be that certain elements of the surrounding environment, primarily living creatures, are acknowledged as not only means to

162. M. Gabriel-Węglowski, *Przestępstwa przeciwko humanitarnej ochronie zwierząt* (Toruń 2008).

achieving particular ends but as ends in and of themselves, possessing inherent value.

Chapter 6. Forest Protection

§1. General Conditions for Protection of Forests in Poland

I. Legal Bases of Forest Protection

496. Forests, as permanent elements of the biosphere and primary components of the natural environment, and also as goods belonging to the entire nation, are the object of particular protection from the state; this is reflected in numerous statutes, regulations, orders, instructions and principles.

497. The protection of forests in Poland is regulated by legal acts of all ranks. Leading statutes regulating the issue include the Environmental Protection, the Nature Protection Act, the Forest Act of 28 September 1991,[163] the Agricultural and Forest Lands Protection Act of 3 February 1995,[164] and the Act of 6 July 2001 on maintaining the national character of the country's strategic natural assets.[165]

II. The Social Objective of Forest Protection

498. Forests have a significant impact on the protection of the natural environment through their protective and social functions, as well as their productive function, all performed in compliance with the principle of stable and sustainable forest management. This activity aims at shaping the structure of forests and their exploitation at a pace and in a manner ensuring the preservation of their biological diversity, high productivity levels and the regenerative potential, vigour and capacity to fulfil, both now and in the future, all of their important protective, commercial and social functions at the local, national and global level without harm to other ecosystems.

The objective of legal and factual activities, commenced to fulfil the protective functions, is to maintain and enhance the productivity of forests, and to secure the beneficial effects of forests on the climate, economy, and the health and culture of communities. In forest protection, of crucial importance are prevention of forests and wooded areas from the damaging effects of environmental pollution, afforestation and the development of concentrations of vegetation, especially when it is necessary due to the need to protect the soil and the animal world, shape the climate and important needs related to ensuring natural balance and satisfying the needs of people in regard to recreation.

163. Dz. U. 2017, item 788 with amendments.
164. Dz. U. 2017, item 116 with amendments.
165. Dz. U. 2018, item 1235 with amendments.

III. State Monitoring

499. The Environmental Protection Act does not define the concept of a forest, nor does it set forth the material scope of forest protection. However, section 4 of the Act does indicate one source of information about the environment, namely state environmental monitoring. This institution consists of the system of measurements, evaluations and forecasts of the condition of the natural environment, as well as the collection, processing and dissemination of information about the natural environment. It supports environmental protection activities through the systematic informing of administrative authorities and society about the quality of components of the natural environment, as well as changes taking place and the causes of those changes. Article 26(1)(6) indicates that the scope of state environmental monitoring includes information concerning the condition of environmental resources, including of forests. Monitoring is performed according to a cyclical schedule, and standardized methods for collecting, collating and processing data are applied, together with the use and registration of spatial data. International agreements oblige Poland to forward the data gathered to interested parties. Forest protection, as defined by Article 127(2)(5–7), is undertaken in particular by such means as protecting forests and wooded areas from pollution and fire, thus leading to restrictions in the cutting down of trees and wooded areas, as well as in the liquidation of green spaces. The maintenance of valuable ecosystems, biodiversity and natural equilibrium are all supported by afforestation and the creation of concentrations of vegetation, particularly in conjunction with the need to protect soil and animal life, to shape the climate, to ensure equilibrium in nature and to meet the recreational needs of humans.

IV. General Conditions of Protection of Forests in the Nature Protection Act

500. The Nature Protection Act does not constitute the direct regulation of forests as a whole but rather addresses the protection of particular elements of that ecosystem. The Act defines the objectives, principles and forms of protection of both animate and inanimate elements of the landscape. Article 2(1) defines nature protection as the maintenance, sustainable use and renewal of resources, creations and elements of nature, particularly wild flora, fauna and fungi, greenery in urban and rural areas, and wooded areas. Section 4 of the Act regulates the protection of green and wooded areas, imposing on communal and municipal councils the obligation to establish green and wooded areas and to maintain them in an appropriate condition.

V. Tree Removal Permit

501. The issue of removing trees and bushes from real property is regulated in detail by Article 83 of the Nature Protection Act, which provides for the possibility of removing trees and bushes subject to the consent of the prefect (mayor) at the request of the real property's possessor with the consent of the owner and/or owner of device, if said trees and bushes constitute a danger to the operation of such equipment. Consent from the owner of the real property is not required in the event of an application submitted by the holder of perpetual usufruct rights to the real property. A permit for the removal of trees and bushes from real property entered into the landmark register is issued by the provincial landmark conservator, whereas the removal of trees in the area around a right-of-way (save for foreign species of poplars) requires thirty days' advance coordination with the regional director for environmental protection. Before a permit may be issued, an inspection is conducted to determine if there are any protected species of trees or bushes present. On occasion, issuance of a permit is dependent on the replanting of trees and bushes in a place indicated by the issuer of the permit, or on replacement of them with other trees and bushes in a quantity at least equivalent to the number of removed trees and bushes. This provision provides for exceptional treatment of trees and bushes growing in forests and trees of under ten years of age removed from areas located between the coastline and a flood levee or natural high shore along which a flood levee has been constructed on the basis of a decision by the appropriate authority, as well as those removed on the basis of a decision by the appropriate authority and which obstruct the view of signalling devices and trains, creating difficulties in the operation of railway equipment, or which lead to the formation of snowdrifts on railways. Similar consideration is also given to fruit trees, with the exception of those growing on real property entered into the landmark register or within the borders of a national park or nature reserve in areas not encompassed by landscape protection, on tree and bush plantations, trees removed in conjunction with the functioning of botanical and zoological gardens, and also those constituting obstructions to air traffic, removed on the basis of a decision by the appropriate authority for purposes related to the maintenance of water amelioration infrastructure. In these cases, a permit is issued by the authority indicated in separate legal acts.

VI. Fees for Tree Removal

502. Pursuant to Article 84(1), every possessor of a real property who wishes to remove a tree or bush shall pay a fee for doing so. The level of the fee and the time of the removal, replanting or planting of other trees and bushes are established in the permit by the authority authorized to issue it. In cases of replanting or substitution of trees and bushes with other ones, the deadline for paying the associated fee is delayed for a period of three years from the date of issuance of the permit in order to determine whether the replanted trees and bushes remain alive. The level of the fee is determined on the basis of the circumference of the trunk, as well as the type and species of the tree. Article 85(2) of the Nature Protection Act indicates how to set the fee for removing the tree. The fees for removal of trees cannot exceed PLN 500 and are subject to a 100% surcharge for the removal of trees from health resort (spa) areas, areas encompassed by health resort conservation areas, real property entered into the landmark register and green areas. If the tree forks at a height below 130 cm, every trunk is treated as a separate tree. The Regulation of the Minister of the Environment of 3 July 2017 on the amount of the rate of fees for removing trees and shrubs,[166] establishes fees differentiated on the basis of particular types and species of trees, as well as multipliers differentiating fees on the basis of trunk circumference.

VII. Exemptions from Fees

503. Article 86(1) of the Nature Protection Act contains a list of situations in which fees are not collected for the removal of trees. These include trees for whose removal a permit is not required when removal is associated with the renewal and upkeep of trees growing on real property entered in the landmark register. Fees are also not collected for the removal of trees constituting a threat to people or property in existing structures or to the functioning of transmission systems, nor of trees that pose a threat to road, railway or seaborne traffic. An exemption from fees is also provided for trees removed in conjunction with the reconstruction of public roads and railway lines. Further rational exemptions for tree removal include those which have died or have no chance of surviving for reasons unrelated to the possessor of the real property they are located on, as well as non-native species of poplars with a trunk circumference in excess of 100 cm as measured at a height of 130 cm. If the removal is associated with the protection of flora, fauna and fungi under species protection or protection of natural habitats, or from a fish pond levee, or if the removal was associated with the regulation and maintenance of the beds of natural watercourses, and with the implementation and maintenance of water amelioration infrastructure involved in the shaping of water resources and flood protection necessary for the implementation and maintenance of such infrastructure, fees are also not collected.

§2. Particular Regulations Concerning Forest Protection

I. The Statutory Definition of a Forest

504. The most extensive regulation concerning forest protection is contained in the Forest Act. This Act applies to all forests, regardless of their form of ownership. It establishes the principles used in the maintenance, protection and augmentation of forest resources, as well as the principles of forest management in relation to other elements of the natural environment and national economy.

As set forth in Article 3 of the Act, a forest is defined as land with a total area of at least 0.10 ha, covered by forest vegetation (forest plantations) – trees, bushes and undergrowth – or temporarily lacking it but designated for forest production or constituting a nature reserve, constituting a portion of a national park, or entered in the landmark register. Included in the definition of forest is land associated with forest

166. Dz. U. 2017, item 1330.

management, occupied by buildings and structures used for forest management purposes, water amelioration infrastructure, forest spatial dividing lines, forest roads, areas under energy lines, plant nurseries, locations for wood storage, forest car parks and tourist infrastructure. Forests may be both non-public (private) property or the property of the State Treasury, which are managed pursuant to Article 4(1) by the SFNFH Pursuant to Article 5(1)(1–2), supervision of forests belonging to the State Treasury is performed by the minister responsible for environmental affairs, while the county commissioner oversees forests owned by other entities than the State Treasury. In the event of forests segmented by the borders of counties, forests are overseen by the commissioner of the county within whose borders the largest section of the forest is located. The county commissioner is authorized, by way of agreement, to entrust the performance of supervisory tasks, including the issuance of decisions in the first instance, to a forest manager of the SFNFH. It should be kept in mind that the management of forests entered into the landmark register and of forests containing archaeological landmarks entered into the landmark register is performed in cooperation with the provincial landmark conservator.

II. Forest Management

505. Administrative authorities of forests and other organizational entities operating in the field of forest management are obliged to conduct rational forest management, with the objective of ensuring that the principles of sustainable development are upheld. Pursuant to Article 7, stable and sustainable forest management is conducted according to a forest management plan for forests constituting property of the State Treasury, while forests not belonging to the State Treasury are managed according to a simplified forest management plan. In particular, these plans encompass activities aimed at maintaining forests and their beneficial impact on the climate, air, water, soil, quality of life and health of humans, and environmental equilibrium. Another of their tasks is to protect forests considered particularly valuable for their biodiversity, genetic resources, landscape virtues or for the needs of science, as well as for the protection of soil and areas particularly threatened by pollution and damage, and areas of social significance. A singularly important element of sustainable forest management is the rational production of wood as well as raw materials and by-products generated from the exploitation of forests. To ensure that all related activities are conducted appropriately, they must follow the principles of general protection of forests, permanence of maintenance of forests, continuity and balanced exploitation of all functions of forests, as well as of augmentation of forest resources.

III. The Principles of Access to Forests

506. Section 5 of the Forest Act defines the principles for providing access to forests, stating in Article 26(1) that forests belonging to the State Treasury are to be made available to the public at large. The only restrictions on entry are those placed on forest plantations of up to 4 m in height, experimental areas and semi-coniferous tree stands, animal refuges, heads of rivers and streams, and areas threatened by erosion. A forest manager may also impose a temporary ban on entering a forest belonging to the State Treasury in the event of destruction or significant damage to tree stands or degradation of forest undergrowth, as well as in cases of significant threat of fire, or when activities are being performed related to forest husbandry, forest protection or wood harvesting. Forests are labelled as 'Entry forbidden' and both the cause and time period of the restriction are indicated. In the case of forests under the management of the SFNFH, the forest manager is obliged to put up and maintain signage, while in the case of other forests it is the owners who are required to do so.

507. Under Article 29(1) of the Forest Act, it is only permitted to operate a motor vehicle, horse-drawn vehicle or motorcycle in a forest along public roads; forest roads may only be used when they are marked with signs permitting traffic to enter. This does not apply to disabled persons using vehicles adapted to their needs. However, horse riding is only permitted along forest roads designated by the forest manager.

Vehicles may be parked along forest roads exclusively in places where signs permit. Restrictions do not apply to individuals performing official duties, such as employees of forest inspectorates, those supervising forest management and managing organizational units of the SFNFH, individuals engaged in firefighting, people involved in saving human life or health, officials of the Border Guard protecting national borders and officials of other authorities responsible for safety and public order, owners of forests in their own forests, and individuals utilizing agricultural lands located around forests.

508. Article 30(1) sets forth a catalogue of activities forbidden to be undertaken in forests. Above all, it is unlawful to pollute soil and water, to litter, to dig up the ground, to destroy mushrooms and spawns, to destroy or damage trees, bushes and other vegetation, to destroy commercial, tourist and technical infrastructure and objects, and to destroy signs and information boards. It is also forbidden to gather produce from forest undergrowth in places where appropriate signs are posted, to rake and gather bedding, to allow farm animals to graze, to camp outside of places designated by the forest owner or manager, to collect eggs and chicks, to destroy dens, bird nests, lairs, and ant colonies, to startle, chase, capture or kill wild animals with the exception of cases requiring the raising of an alarm, to stir up fire beyond areas designated by the forest owner or manager, to start an open fire, and to burn off the top layer of soil and vegetation. Within 100 m of the border of a forest it is forbidden to engage in activities that may cause danger.

509. Under Article 29(4), sporting events and other mass events may be organized in a forest, with the prior consent of the forest's owner.

Wood harvested in forests is subject to stamping (grading) under the provisions of Article 14a(1). The obligation to stamp wood rests on forest owners. Wood harvested in forests not belonging to the State Treasury is stamped by the county commissioner, who issues the owner of the forest with a document ascertaining the legality of the wood's harvest.

510. Forests are not subject to re-privatization. It is permissible to change the status of a forest to that of agricultural land only in the case of particularly justified needs of the forest's owner. Decisions in such matters are issued by the director of the regional directorate for the SFNFH upon the request of the forest manager responsible for forests belonging to the State Treasury. In respect of forests not owned by the State Treasury, such a decision is issued by the county commissioner upon the request of the forest's owner.

IV. Protective Forests

511. Pursuant to Article 15(1), forests afforded an enhanced level of protection, referred to as 'protected forests', may be those forests which protect the soil from being washed away or depleted, prevent landslides, rockslides or avalanches, protect surface water and groundwater, regulate hydrological relations in basins and watersheds, and also forests which limit the formation or expansion of quicksands, those permanently damaged as a result of industrial activity, forests constituting semi-coniferous tree stands, animal refuges or colonies of vegetation under species protection, those with special natural or scientific significance, and those important to national defence and security. Other protected forests are those located within the administrative borders of cities and within 10 km of the administrative borders of cities containing over 50,000 residents, in health resort conservation zones as set forth in the Act of 28 July 2005 on health resort medicine, health resorts and health resort conservation zones and on health resort communes, and those at a tree line. A forest belonging to the State Treasury is made a protected forest by way of a decision of the minister responsible for environmental affairs upon submission. In respect of other forests, the county commissioner is authorized to issue a decision awarding or taking away protected status following consultation with the forest's owner and the municipal council. The municipal council should express its opinion within two months of receipt of a request for it to do so. If this period elapses without action by the council, it is considered that the council has no objections.

V. Sale of Forests

512. The sale of forests, land and other real property of the State Treasury under the management of the SFNFH is tightly restricted and takes place exclusively in situations described in Article 38(1)(1–5) of the Forest Act. These comprise situations such as the sale of the State Treasury's shares in forests constituting jointly-owned property, adjustment of field and forest borders, ascertainment by the forest manager of the unsuitability of land, buildings and structures for the needs of forest management, and also changes in designation for non-forestry and non-agricultural purposes as well as those dictated by important economic or social considerations, insofar as it does not damage the interests of the State Treasury. A forest manager may independently sell forest and non-forest land of an area up to 1 ha if it constitutes an enclave among lands with other forms of ownership. The sale of forests, land and other real property under the management of the SFNFH following two failed tender proceedings may be conducted by way of price negotiations, and the commune has a right of pre-emption.

VI. SFNFH as a State Organizational Entity Without Legal Personhood

513. Section 6 of the Forest Act establishes the SFNFH and sets forth the subjective and objective scope of that state organizational entity. The SFNFH, as a state organizational entity without legal personhood, represents the State Treasury in the management of assets. It is run by its General Director, who is assisted by the directors of SFNFH regional directorates. The competencies of a forest manager as outlined in Article 35 of the Forest Act include independent forest management in a forest inspectorate on the basis of a forest management plan, responsibility for the condition of the forest, organization of the protection of property and combating sabotage to the forest. The forest manager provides assistance on request to the owner of a forest that does not belong to the State Treasury with consultation in the areas of afforestation and forest management, and also provides, for a fee, access to saplings and bushes for planting together with specialist forestry equipment. Article 39a allows the forest manager, upon receiving the consent of the director of the regional directorate for the SFNFH, to set up a road or transmission line easement (for remuneration) on real property under the management of the SFNFH, taking into account the principles of forest management. Remuneration from the easement constitutes income of the SFNFH. Fees for the establishment of a transmission line easement on behalf of an enterprise engaged in the transmission or distribution of electrical energy are set at an amount equivalent to the value of taxes and fees borne by the SFNFH for the portion of the real property whose use is restricted in conjunction with the easement. An entrepreneur benefiting from the transmission line easement is obliged to remove trees, bushes and branches threatening the functioning of the enterprise's equipment.

VII. The Forest Ranger Service

514. Under Article 45(1)(1–4) of the Forest Act, the Forest Service functions within the SFNFH, and is composed of employees involved in matters of forests managed by the SFNFH, forest management and forest protection, combating crimes involving forest sabotage, and performing other tasks related to the protection of property. On the basis of Article 2, an employee of the Forest Service must be a Polish citizen of at least 21 years of age, enjoying full civil and civic rights, who holds appropriate professional qualifications, enjoys the impeccable opinion of others, is employed on a full-time basis, is in good health, and has not been sentenced by a court for crimes stemming from the desire to profit or from other 'low' motives. The Forest Service is headed up by the Chief Inspector for Forest Service, who is subordinated to the General Director.

According to Article 47(2)(1–10), in the performance of their functions forest rangers are authorized to request identification from individuals suspected of committing a crime or petty offence, as well as from witnesses to a crime or petty offence, in order to establish their identity. They may issue and collect penal fines in matters set forth in other regulations. Forest rangers are authorized to stop vehicles and other means of transport in forest areas and immediately adjacent areas in order to search them in the event of a justified suspicion of the commission of a crime, as well as to search premises and other places for the same reason, pursuant to the relevant regulations of the Code of Criminal Proceedings. Additionally, forest rangers are authorized to carry firearms, handcuffs, truncheons, hand-held delivery systems of incapacitating substances and devices designed to incapacitate people using electrical energy. Forest rangers are authorized to audit commercial entities involved in trade and the processing of wood and other forest products in order to determine the legality of origin of raw materials and other forest products.

VIII. Forests and Management of Strategic Natural Resources

515. An incidental but also important act regulating forest protection is the Act on maintaining the national character of the country's strategic natural assets. This Act counts state forests among the country's strategic natural assets. Under Article 3 of the Act, the management of strategic natural assets is conducted in accordance with the principle of sustainable development, with a view to the common good. Access to the State Treasury's natural assets with a view to satisfying needs of the general population other than those related to production, such as recreation and non-commercial gathering of forest fruits, is provided for free. The claims of natural persons, former owners and their descendants arising out of loss of ownership of assets are satisfied in the form of financial compensation paid out of the State budget.

516. Lastly, it is worth mentioning the contribution to the protection of Polish forests provided by its organizational system, by the existence and functioning of forest protection teams, their cooperation with scientific institutions (in particular the Forestry Research Institute), and a systematic scheme of forecasting activities.

Chapter 7. Protection of Agricultural and Forest Land

517. The Agricultural and Forest Land Protection Act defines forest lands as lands defined as forests, lands recultivated in conjunction with forest management, and lands under access roads to forest lands. Forest lands and forests themselves are subject to protection. Under Article 3(2), the protection of forest lands consists of restricting the possibility to designate them for non-forestry or non-agricultural purposes, preventing the degradation and devastation of forest lands and damage to tree stands and forest production resulting from activities unrelated to forestry as well as from large movements of earth, and restoring the land-use value of lands that have lost their character as forest lands resulting from activities unrelated to forestry while improving their use value and preventing a decline in their productivity. The director of the regional directorate for the SFNFH is the appropriate authority in matters of forest lands protection, with the exception of national parks, where the park director is the appropriate authority.

518. Pursuant to Article 6(1) of the Agricultural and Forest Land Protection Act, agricultural and forest lands may be designated for non-agricultural and non-forestry purposes with prior consent expressed in a local spatial management plan drawn up in accordance with provisions on spatial planning and management. The agreement of the minister responsible for environmental affairs or an individual authorized by the minister is required to reassign forest lands owned by the State Treasury for non-agricultural and non-forestry purposes. Changes in the designation of other forest lands require the consent of the provincial marshal, expressed after receiving an opinion from the chamber of agriculture. Consent is expressed following an application from the prefect (mayor), who must attach the opinion of the director of the regional directorate for the SFNFH to an application concerning forest lands owned by the State Treasury, or the opinion of the park director in respect of lands in national parks. The application is then submitted to the minister within thirty days of its submission by the prefect (mayor).

519. Article 9(2) of the Agricultural and Forest Land Protection Act also establishes the conditions for erecting buildings and structures in protected forests that will serve the needs of forest management, national defence and security, navigational or geodesic signage, the protection of health, and equipment designed to serve tourists. In cases justified by important social considerations and in the absence of other lands, protected forests may be designated for other purposes than those given above upon receiving the consent of the minister responsible for environmental affairs. The appropriate director of the regional directorate for the SFNFH may issue a decision ordering the owner of lands to plant trees and bushes or to install permanent grassland, when justified by the need to protect soil from erosion and mass earth movements. If execution of the decision results in damage from reduced production of vegetation, the owner of the lands is entitled to compensation from the provincial budget over a period of ten years.

520. Pursuant to Article 16(1), management plans for lands located in restricted use areas around industrial facilities are developed and funded by those facilities. If the owner of lands incurs damage in the form of reduced agricultural or forest production, compensation must be paid by the industrial facility. In the event of a reduction in productivity levels by one-third for a period of three years, upon submission of an application by the owner the facility is obliged to purchase those lands either in full or in part, at market prices. If a change in the profile of agricultural or forest production is necessitated by the execution of the plan, the industrial facility is obliged to refund the owner of the lands the associated costs, as well as to pay full compensation for damage resulting from the change in production profile.

Chapter 8. Mineral Resources Management

§1. Sources of Law in Mineral Resources Management

521. The protection of mineral resources is mainly regulated by two pieces of legislation: the Environmental Protection Act of 27 April 2001 and the Geological and Mining Act of 9 June 2011.[167]

§2. General Principles of Mineral Resources Management

522. Sections II and VII of the Environmental Protection Act establishes framework principles for geological and mining regulations, and one of its primary elements is the protection of mineral deposits. This protection consists of the rational management of mineral resources, as well as their comprehensive exploitation. This also applies to accompanying minerals extracted together with the primary mineral.

523. The principle of sustainable development is implemented by Article 5 of the Constitution of the Republic of Poland of 2 April 1997.[168] The Constitution expresses the necessity of ensuring the protection of the natural environment, guided by the principle of sustainable growth. This principle is defined as social and economic growth that involves the process of integrating political, economic and social activities while maintaining equilibrium in nature as well as the stability of natural processes in order to ensure it remains possible to meet the basic needs of individuals and societies of both the current and future generations. This legal definition was introduced in Article 3(50) of the Environmental Protection Act. Under Article 126 of the Environmental Protection Act, the exploitation of mineral deposits is to be conducted in an economically appropriate manner, applying means and methods that limit damage to the environment and ensuring rational extraction and management. An entity commencing or engaged in an activity regulated by this Act is obliged to undertake actions necessary for the protection of natural resources, the surface of the Earth, as well as both surface water and groundwater. It places the obligation on such an entity to conduct continual reclamation of mined lands, as well as to restore components of the natural environment to their proper condition if they have been damaged by the activity performed.

§3. Principles of Conducting Geological and Extraction Activity

524. The Geological and Mining Act regulates material concerning the principles and conditions of conducting geological and extraction activity, as well as the storage of their output. Additionally, it sets forth requirements addressing the protection of mineral deposits, groundwater and other elements of the natural environment that may be threatened by the conducting of activity regulated under that Act.

---

167. Dz. U. 2017, item 2126 with amendments.
168. Dz. U. No. 78, item 483 with amendments.

Mineral resources are defined as naturally occurring deposits of minerals, stones and other substances whose extraction may generate economic benefits. In order to serve the purposes of the Act, the category of mineral resources also includes medicinal, thermal and salt spring waters. The previous Geological and Mining Act of 4 February 1994,[169] in force until 31 December 2011, divided mineral resources into primary and common ones under Article 5(1–3). Primary mineral resources included natural gas, crude oil and its natural derivatives, lignite and anthracite coal, precious metals, metal ores and asbestos. Common mineral resources thus *a contrario* were considered all other deposits not enumerated in Article 5. An exhaustive list of deposits that can be considered mining property is contained in Article 10 of the Geological and Mining Act currently in force. In particular, it lists deposits of hydrocarbons, anthracite coal, methane occurring as an accompanying mineral, lignite, metal ores (except turf iron ore), ores of radioactive elements, gypsum, precious stones, and the aforementioned medicinal, thermal and salt spring waters. Deposits of mineral resources that are not constituent parts of real property are the property of the State Treasury, which holds the exclusive right to make use of them as well as to dispose of rights to them by awarding mining rights. The establishment of mining rights takes place by way of a written contract, as other forms of contract are null under the statute. This remuneration constitutes revenue of the State budget. The Act provides for the possibility of awarding exclusive mining rights to the entity that first discovers a given deposit. Within the boundaries set forth in the Act and the contract establishing mining rights, the rights holder may conduct an activity regulated under the Act to the exclusion of other persons in the area encompassed by such rights. In particular, the rights holder may perform a geological activity, extract minerals from deposits, conduct activity including the underground non-tank storage of substances, underground storage of waste and underground storage of carbon dioxide.

525. Mining rights are established by way of concession. The concession is a fundamental instrument of regulation. The rules governing concessioning are set forth in section III of the Geological and Mining Act.

526. Geological work involving the use of geological surveys may only be conducted on the basis of a plan. In addition to outlining the objective, type and schedule of work, a plan for a geological survey should state the activities that must be undertaken with a view to protecting the environment, the manner in which excavations and wells will be liquidated, the means by which land will be reclaimed, and also actions to be taken in order to prevent damage that may result from the planned work. The competent minister for environmental matters is obliged to issue a regulation detailing the requirements for such plans whose execution requires the receipt of a concession. In doing so, the competent minister is to observe the needs of environmental protection, the necessity of ensuring proper geological identification, and the observance of relevant safety regulations. Approval of construction plans requires obtaining the opinion of the local prefect (mayor). Such approval is refused

169. Dz. U. No. 27, item 96.

in the event of a plan that would violate the requirements of environmental protection. The new version of Article 83 allows for the possibility of ordering an entity that has received a concession to perform additional activities (with compensation), including tests, measurements and collecting extra samples. This is justified in the event of the need to ensure general safety, to protect the environment, or to further knowledge of the country's geological construction so as to fulfil the postulate of rational management of mineral resource deposits. Within the scope of the aforegoing, the competent authority is that responsible for geological administration which issues a decision superseding a concession or plan for geological work. Geological work can commence if the county commissioner fails to issue a formal decision containing an objection within thirty days of presentation of the geological survey plan. The county commissioner may raise an objection in the event the manner in which the intended geological survey is to be carried out constitutes a threat to the natural environment.

527. Enterprises are required to fulfil a broad range of formalities, including maintenance of documentation detailing their activities. Geological documentation should include such elements as a forecast of changes to the environment that may be brought about as a result of the performance and liquidation of planned undertakings. Such documentation is approved by the competent authority for geological administration which issues an administrative decision. Records of mineral resource deposits as detailed in Article 101 are maintained by the enterprise, with the purpose of determining changes caused by such factors as environmental protection. In addition, the enterprise is obliged to prepare and submit a report detailing changes in the balance of mineral resource deposits on the basis of a current inventory, to be filed not later than 15 March to the competent concession authority and the Polish Geological Institute. The latter, in the event of justified reservations associated with a violation of environmental protection regulations, can issue a decision ordering a survey of excavations and submission of a current inventory at a later date. In the event of the liquidation of a mining plant, the enterprise is obliged to engage in undertakings necessary to protect the natural environment and to reclaim lands following the conclusion of mining activity. Land reclamation is governed by the relevant provisions of the Agricultural and Forest Lands Protection Act of 3 February 1995.[170] Approval of a liquidation plan requires consultation with the competent prefect (the mayor). The criterion for this consultation is compliance of the manner in which liquidation will be performed with the land's designation. In justified cases, the competent mining supervision authority may issue a decision ordering the enterprise to liquidate a mining plant or designated portion of it. Liability for damage caused by a mining plant is borne by the enterprise performing mining activity that has caused such damage. If damage occurs for reasons other than mining activity, the liability of those entities is solidary. The obligation of *restitutio in integrum* rests with the entity liable for the damage, and it may be performed by supplying land, buildings, equipment, premises, water or other goods of the same type. Compensation for damage to agricultural or forest land that has been degraded or devastated by mining activity is to be rendered in the manner set forth in legislation

170. Dz. U. 2017, item 1161 with amendments.

addressing the protection of such land. Upon the consent of the entity liable for the damage, the aggrieved may perform the obligation in exchange for payment of an appropriate sum of money. In order to prevent imminent damage and/or its further effects, a court may order necessary action to be undertaken. If this obligation is borne by the aggrieved, a court may order the entity against whom the claim is directed to pay an appropriate sum of money with immediate effect. In the event of damage resulting from loss of water or loss of its utility, the entity against whom a claim is directed is obliged to deliver the necessary amount of water free of charge to the aggrieved until such time as the damage is repaired.

528. For the purposes of performing oversight and review, upon presentation of their official identification card authorized employees of public administration may exercise a wide range of powers. Article 153 provides an exhaustive list of these powers, including the right to enter a mining plant at all times of the day, the right of access to all necessary information, equipment and documents, the right to demand information in written or oral form, the right to demand the presentation of documents and access to necessary data, as well as to take samples. In addition, there is also the possibility of conducting necessary tests or other oversight activities in order to determine the state of the environment and assess that state pursuant to environmental protection regulations. Directors of entities being inspected are required to facilitate the performance of necessary activities. The President of the State Mining Authority is the competent authority for issuing decisions assessing financial penalties on an enterprise that does not fulfil its obligations in respect of identifying threats resulting from the operation of a mining plant and taking steps to prevent and eliminate such threats. A fine is also levied against an enterprise that fails to execute the decisions of a competent mining authority in respect of the total or partial stoppage of that enterprise and/or its machinery in spite of the potential to cause a direct threat to the mine, to its employees, to general safety and security, and/or to the natural environment. This also concerns situations in which the enterprise fails to perform required tests serving to assess the condition of the facility's safety, general safety and environmental safety in relation to the functioning of that enterprise. The Act also introduces criminal liability alongside financial penalties in order to ensure that its provisions are observed. This regulation is contained in section XI of the Act, which contains detailed regulations concerning liability for behaviour and omissions that contradict its provisions.

529. The management of mineral resource deposits and exploitation of those deposits are, and will continue to be, the object of particular legislative attention in Poland due to the very significant role played in the country's economy by the extraction and processing of mineral raw materials. For this reason, it can be expected that the legislator, aware of Poland's industrial culture, will continue to update the relevant laws with a view to the development of ecological forms of power generation and the limitation of carbon dioxide emissions into the atmosphere.

Part III. Zoning and Land-Use Planning

530. The basic regulations pertaining to zoning and land-use planning in terms of environmental protection can be found in two acts, as a result of which we can refer to the duality of environmental protection in land-use planning. The first of these acts is the 27 March 2003 Act on Zoning and Land-Use Planning.[171] The second is the Environmental Protection Act, section VII of which deals with environmental protection in zoning and realization of investments. The sources of law in this regard also include other special acts dealing with environmental protection. They contain the environmental protection requirements in accepting zoning acts.

531. A good starting point would be the principle of planning expressed in Article 8 of the Environmental Protection Act. According to this principle, policies, strategies, plans or programmes which pertain especially to industry, power engineering, transportation, telecommunication, water management, waste management, zoning, forestry, agriculture, fishing, tourism and exploitation of territory should duly take into consideration the principles of environmental protection and sustainable development. Article 71 of the Environmental Protection Act explains this principle with regard to land-use planning. The principles of sustainable development and environmental protection constitute the basis for drafting and updating the national zoning concept, development strategies for provinces, zoning plans for provinces, research on the conditions and directions of zoning in counties as well as their local land-use planning. These concepts, strategies, plans and research play the following roles: (1) they define solutions necessary to prevent pollution, ensure protection from emerging pollutants as well as restore the environment to its original state; (2) they define the conditions for realizing undertakings which make it possible to achieve optimal effects with regard to environmental protection. Furthermore, the purpose marked out for a certain territory, as well as the manner of its management, should, as much as possible, ensure that its landscape qualities are preserved.

532. The basic statute which regulates the process of zoning is the Act on Zoning and Land-Use Planning. It covers regulation of two basic areas: (1) defining the principles by which zoning policy is shaped by administrative bodies; and (2) defining the scope and manner of conduct in devoting certain areas for specific purposes

171. Dz. U. 2018, item 1945 with amendments.

and establishing the principles for their zoning and building. The protection of two fundamental values – spatial planning and sustainable development – is to constitute the basis for the above activity.

533. Land-use planning takes place at three fundamental levels: commune, regional (provincial) and national. At the county level, land-use planning is of an informal nature and is subsidiary to commune, regional and national planning.

534. The land-use planning system includes the following planning acts:

(1) A study of the conditions and directions of commune zoning as well as the local zoning plans (local law);
(2) An analysis and study of the scope of zoning with regard to the county area;
(3) A framework study of the conditions and directions of zoning within the metropolitan union (if such has been established), prepared for the entire metropolitan area;
(4) The provincial zoning plan (local law), analysis and study, concepts and programs with regard to zoning areas and problems according to the needs and objectives in this area of work (regional and subregional programs), landscape audit;
(5) The national zoning concept.

535. The competent authorities are as follows: commune authorities, county authorities, authorities of the metropolitan union, authorities of the provincial government and the Council of Ministers.

536. Environmental protection is one of the highly esteemed values during land-use planning (Article 1 of the Act on Zoning and Land-Use Planning). The subject scope of the Act outlines the fact that in land-use planning, the following is considered: (1) landscape values, (2) environmental protection requirements, including water management and protection of agricultural and forest land.

537. As to landscape values, it is noteworthy that the provisions of the 16 April 2004 Act on Protection of Nature and other acts (including the Landscape Act) have an impact on shaping landscape values as well as on the interpretation of this undefined concept. They introduce the definition of the concept of 'landscape protection' (Article 5(8)), which means 'maintaining the characteristic traits of a given landscape'. The Act also introduces legal forms of landscape protection: nature reserves, landscape parks, protected landscape areas. They also introduce solutions which regulate planning activities in these areas (e.g., the obligation to consult drafts of local ordinances with the nature protection authorities, the obligation to consider the provisions of protection plans in local ordinances etc.).

538. When it comes to the requirements of environmental protection, the provisions of the Environmental Protection Act, especially Articles 71–73 provide a reconstruction of the concept as well as a supplementation to the general provisions of Article 1(2–3) of the Act in question. They outline detailed arrangements and solutions which should be considered in prepared planning acts.

539. Furthermore, Articles 113 and 114 of the Environmental Protection Act introduce the principles of protection from noise in land-use planning. According to Article 112, protection from noise involves ensuring as good an acoustic state of the environment as possible especially by keeping the noise level below the limit, or at least at the limit, or generally reducing the noise level. The commune, in its eco-physiographic study, outlines the requirements with regard to protection from noise (Article 72(1)(6) of the Environmental Protection Act). Furthermore, in preparing the local land-use plan, it is required that there be a differentiation of different terrains with different functions or different principles of management (e.g., terrain for residential buildings, hospitals and nursing homes, terrain for recreational purposes as well as for residential-commercial purposes (Article 114(1) of the Environmental Protection Act). The local land-use plan, as well as the decision of the county regarding the conditions of building and management of the territory, take into consideration restrictions resulting from the designation of quiet areas within as well as outside of an agglomeration (Article 73(2a) of the Environmental Protection Act).

540. Article 135 of the Environmental Protection Act provides for the possibility of creating areas of limited-use and introducing, within such areas, restrictions related to the purpose of the areas, the method of using them, as well as the technical requirements regarding buildings in such areas. Limited-use areas are established for certain kinds of investments, such as sewage treatment plants, municipal waste landfill, composting, communication routes, airports, electroenergetic stations as well as radio communication and radio navigation installations. The aim is to establish a safe distance from buildings and areas which have a negative impact on the environment, or from buildings and areas which should be protected from such negative impact. If such an area has been established, it is duly noted in the planning acts created. Such documents should outline the boundaries of the area as well as the restrictions and requirements related to the establishment of limited-use in the said area.

541. When it comes to water management, the requirements which need to be adhered to in zoning are outlined in the Water Law. This Act includes provisions for the possibility of establishing protected zones for water intake as well as protected areas for inland water reservoirs. For such zones and areas, the Act outlines the permissible restrictions in relation to the purpose of the area, the method of using it as well as technical requirements regarding buildings in such areas. These provisions are considered in created planning acts. The provisions of the 21 March 1991 Act on Sea Areas of the Republic of Poland and Maritime Administration[172] are also significant.

542. Protection of agricultural and forest land is regulated first and foremost in the Act on Protection of Agricultural and Forest Land. Apart from the definition of

172. Dz. U. 2013, item 934 with amendments.

agricultural and forest land as well as the list of protection measures introduced in Articles 2 and 3 of the Act, Articles 6 and 8 are also worthy of note, as they bring to bear the principles of designating agricultural and forest land for non-agricultural and non-forest purposes. The rule is to restrict the designation of agricultural and forest land for non-agricultural and non-forest purposes. Lands categorized as barren or fallow in the lands register can be used for non-agricultural and non-forest purposes, and in the absence of such, lands with the lowest production suitability can be used. Since 2008, all agricultural lands located in administrative towns have been deprived of agricultural status, regardless of their class. These regulations are binding on authorities which create planning acts.

543. The Act on Zoning and Land-use Planning confirms the principle of general (assumed) competence of the commune in the public administration system with regard to authority to designate areas for certain purposes as well as outline the conditions for their management (planning authority of the commune). This implies the binding principle of the planning authority (planning independence) of the commune.

544. It is the responsibility of the commune to ensure spatial order. Article 7 of the 1990 Act on the Municipal Government mentions the scope of ensuring spatial order in the ecological sense (ecological order): protection of the environment and nature as well as water management (point 1), water supply, sewage system, removal and treatment of municipal wastewater (point 1 in fine), maintenance of cleanliness and of sanitary facilities, landfills and disposal of municipal waste (point 3) and communal greenery and tree stands (point 12).

545. The land-use planning process in the commune has many stages; it is made up of acts (resolutions of the commune council) in which 'the conditions of maintaining balance in nature as well as rational management of the resources of the environment are ensured' (Article 72 of the Environmental Protection Act), in particular, by: (1) Establishing programmes for rational use of the earth surface, including areas of exploitation of mineral deposits and rational management of lands; (2) Considering areas of mineral deposits as well as present and future needs for mining these deposits; (3) Providing a complex solution to building problems in towns and villages, with particular consideration for water management, wastewater disposal, waste management, public transportation and communication systems as well as arranging and shaping green areas; (4) Considering the necessity of protecting water, soil and earth from contamination due to farming; (5) Ensuring the protection of the landscape values and climatic conditions of the environment; (6) Considering the need to prevent mass movement of the earth and its effects; (7) Considering other needs with regard to protection of air, water, soil, earth, noise, vibrations and electromagnetic fields. This provision corresponds with the regulation contained in the Act on Zoning and Land-use Planning

546. The planning acts of the commune include:

(1) A study of the conditions and the direction the commune is taking in zoning – this study considers the conditions resulting from the state of the environment including the state of the agricultural and forest production space, the quantity and quality of water resources, environmental protection requirements, nature and the cultural landscape, 'the occurrence of buildings and lands protected based on separate provisions' (including the Act on Protection of Nature for instance), 'the occurrence of natural geological hazard areas', 'the occurrence of documented mineral deposits as well as groundwater resources', 'the occurrence of mining areas marked out based on separate provisions', 'the state of communication systems and technical infrastructure, including the degree of ordering water and sewage management, energy management and waste management' as well as 'requirements with regard to anti-flood protection' (Article 10).

(2) With regard to the commune zoning plan, the Act on Zoning and Land-use Planning places an obligation for the local zoning plan to define the 'principles of the protection of the environment, nature and the cultural landscape', 'the boundaries and methods of managing protected areas and buildings, established based on separate provisions, including mining territories and territories vulnerable to flood and mass earth movement', 'special conditions for managing terrains as well as restrictions in their use, including a ban on building', 'the principles of modernisation, building and expansion of communication systems and technical infrastructure', as well as – where the need arises – 'the boundaries of areas which require conversion or reclamation' (Article 15).

547. Before preparing the study and the local plan, an ecophysiographic study is required. This obligation was imposed by Article 72(4) of the Environmental Protection Act. The term ecophysiographic study refers to documentation prepared for the purpose of studying the conditions as well as the direction taken by the commune in zoning, the local zoning plan as well as the provincial zoning plan which describe particular natural elements within the area covered by the study or plan as well as their mutual connections. This study is of a subsidiary nature in relation to planning documents but cannot be overlooked. It plays an informatory role during work on planning acts and cannot replace such acts or perform a decisive function. It constitutes the basis for creating space with full consideration of the natural environment and the landscape. The information about the environment contained in the study affects not only future planning resolutions but also the prognosis of the impact of various elements on the environment.

548. In areas without a local zoning plan, environmental protection requirements are taken into consideration in the decision regarding the conditions of building and management of the area (private investments) or in the decision establishing the location of the public purpose investment (public investments).

549. The requirements for environmental protection in land-use planning based on the Environmental Protection Act come down to restrictions of a certain kind, related to the category of a special area in question. These restrictions are not uniform, due to the number of values in question, and are scattered over various legal acts. These restrictions are considered in the local zoning plan and in the absence of such, in the decision regarding the conditions of buildings and managing the terrain (Article 73 of the Environmental Protection Act). They result from establishments as to the form of protection of nature and conservation area, creation of limited-use areas or industrial zones, marking out quiet areas within and without agglomerations and establishing protected water intake zones as well as protected reservoirs of inland waters.

550. In special areas, there is a specific public law regime, related to the realization of a defined public purpose and established by an act of law. These can be endangered areas (e.g., areas of restricted use, or industrial zones), valuable natural or spa areas or other areas, for instance, connected to the creation of protected zones for water intake. The concept of special areas is independent of the territorial division within the state. The motivation for distinguishing special areas is always public interest, related to the protection of fundamental values like life, health, the environment or safety. In this regard, restrictions on the rights and freedoms of the individual are allowed if that is the only way to safeguard public interest. For instance, there are numerous investment restrictions in the spa protection zone 'A', in which it is forbidden to build industrial plants, single-family and multi-family residential buildings and garages, petrol stations and distribution points for petroleum products, highways and expressways, mobile telephony base stations and other buildings which emit electromagnetic waves as well as others which may have a significant impact on the environment.

551. The system of arrangements made with competent authorities for environmental protection (e.g., the director of the national park), provided for in the Act on Zoning and Land-use Planning is aimed at ensuring that planning documents properly consider certain issues essential to environmental protection. Where these requirements are violated, legal measures (control and supervision) provided for in the Act on Municipal Government are applied. According to Article 91, resolutions or orders of the commune body which are contrary to the provisions of the law are invalid. The supervisory body (the Province Governor/Voivode) decides as to the partial or complete invalidity of an order or resolution within thirty days from when the order or resolution in question is presented by the commune. Furthermore, the legal measures provided for in Article 101(1) of the Act on Local Government according to which: 'Anyone, whose legal interest or rights have been violated by an order or resolution of a commune body within the scope of public administration can, after unsuccessfully appealing to the commune for a rectification of the violation, appeal against the order or resolution to the administrative court'.

552. In order to compile all the planning documents listed in Article 71(1) of the Environmental Production Act, it is necessary to carry out a strategic environmental impact assessment according to the provisions of the Act on the Sharing of Information on the Environment and its Protection, Public Participation in Environmental Protection and Environmental Impact Assessments. The aim of this procedure is for the administrative body to obtain the required information as to whether and in what manner a given strategic document (for instance, a local zoning plan) impacts the environment. Furthermore, the aim is to identify – at the planning stage – the dangers to the environment and minimize potential negative impact as well as make amendments at the earliest stage, that is, during the preparation of plans and programs which often constitute the bases of future investment ventures.

553. In the special cases described in Article 48 of the Act on the Sharing of Information on the Environment and its Protection, Public Participation in Environmental Protection and Environmental Impact Assessments it is possible to forego the carrying out of the strategic environmental impact assessment. The body preparing the project is obligated to inform the public of this fact without delay.

554. Elements of the strategic environmental impact assessment are:

(1) The first stage is agreeing on the scope and level of detail of the information required in the environmental impact prognosis. The body which prepares the draft of the document, depending on the kind of document it is, consults with the appropriate environmental body, that is, the Director General for Environmental Protection or the Regional Director for Environmental Protection; the appropriate body for sanitary inspection, that is, the Chief Sanitary Inspector, the State Provincial Sanitary Inspector or the Chief County Sanitary Inspector; the appropriate Director for the Maritime Office in cases where a certain document is to be carried out within sea areas.
(2) Prognosis of Environmental Impact – this prognosis is prepared by the administrative body responsible for preparing the draft of the document. In the formal sense, this prognosis is not an integral part of the plan and is not normative in nature. As an informational-prognostic document, it is not binding on the citizens, neither on the commune bodies. However, it can significantly influence the content of the plan as well as its realization. Among other things, it defines the state of the environment in the area covered by the document in question, what problems or impact on the environment could occur within said area, how to counter negative effects of the establishments in the document on the environment and it also contains solutions aimed at preventing, limiting or naturally compensating for negative impacts on the environment. Reducing the effect on the environment can take place by refraining from certain actions, changing the manner of carrying them out as well as providing alternatives.[173]
(3) Assessment and consultations – the body preparing the draft of the document presents the draft, along with the environmental impact prognosis for assessment or consultation by the appropriate bodies. Assessments are prepared by the same bodies which took part in consultations as to the scope and level of detail of information required in the prognosis. Special laws determine which body is competent to carry out particular actions. The competent bodies issue their assessments within thirty days of receiving the application for assessment.

173. Verdict of the Supreme Administrative Court of 10 June 1998, IV SA 2261/97.

(4) An essential and mandatory component of the strategic environmental impact assessment is public participation. The general rule is that everyone has the right to submit comments and requests in proceedings where members of the public are required to play a role. The scope of information includes: information regarding starting to work on the draft of the document as well as regarding its subject, the possibility of getting acquainted with the draft of the document, the prognosis as well as the positions of other bodies to the degree that they are available at a certain stage of proceedings as well as the place where they are available for inspection; the possibility of submitting comments and requests, the place of their submission and the deadline for their submission (at least twenty-one days); the appropriate body for the consideration of such requests and comments; proceedings with regard to cross-border environmental impact if such is being carried out.

555. Certain principles for making comments and requests in proceedings involving the public are obligatory with regard to drafts of local zoning plans as well as studies of the conditions and directions of the zoning plan of the commune. They are based on the 27 March 2003 Act on Zoning and Land-use Planning.

556. Comments and requests can be submitted in writing, orally to the protocol, by electronic means of communication without the necessity of a qualified electronic signature.

The body which prepares the draft of the document involving the public:

(1) considers comments and requests;
(2) attaches a substantiation laying out the grounds for the adopted document, including information as to how those grounds were taken into consideration.

The body which prepares the draft of the document is obligated to monitor the effects of the realization of the provisions of the adopted document with regard to environmental impact.

Part IV. Liability Questions

557. In environmental law, legal liability comes into play when the law outlines the negative consequences of inappropriate conduct of a given entity. Such provisions regarding liability outline the following:

(1) The liable entity, that is, a physical person, a legal person or an organizational unit without legal personality.
(2) An incident or state (most often brought about by the action or omission of the liable entity) which has been defined as negative in the law, for instance, damage to the environment or the threat of its occurrence, as well as a violation of the requirements for environmental protection.
(3) The objective attribution of the incident or state to the body responsible for it, and a principle, based on which a certain incident or state has been attributed to the liable entity, for instance, the principle of guilt, the principle of risk or the principle of illegality.
(4) Negative consequences of a personal or material (fiscal) nature which affect the liable entity.

558. Legal liability in environmental protection, just like in every other branch of law has three functions:

(1) Preventive – aimed at preventing damage to the environment.
(2) Compensatory – aimed at compensating for damage to the environment.
(3) Repressive – aimed at punishing the entity causing damage to the environment.

559. There are various areas of law and this provides the basis for distinguishing different kinds of legal liability. This criterion for division is also applied in the provisions of the Environmental Protection Act (Title VI). We distinguish three different kinds of liability for failure to abide by the requirements of environmental protection: civil, criminal, and administrative. Each of them plays a different role and is characterized by different methods and legal instruments. They are independent of one another but are not mutually exclusive, and they fully complement each other.

Chapter 1. Administrative Liability

560. According to Jan Boć, administrative liability in environmental protection is the activation of legal measures with regard to a certain entity due to actions taken by the said entity which have violated the state of the environment.[174] In terms of their forms and procedures, these measures are peculiar to public administration. The forms of administrative liability (various administrative measures), which can be applied by administrative bodies in response to the violation of the requirements of environmental protection, negative impact on the environment, as well as in case of the violation of the provisions of general and individual legal acts pertaining to environmental protection are varied, and regulated in several legal acts.

§1. Sanction Decisions (Administrative Compensation)

561. Administrative liability is regulated in title VI section III of the Environmental Protection Act dedicated to that subject (Articles 362–375).[175] The provisions contained in Article 362 deal with the liability of an entity who exploits the environment (according to the legal definition), Article 363 provides for the possibility of issuing a decision addressed to a physical person who is not an entity exploiting the environment.

562. Based on the aforementioned laws, we can distinguish material sanction decisions, as well as financial sanction decisions.

563. If the entity exploiting the environment (or a physical person) has a negative impact on the environment, the body responsible for environmental protection can, by way of a decision, can impose sanctions of a material nature: (1) limiting the entity's impact on the environment and the consequent dangers and/or, (2) restoring the environment to the right state. In such a decision, the body responsible for the protection of the environment can also define: (1) the scope of the limitation of the entity's impact on the environment or the state to which the environment is to be restored; (2) actions aimed at limiting the entity's impact on the environment or at restoring the original state of the environment; (3) the time limit for carrying out these obligations. These are known as the optional elements of the decision.

564. The Act does not demand that the conduct of the offending entity be culpable, or even illegal. The point is the objective state of having made a negative impact on the environment. It is noteworthy that such a decision is issued in cases of 'negative impact' on the environment, which concept was not clearly defined in the Act. It is generally accepted that this negative impact refers to any change in the environment or its elements that is disadvantageous when compared to the state of the environment before the said change was made.

---

174. Boć, Nowacki, Samborska-Boć,*Ochrona środowiska*, 361.
175. Górski et al., *Prawo ochrony środowiska.*

565. On the other hand, there are negative impacts which are not harmful to the environment. The provisions of the Environmental Damage Prevention and Amelioration Act are applicable to negative impacts which are harmful to the environment. The enforcement of liability due to the violation of the principle of prevention by entities whose actions are harmful to the environment takes place through similar decisions, issued based on Article 15(1) of the Act.

566. The proceedings for the issue of such a decision are carried out ex officio, and the conclusion reached by the body is left to its discretion. Such a decision is basically comprised of two obligations, material in nature, which can be imposed on the liable entity jointly or alternatively.

567. Article 362(3–5) of the Environmental Protection Act deals with a concept knows as quasi-administrative compensation which also involves sanction decisions, but which impose financial obligations. The premise for their issue is the absence of a possibility of imposing the obligation to take the aforementioned actions. The body responsible for environmental protection can obligate the entity exploiting the environment (or a physical person) to pay a certain sum of money to the appropriate local county, which sum of money corresponds to the degree of damage resulting from the violation of the state of the environment. The authority issuing the decision has to assess the scope of damage and estimate the corresponding sum of money. However, the Act on Environmental Protection does not provide clear-cut parameters for estimating the sum of money to be paid.

§2. Decision to Suspend Actions That Are Harmful to the Environment

568. One of the basic instruments of administrative liability is the decision to suspend actions which are harmful to the environment and the decision to stop the use of the building or installation in question. The basis for the application of this kind of sanction is an administrative decision which issue must be preceded by an ascertainment that one of the basic environmental protection obligations has been violated. The order to suspend the use of such building is of a temporary nature, the aim of issuing such a decision is to prevent the occurrence of damage or the broadening of its scope. It is possible to resume the suspended action if the reasons for its suspension have been eliminated. This is why such decisions to suspend in essence do not have the character of a sanction banning certain actions but are aimed at bringing the entities involved to the point of abiding by the requirements regarding environmental protection. This form of administrative responsibility is provided for in various laws pertaining to environmental protection, especially in the Act on Environmental Protection, the Waste Act, the Geological and Mining Act and the Water Act.

569. The Environmental Protection Act deals with this sanction as an obligatory or optional consequence of various behaviours that are harmful to the environment. An example is the provisions of Article 364, which state that if the actions of an entity exploiting the environment, or a physical person lead to significant deterioration in the state of the environment or endanger the life or health of people (the culpability or illegality of such actions are not relevant at this point), the Provincial Inspector for Environmental Protection issues a decision suspending this action to the degree that is necessary to prevent deterioration of the state of the environment. When it comes to installations which require an integrated permit, the fact that they are used without the required permit constitutes sufficient grounds for the issuing of such a decision (Article 365 of The Environmental Protection Act). In such cases, the administrative body does not consider the degree of danger as mentioned above. A similar situation takes place in relation to newly built or reconstructed buildings, groups of buildings or installations considered capable of significantly impacting the environment, if the administrative body finds irregularities related to environmental protection or failure to comply with the emission standards during booting (Article 365(2) of the Environmental Protection Act). In all the above-mentioned cases, decisions issued by the Provincial Inspector for Environmental Protection are of an obligatory nature (issued in strict accordance with the provisions of the law) and are immediately enforceable. When there is an improvement in the impact on the environment after it has been determined that the reasons for suspending certain activity no longer obtain, the authorized body, by way of decision, allows for the continuance of the suspended actions. This decision is based on the application of an interested party.

570. In turn, optional suspension of activity (or use of certain buildings or installations) takes place in the following cases: (1) Where the entity exploiting the environment introduces substances or energy into the environment without the required permit, or in violation of its conditions, (2) Violation by the entity exploiting the environment of the conditions of the decision stating the requirements as to the functioning of the installation where it is generally required that the authorities be notified of such installation, (3) Failure to notify the appropriate body of the installation or failure to notify aforementioned body of the use of the installation in a manner contrary to the information contained in the notification (Article 367 of the Environmental Protection Act).

571. Also, a ban on production, importation and circulation of products that fail to meet the requirements of environmental protection can be imposed by way of decision (Article 367 of the Act on Environmental Protection).

§3. Administrative Fines and Increased Fees

572. Administrative fines and increased fees were not explicitly categorized by the legislator as measures of administrative liability but are regulated in title V of the Environmental Protection Act, which deals with legal-financial measures. However, they are widely considered as legal liability measures of an administrative nature (administrative sanctions), and their omission in the section of the Act dealing with liability is considered a theoretical and conceptual error.[176]

573. Financial-legal measures in environmental protection are as follows: (1) Payment for exploiting the environment; (2) Administrative fines; (3) Varied tax rates and other public tributes for environmental protection. Among them, administrative fines and increased fees are characteristic of financial sanctions.

574. Fines are incurred in cases of violation of the conditions for exploiting the environment defined in permits or resulting directly from the law, as well as with regard to storage of waste and noise emission in the environment. Additionally, the provisions of the Nature Conservation Act, the Geological and Mining Act as well as other statutes (e.g., the 20 April 2004 Ozone Layer Depleting Substances Act, the 28 April 2011 Act on the Greenhouse Gas Emission Allowance Trading Scheme, the 24 April 2009 Act on Batteries and Accumulators, the 29 June 2007 Act on International Shipments of Waste) define particular cases and principles for incurring fees for exploitation of the environment as well as administrative fines. In Article 276(2) of the Environmental Protection Act, the legislator dealt with the issue of cumulative or alternative application of environment exploitation fees and fines. In cases of exceeding or violating the conditions defined in the permit or another decision, sanctions occur as well as fees. This means that if the law provides for both fees and fines for certain actions, the fees are paid in full for the permissible and forbidden activity, and in addition, a fine is paid for the forbidden activity.

575. Administrative fines are imposed by way of decision issued by the Provincial Inspector for Environmental Protection. The amount of money to be paid depends on respectively: (1) The amount and the kind of gas or dust released into the atmosphere; (2) The amount and kind of stored waste as well as the time of their storage; (3) The time of day and the level at which permissible noise levels are exceeded. For instance, the sanction for releasing gas or dust into the atmosphere is calculated as twenty times the value of a unit of payment.

576. An entity exploiting the environment without gaining the required permit or another decision pays an increased fee for exploiting the environment (Article 276(1) of the Environmental Protection Act). For instance, for emitting gas and dust into the atmosphere without the required permit, the entity exploiting the environment pays a fee that is increased by 500%. Considering the fact that the increase is so severe, such an increased fee can justifiably be considered as a sanction of a repressive nature.

577. Increased fees are the subject of lively discussion and rich case-law. Literature indicates that there are two distinguishable situations: (1) An organizational entity has not received a decision permitting emission, as it has not applied for the

176. *Ibid.*

issuance of such. (2) An organizational entity has not received a final decision permitting emission, but: (a) has applied for the issuance of such a decision;, (b) has received a decision that is yet to become final; or (c) has appealed against the decision to the administrative court.

578. In literature, it is emphasized that paying increased fees would be dependent on the efficiency or rightness (legality) of administrative actions. The Citizen's Ombudsman took an interest in the issue of increased fees, and after noticing discrepancies in case-law and literature, applied to the SAC for a court resolution on the issue. The SAC released a resolution stating that 'In cases of imposing increased fees for the exploitation of the environment without the required permit or another decision, based on Article 276(1) of the Environmental Protection Act, the reason for the lack of a permit might be significant if the entity exploiting the environment in line with permission applies for a permit for a subsequent period'.[177] In providing grounds for this resolution, the Court stated that two situations are distinguishable: (1) The entity exploiting the environment on the basis of the required permit, applies for another permit for a subsequent period but does not receive it before the validity period of the previous permit expires. (2) The entity does not possess the required permit and exploits the environment without such permit or decision. In this second situation, the state of things is clear, but with regard to the first situation, it has been accepted, that if the applicant, before the expiry of the validity period of the present permit, applied for a new permit within the time limit required for such applications, and the administrative body (due to its inaction or unnecessary delay) fails to issue the new permit before the expiry date of the previous permit, during the period between the expiry of the previous permit and the issuance of the new permit, the fee for exploitation of the environment should be the same as hitherto, that is, the amount that was required during the validity period of the previous permit. It is unacceptable for the entity exploiting the environment to bear the consequences of inefficient or protracted administrative proceedings in the form of increased fees for environment exploitation.

579. Proceedings regarding fees for environment exploitation as well as administrative fines are commenced ex officio or on the application of an entity exploiting the environment who is to pay the fee or fine. Proceeds from fees and fines constitute revenue of the National Fund for Environmental Protection and Water Management, provincial funds for environmental protection and water management as well as budget income of local communes and counties.

580. A separate section of the Environmental Protection Act was dedicated to the issue of fines for lapses in the preparation and realization of air protection programs, as well as short-term plans of action. The environmental protection body bears the liability for this, which is why legal literature deals with the issue of the nature of the legal remedy applied in such situations. There are two positions: (1) It is a form of supervision by the Provincial Inspector for Environmental Protection in relation to a group of environmental protection bodies, as well as other entities; (2)

177. Resolution of 12 December 2011, II OPS 2/11, ONSAiWSA 2012, Nr 2 (22).

It is one more form of legal liability because, in Article 315A, we easily find all the elements which, in the theory of law, make for legal liability, including administrative law liability. In terms of its legal characteristics, it does not differ in any way from liability in the form of paying increased fees due to the lack of a required permit or decision and administrative fines for violating or exceeding the conditions of the permit or decision.

581. According to Article 315A(1) in cases: (1) Where the body being inspected fails to carry out the post-inspection recommendations with regard to the deadline set for adoption of environment protection programs as well as short-term action plans, (2) Of failure to meet the statute-based deadline for adoption of air protection programs as well as short-term action plans, (3) Of failure to meet the deadlines for realizing tasks outlined in air protection programs as well as short-term action plans – the body responsible for this is subject to a fine of PLN 50,000 – PLN 500,000. This fine is imposed, by way of decision, by the Provincial Inspector for Environmental Protection, taking into consideration the amount and seriousness of discovered lapses and the duties violated by the body in question. Such a decision imposing the fines provided for in Article 315A can be appealed against to the Chief Inspector for Environmental Protection.

582. The Environmental Protection Act also deals with the rules for adjournment, reduction as well as annulment of increased fees for environment exploitation as well as fines. This option is one of the most effective ways of fighting violations of environmental protection requirements.[178] The competent authority in cases regarding the adjournment of the deadline for paying increased fees environment exploitation as well as for their reduction and annulment is the Province Marshal, and in cases regarding administrative fines, the Provincial Inspector for Environmental Protection.

583. The deadline for paying the fee for environment exploitation as well as administrative fines can be postponed in response to the application of an entity exploiting the environment, who is obligated to make the above payments, if such entity undertakes action within the prescribed time to ensure the removal of the reason for the imposition of the increased fees or fines. Such action should be undertaken within five years from the date of the application. The deadline for payment can be postponed with regard to a part or the whole of the fee or fine, but the postponement can pertain only to the difference between the increased fee demanded of the entity involved and the usual fee the entity exploiting the environment would have paid had it possessed the required permit or decision. The deadline for payment can be postponed only for the period necessary to undertake action, which realization will ensure the removal of the reason for the increased fee or fine.

584. The application should be made to the competent body before the deadline for the payment of the fee or fine. Application for postponement of the deadline for payment does not release the entity from the obligation to pay the part of the fee or

178. Jendrośka, Bar, *Prawo ochrony środowiska*, p. 1021.

fine for which the payment deadline was not postponed. The decision to postpone the deadline for payment of fee or fine outlines: (1) The fee or fine which deadline for payment has been postponed, as well as the amount of money to be paid; (2) The actions undertaken by the applicant; (3) The timetable for the realization of these actions; (4) The time till which the deadline for payment of fine or fee is postponed.

585. The competent body, by way of decision, can refuse an application for the postponement of the deadline for payment of fine or fee, if the requirements for such postponement, as outlined in the statute, have not been met.

586. In cases where the timely realization of the actions which constitute the basis for the postponement of payment remove the reason for the imposition of the fine or fee, the competent body, by way of decision, reduces the payment to be made at the postponed time by the sum of money spent by the entity involved to undertake the required actions. On the other hand, if the actions which were the basis for the postponement of the deadline for payment have not been undertaken on time or have failed to remove the reason for the imposition of the fee or fine, the competent authority rules that the entity involved is obligated to pay the postponed fee or fine.

§4. Prevention and Amelioration of Damage to the Environment

587. The issue of prevention and reparation of damage to the environment is dealt with in the 13 April 2007 Act on Environmental Damage Prevention and Amelioration. The most general aim of this statute is the realization of the principle that 'the polluter pays'. The provisions of the statute are applied to direct danger of damage to the environment or to damage to the environment caused by actions of the entity exploiting the environment which create a risk of damage, or actions which directly cause damage, if this damage affects protected species or protected natural habitats, or if the damage is the fault of the entity exploiting the environment. The provisions of the statute are also applied to the direct danger of damage to the environment or to damage to the environment caused by diffuse emissions from various sources, where it is possible to establish a direct connection between the activities of the entity exploiting the environment and the direct danger of damage or the actual damage to the environment.

588. Activities that create a risk of damage to the environment include (Article 3): (1) Activities pertaining to the collection of municipal waste from property owners, which require entry in the register of regulated activity; (2) Exploitation of installations which requires an integrated permit or a permit to emit gas and dust into the atmosphere; (3) Collection and treatment of waste, where a permit is required for said collection and treatment; (4) Activities which require a permit under the Act: (a) transferring sewage into water or land, (b) collection and drainage of surface water or groundwater, (c) retention of inland surface waters; (5) Closed use of microorganisms and GMO, deliberate release of GMO into the atmosphere or into circulation; (6) International waste management; (7) Management of extractive waste based on the decision ratifying the program for management of extractive waste; (8) Underground storage of carbon dioxide as well as activities aimed at seeking, recognizing and extracting hydrocarbons from deposits within the boundaries of sea areas in the Republic of Poland.

589. An entity responsible for pollution which does not carry out this sort of business activity is not liable on the basis of the statute. In such cases, general statute provisions are applied, in particular, Article 362(1) of the Environmental Protection Act, unless the activity is one of those mentioned above, where the entity involved is culpable. The provisions of the Act are also not applicable to: (1) direct threat of damage to the environment which occurred before the 30 April 2007, or results from activities which ended before the 30 April 2007, as well as in cases where over thirty years have passed since the emission or event which caused a direct threat of damage or actual damage to the environment, including historical pollution of the earth's surface; (2) if the direct threat of damage to the environment or damage to the environment was caused by: (a) military conflict, war, civil war or armed uprising, (b) natural disaster, (c) activity aimed at ensuring the defence and security of the state, international security or activity aimed at protection from natural disasters. The provisions of the Act are also not applied to nuclear damage within the scope in which it is regulated in the 29 November 2000 Nuclear Law Act.[179]

590. In this act, the concept of damage was defined for the first time (as ecological damage). It differs from the concept of damage used by the lawmaker in civil law. Doubtlessly, it is of a more narrow scope and includes three basic elements: protected species and habitats, the surface of the earth and water. The term damage is used to define 'negative, measurable change in the state or functions of natural elements, in comparison to their original state, where such change was caused directly or indirectly by the activity of an entity exploiting the environment: (a) in protected species or natural habitats, changes which have a significant impact on achieving or maintaining the right state of protection of these species or natural habitats. Damage to protected species or natural habitats does not include earlier identified negative impact, resulting from the actions of an entity exploiting the environment, (b) in waters, changes that have a significant, negative impact on the ecological potential, ecological state, chemical state or quantity of water; or the environmental state of waters in sea areas, (c) on the earth surface, changes that cause pollution of the soil or land, especially pollution which can endanger the health of people'.

591. The competent body in cases pertaining to responsibility for preventing damage to the environment and reparation of damage to the environment is the Regional Director for Environmental Protection. The higher-instance body is the General Director for Environmental Protection. In cases where there is a direct threat of damage to the environment or actual damage to the environment, caused

179. Dz. U. 2014, item 1512 with amendments.

by activities related to GMO, the competent body is the Minister of the Environment. Administrative bodies undertake necessary action ex officio. Victims and ecological organizations can only apply to the appropriate authority for necessary action to be taken. The competent authority for environmental protection is required to process every notification of the incidence of direct threat of damage to the environment, or actual damage to the environment.

592. The obligations of the perpetrator of damage to the environment or the danger of its occurrence come down to remedial or preventive actions. In cases where there is a direct threat of danger to the environment, the entity exploiting the environment is required to immediately undertake preventive action. Preventive action is the activity taken with regard to an event, action or omission which causes a direct threat of damage to the environment, aimed at preventing or reducing said damage, especially eliminating or limiting emission.

593. In cases where damage to the environment occurs, the entity exploiting the environment is obligated to: (1) take action aimed at reducing the damage to the environment, preventing further damage and negative impact on people's health or further weakening of the functions of natural elements, including immediate control, restraint, removal or reduction of the pollution or other harmful elements in some other manner; (2) undertake action aimed at reparation (all action, including temporary or restrictive activities, taken with the aim of repairing, or equivalently replacing natural elements or their functions which were damaged, as well as compensatory actions. Actions aimed at reparation especially include carrying out remediation, restoring the natural terrain, afforestation, forestation or creation of concentrations of vegetation, reintroduction of destroyed species, leading to the removal of danger to the health of people as well as the restoration of the natural balance within a certain territory).

594. The entity exploiting the environment bears the costs of the preventive or remedial activity. This obligation can be waived if this entity proves that the direct threat of damage to the environment or actual damage to the environment: (1) was caused by another entity or that it occurred despite the use of the appropriate safety measures. The entity on whom the burden of proof lies is obligated to indicate the entity responsible for the damage; (2) was caused by obedience to an order issued by a public administration body, unless this order resulted from emission or an event caused by the activity of the entity exploiting the environment. In cases where such an entity bears the costs, the said entity can seek compensation from the appropriate quarters (the perpetrator of the damage, the administrative body).

595. The entity exploiting the environment is obligated to consult the conditions for the remedial activities with the environmental protection body. Such proceedings are initiated by an application to determine the conditions for the remedial activities. The said conditions are determined by way of decision. The draft of the decision is subject to the opinions of other competent administrative bodies, according to their functional competence. For instance, the Director for the Maritime Office, the Regional Director for State Forests or the Director for the National Park.

596. When it comes to damage to protected species or natural habitats or in waters, the decision outlines: (1) the state to which the environment is to be restored, (2) the scope and manner of carrying out remedial activity, (3) the time for beginning and ending the remedial activity, (4) the manner of confirming that the planned ecological effect has been achieved.

597. When it comes to damage to the earth's surface, the decision establishing the plan for reparation outlines: (1) the territory on which reparation has to be carried out, by stating the address and the numbers of the land plots in question, as well as their total area, (2) the risk-causing substances as well as the effect of the remedial activity in terms of the amount of said substances that should be present in the soil and land after the remedial activity, (3) the manner of remediation, (4) the time of starting and finishing the remedial activities, (5) the manner of notification of completion of remedial activities as well as the time for submitting the required documents pertaining to the carrying out of these activities.

598. In cases where more than one kind of damage to the environment occurs, in such a way that remedial activities cannot be undertaken in relation to all the damages, the environmental protection body can specify, by way of decision, the order in which the remedial activities are to be undertaken.

599. If the responsible entity does not take preventive action or attempt to establish the conditions of the remedial activities, the environment protection body: (1) summons the entity to submit within a prescribed time, an application to determine the conditions for carrying out the preventive or remedial activities; (2) if said application is not made in accordance with the summons, the competent body, by way of decision, imposes on the entity, an obligation to carry out said activities.

600. The body for environmental protection undertakes preventive or remedial action if: (1) the entity exploiting the environment cannot be identified, or it is impossible to initiate enforcement proceedings, or the enforcement proceedings were ineffective; (2) due to the danger to health and the possibility of irrevocable damage to the environment, it is necessary to immediately take these actions (substitute activities). According to the principle that the 'polluter pays', the environmental protection body demands of the entity exploiting the environment, a refund of the costs it has taken to carry out the preventive and remedial activities. The obligation to bear the costs of preventive and remedial activities, the amount of money to be paid as well as the manner of payment are outlined by way of decision by the environmental protection body. The Act also outlines the premises under which the entity in question is not required to refund some or all the costs, as well as the time when the claim expires.

Chapter 2. Criminal Liability

§1. Criminal Liability in the Criminal Code

601. The legal foundations for criminal liability in matters of environmental are to be found in a wide range of regulations, among which the CC performs neither an exclusive nor fully sufficient role.[180] Grounds for criminal liability, including liability for petty offences, can be found in *inter alia* the CC of 6 June 1997.[181] Offences against the natural environment are regulated in section XXII of the CC, which provides for penalizing the commission of criminal acts with fines, non-custodial sentences and imprisonment. Unintentional acts are penalized less harshly than wilfully perpetrated ones.

602. The CC proscribes a fine, non-custodial sentence or imprisonment for up to five years for damaging or destroying vegetation and/or animal life in both protected areas and independently of the place of commission of the act (Article 181).

603. Polluting the water, air or soil with a substance or radioactive material in quantities threatening the health or life of humans, or causing significant degradation in the quality of water, air or soil and/or large-scale destruction to plant and/or animal life, may result in a fine, non-custodial sentence or imprisonment of up to eight years (Article 182).

604. Acts consisting of storing, removing, processing, recycling, neutralizing or transporting waste or substances in such conditions and in such a manner that causes a threat to the life or health of humans and/or significant degradation in the quality of water, air or soil and/or large-scale destruction to plant and/or animal life are also criminalized. Such action taken unlawfully may be punished by a fine, non-custodial sentence or imprisonment of up to two years, imprisonment of between three months and five years, or imprisonment of between six months and eight years (Article 183).

605. Producing, processing, transporting, importing from abroad, exporting abroad, gathering, warehousing, storing, possessing, using, employing, eliminating, discarding and/or leaving atomic material or another source of radioactivity without appropriate safeguards in such conditions or in such a manner that may cause a threat to the health or life of humans and/or significant degradation in the quality of water, air or soil and/or large-scale destruction to plant and/or animal life is subject to imprisonment for a period of between three months and five years; if done unintentionally, such acts are subject to a fine, non-custodial sentence or imprisonment of up to two years. If the aforementioned acts lead to large-scale destruction to plant or animal life, or to significant degradation of the quality of water, air or soil, the culprit is subject to imprisonment for a period of between six months and eight years, or in the event of serious harm to the health of a human, for a period of

180. Boć, Nowacki, Samborska-Boć *Ochrona środowiska*, 381.
181. Dz. U. 2017, item 1600 with amendments.

between one to ten years. However, when the result is the death of a human or serious harm to the health of many people, the potential penalty is imprisonment for a period of between two and twelve years (Articles 184 and 185).

606. Anyone who, acting in a manner inconsistent with their duty, fails to maintain in proper condition and/or to employ equipment to protect water, air and/or soil from pollution, or equipment providing protection against radioactive contamination or ionizing radiation, is subject to a fine, non-custodial sentence or imprisonment of up to two years. Similar penalties may be imposed on anyone who, acting in a manner inconsistent with their duties, commissions or otherwise permits the use of a structure or group of structures lacking legally required infrastructure (Article 186).

607. Destruction, serious damage or significant diminishment of the natural value of a legally protected space or facility is punishable by a fine, non-custodial sentence or imprisonment for a period of up to two years; if the perpetrator acted unintentionally, the penalty may be either a fine or non-custodial sentence (Article 187).

Lastly, anyone who erects a new structure, expands an existing structure or conducts commercial activity constituting a threat to the natural environment contrary to regulations in an area protected for its natural beauty and/or landscape, or in the buffer zone of such an area, is subject to a fine, non-custodial sentence or imprisonment for a period of up to two years (Article 188).

§2. Criminal Liability in the Environmental Protection Act

608. Another source of criminal liability in matters of environmental protection is the Environmental Protection Act, which provides for fines for the majority of activities defined as undesirable and harmful in respect of environmental protection. Such regulations apply in the event of failure to perform the obligation to collect and process data, and to provide free of charge access for the purposes of state-conducted environmental monitoring (Article 329), failure to provide for the needs of environmental protection in an area where construction works are being performed (Article 330), and failure to inform the provincial inspector for environmental protection of the planned commissioning date of a structure, group of structures or installation, or of the planned completion of an installation's start-up (Article 331). A fine may also be assessed for advertising or promoting a product without providing clear information on environmentally safe use of the product (Article 332a). Failure to take measurements of airborne substances and/or failure to retain the results of such measurements for the period set forth in a decision (Article 333), the use of soil or earth that fails to meet quality standards (Article 336) and violation of the terms of a decision on acceptable noise levels (Article 337a) are punishable by a fine, and in the last of the aforementioned infractions the legislator has also provided for the sanction of short-term imprisonment or a non-custodial sentence.

609. Short-term imprisonment and a non-custodial sentence may also be imposed as alternatives to a fine for failure to fulfil the obligation to perform measurements of magnetic fields (Article 338a), failure to decontaminate or neutralize installations or devices containing or having contained substances posing a serious threat to the environment or in respect of which there is a reasonable suspicion that such substances have been used in them (Article 345). Short-term imprisonment or a non-custodial sentence may be imposed on anyone who operates an installation without a required permit or in violation of its conditions or if an installation is operated without providing the required security (Article 351(1–2)). Exceptionally, the legislator allows for the imposition of short-term imprisonment as an alternative to a fine in respect of disclosure of information acquired in conjunction with the performance of the duties of an environmental verifier (Article 351a). Other situations in which short-term imprisonment or a non-custodial sentence may be used as an alternative to a fine are those involving failure to perform one's duties as the head of an elevated-risk or high-risk facility, including in the event of an accident (Article 354(1–2)). The same catalogue of punishments is applicable in cases when the head of a high-risk facility fails to develop or to implement a safety system, commences the operation of a facility without possessing an approved safety report, fails to analyse and introduce justified changes into a safety report, or fails to perform other obligations set forth in the Environmental Protection Act (Article 355). Lastly, penalties other than fines are applicable to anyone who fails to adhere to a decision ordering the suspension of activity or commission of a structure, group of structures, installation or device or forbidding the use of such, a decision forbidding the production, import or bringing to market of products that fail to satisfy environmental protection standards, and a decision ordering the removal of identified defects within a specified period of time or suspending the activation or operation of an installation (Article 360).

610. In other cases involving violations of the law, the legislator provides only for the imposition of a fine. Primarily these are situations involving the introduction of a substance or of energy into the environment exceeding acceptable emissions standards, failure to observe requirements concerning the proper operation of an installation or device, or failure to fulfil statutory requirements in the event of an accident or event involving an installation (Article 339(1–2)). Similar action can be taken in the event of failure to perform one's obligation to conduct periodic, continual or initial measurements of emissions volumes or failure to retain the results of measurements for the required period, as well as in situations involving the failure to ensure emissions volume measurements are conducted by a laboratory that meets the criteria set forth in statute (Article 340(1–2)). Violation of a ban on using public address installations or devices, or failure to observe restrictions, orders or restrictions contained in a resolution of the municipal council, is subject to a fine (Article 343(1–2)). The use of substances posing a serious threat to the natural environment without regularly providing the appropriate authorities with information about their types, quantities and places in which they are located, as well as failure to document the types, quantities and places in which such substances are located within the scope required by law, is subject to the same penalty (Article 346(1–2)). Lastly, mention should be made of penalties applicable in the event of bringing products to market made of artificial materials (e.g., single-use dishes and cutlery) without providing information on their negative environmental impact (347(1–2)), as well as the unlawful use of symbols denoting participation in the domestic Eco-Management and Audit Scheme (EMAS) (Article 351b), or situations in which someone who has observed an accident fails to inform without undue delay people located within the danger zone and the State Fire Service or the prefect (mayor) (Article 352).

§3. Criminal Liability in the Nature Protection Act

611. Criminal liability for offences against the protection of nature is also established under section 11 of the Nature Protection Act. In penalizing particular behaviours described in the Act, apart from fines the legislator has also provided for such punishments as short-term imprisonment, non-custodial sentences and imprisonment for a period of up to five years. The most severely-punished offences are those consisting of coming into possession of specimens of protected species of plants, animals and fungi in greater than negligible quantities, in such conditions or in such a manner that it negatively impacts the protection of the species. In such cases the legislator has provided for a punishment of imprisonment for a period from three months to five years unless the perpetrator acted unintentionally – in such cases the period of imprisonment may be up to two years (Article 127a(1–2)). A penalty of imprisonment for a period from three months to five years is also envisioned for transporting (without the appropriate permit or in violation of its conditions) across the EU border a specimen of a protected species, for trade in specimens of protected species, and for violating EU regulations concerning trade in protected wild plant and animal species. If the perpetrator acted unintentionally, a non-custodial sentence or imprisonment for two years may be imposed (Article 128 and 128a(1–2)).

612. Other behaviours forbidden under the Nature Protection Act are punishable by short-term imprisonment or by a fine. In particular, such behaviours include the wilful violation of orders in place in national parks, landscape parks, protected landscape zones and Natura 2000 zones. Similar penalties can be imposed for infringing restrictions related to natural monuments, documentation stations, ecological lands and areas of outstanding natural beauty. Mention should also be made here of failure to register with the relevant county commissioner animals possessed or raised as listed in Annexes A and B of Council Regulation (EC) No. 338/97 of 9 December 1996 on the protection of species of wild fauna and flora by regulating trade therein (OJ L 67, 3.3.1997, pp. 1–65 with amendments), as well as bringing to market seal products in violation of the conditions set forth in Article 3 of Regulation (EC) No. 1007/2009 of 16 September 2009 on trade in seal products (OJ L 286, 31.10.2009, p. 36) – (Article 127). A similar approach is applied in the case of conducting commercial activity (without possessing or forwarding the proper documentation establishing the legality of an animal's origin) in respect of trade in protected species, as well as the capture or killing of wild animals using devices, means or methods that may cause the loss of a local animal population, and also maintaining a botanical or zoological garden without possessing the proper permit or in violation of its terms and failure to provide animals found there with appropriate living conditions during the liquidation of the garden. Also worthy of mention is the transfer of an endangered plant or animal species from a botanical or zoological garden to the natural environment without a permit or in violation of its terms. This category also includes acts related to animals considered a danger to human health and life consisting of violating restrictions concerning those animals and failure to exercise due caution resulting in such animals escaping captivity. Introducing into the environment, transporting and importing without a permit, keeping, raising, breeding and selling foreign species all constitute activities subject to punishment by short-term imprisonment or a fine. Criminal penalties are also applicable for infringing the protection afforded to plants, animals and fungi encompassed by species protection; the burning of grasslands, pastures, ditches and railway paths is also forbidden. The same penalty is envisioned for failure to report to the appropriate authorities the discovery of fossilized plant or animal material, as well as for killing animals and destroying plants and fungi and/or their habitats (Article 131).

613. The imposition of criminal punishment for the aforementioned actions is also often associated with the forfeiture of instruments used in the commission of the forbidden acts, the obligation to provide *restitutio in integrum*, the handover of specimens of species to entities authorized to care for them, and the forfeiture of animals posing a danger to the health and life of people together with handing them over to entities authorized to care for them appointed by the regional director for environmental protection (Articles 129 and 131a).

§4. Criminal Liability in the Act on Preventing and Repairing Damage to the Natural Environment

614. In the Act of 13 April 2007 on preventing and repairing damage to the natural environment,[182] only the punishment of a fine may be assessed for failure to undertake preventative measures by a person using the natural environment in the event of the occurrence of a direct threat to the environment, as well as of failure to report such a threat to an environmental protection authority and the provincial inspector for environmental protection (Article 28(1–2)).

§5. Criminal Liability in the Water Act

615. The Water Act contains provisions establishing criminal liability in section 9. The most severe criminal sanctions are reserved for actions consisting of preventing or hindering the use of water for combating serious emergencies, natural disasters, fires or other localized dangers or for preventing a serious threat to the life and health of people and/or to property of significant value. In such cases the

182. Dz. U. 2018, item 954 with amendments.

perpetrator is subject to a fine, a non-custodial sentence or imprisonment for a period of up to one year; if the actions of the perpetrator lead to the death or serious damage to the health of a person or to significant loss of property, they are punishable by a fine and imprisonment for a period of up to five years (Article 473(1–2)). Less severe penalties are applied in situations involving the conducting of activities near water or measurement installations that pose a threat to those devices. In such cases a fine, non-custodial sentence or imprisonment for a period of up to one year may be imposed; if the act results in significant damage, the perpetrator may be punished with a fine and imprisonment for a period of up to two years (Article 474(1–2)).

616. A fine, non-custodial sentence or imprisonment for a period of up to one year may be imposed on those who destroy or cause damage to the shorelines of inland surface waters, structures or walls comprising a shore and land under inland surface waters (Article 475).

617. An individual who uses water, installs water infrastructure or performs other activities requiring a water law permit without such a permit or in violation of its conditions is subject to short-term imprisonment, a non-custodial sentence or a fine. The same punishment may be imposed on an individual who fails to perform obligations set forth in a decision ascertaining the expiration or revocation of a water law permit (Article 476(1–2)).

618. A fine may also be imposed on those who fail to perform their duty to maintain waters and/or water infrastructure in proper condition, prevent access to public waters, or fail to perform such actions as measuring the quantity and quality of effluent intended for agricultural applications (Article 477). The same penalty is imposed on the one who in particular changes the direction and intensity of outflow of rainfall or snowmelt on his land, or the direction of water outflow from springs, or discharges water or introduces sewage into neighbouring land. Similarly treated would be the activity of fencing the properties adjacent to public inland surface waters or to the shore of sea waters or the territorial sea, at a distance of less than 1.5 m from the shoreline, and not providing data falling within the scope of information collected in the water management information system, or the owner of the land, who is entitled to the ordinary use of waters, performs the abstraction of waters or the introduction of sewage into waters or to the ground, does not provide access to the property to the extent necessary to equip measuring instruments. The same applies to those who release sewage into waters or to the ground, release waste or liquid animal manure into waters, transport snow from contaminated areas to waters, or store it in areas located between the embankment and the waterline or at a distance of less than 50 m from the water's line. The same penalty applies to those who, in areas of particular flood hazard, collect sewage, animal waste, chemicals or other substances or materials that can pollute water, recycle or dispose of waste, or locate new cemeteries, clean vehicles in surface waters or on the banks of these water, extracts from the surface water directly to agricultural sprayers or cleans agricultural sprayers in these waters, uses paints produced on the basis of organic-tin compounds (TBT) for the maintenance of technical underwater structures, uses vehicles in surface waters or on land covered with waters. The fine is also applied to the person who does not ensure protection of waters against pollution, being the owner or manager of a flood embankment, does not impose a temporary ban on moving over flood barriers, dilutes sewage in order to obtain their condition, composition or minimum percentage reduction of pollutants, does not remove sewage from a ship to an onshore reception device, does not mark the boundaries of an area of indirect protection or direct protection, does not apply to prohibitions, orders or restrictions in force in the protection zone, in the protection area or in the protection zone of public service measuring devices. Finally, the same sanction is applied to those who destroys, damages or moves tables containing information about the establishment of a protection zone or permanent standing or floating signs, or tables containing information about the establishment of a protection zone and prohibiting unauthorized access and who discharges state-surveying equipment and does not perform the obligation of water-legal permit to make devices to prevent damage or reduce negative effects of the permit.

§6. Criminal Liability in the Animal Protection Act

619. Criminal liability in respect of animal protection is provided for in section 11 of the Animal Protection Act of 21 August 1997,[183] in which the most severe penalty is foreseen for murdering or killing animals (save for exceptions set forth in statute regarding the slaughter and killing of farm animals) in an inhumane manner consisting of inflicting physical and psychological pain, or slaughtering without taking measures to render the animal unconscious. A person guilty of such an act may be punished by imprisonment for a period of up to two three. The same penalties may be imposed on anyone who abuses an animal; if any of the aforementioned acts are performed with extreme cruelty, the guilty party may be imprisoned for a period from three months up to five years.

620. Short-term imprisonment and a fine may be imposed for acts consisting of breeding or keeping a dog of a breed acknowledged as aggressive without the required permit, transporting animals by a carrier without the required documents, licences or verifications, and failing to ensure proper conditions for animals in transport. The same penalties may be imposed on anyone in possession of a chicken coop who fails to provide care for broiler chickens by persons fulfilling the necessary criteria, increases the population of broiler chickens in violation of regulations, or fails to record, maintain or store the required documentation (Article 37a, Article 37b and Article 37d). In the event of a conviction for the aforementioned crimes, the court may also order forfeiture of the animal(s), forbid the possession of animals for a period of between one and fifteen years, forbid the performance by the convicted person of a specified trade, profession, commercial activity and/or activities requiring a permit and associated with the use of animals or having an impact upon them; the court may also order the forfeiture of tools or other objects deriving from the offence, and exemplary damages at an amount between PLN 1,000 and PLN

183. Dz. U. 2017, item 1840 with amendments.

100,000 to benefit an objective associated with animal protection as indicated by the court. Social organizations whose statutory objective is animal protection may collaborate with the appropriate state and local self-governmental institutions in exposing and prosecuting the crimes and misdemeanours defined in statute (Article 40).

§7. Criminal Liability in the Geological and Mining Act

621. Another source of environmental protection in Polish criminal law is the Geological and Mining Act of 9 June 2011.[184] Regulations concerning criminal liability are contained in section 11, which imposes a punishment of imprisonment for a period of up to three years on an individual who has caused significant damage to property or serious damage to the natural environment in searching for or extracting mineral deposits without the required licence or approved plan for geological works; if the act was committed unintentionally, the punishment may be a fine, non-custodial sentence or imprisonment for a period of up to a year (Article 176(1–3)).

622. Short-term imprisonment or a fine may be imposed on an individual who searches for or extracts mineral deposits without the required permits, or who stores or warehouses waste underground without the use of a cistern (Article 177). The same penalty may be imposed on an individual who, in the operation of a mining facility, performs activities in conditions involving the risk of fire, rock bursts or gas explosions, or other risks involving dust, climate or water, as well as risks associated with the transport of people through a mineshaft or with the storage or use of blasting materials and equipment in a manner that may create danger for the life and health of people and/or the activity of the mining facility. If the individual responsible acted unintentionally, a fine is imposed (Article 184(1–2)). Similar consequences are borne by the head of operations of a mining facility who fails to inform the appropriate mining supervision authority of an accident or natural death occurring at the mining facility, as well as of unsafe events associated with the operation of a mining facility creating a threat to human health and life and/or to public safety (Article 186).

623. In other situations the legislator has provided a fine, which is to be imposed in situations such as when geological works are overseen or supervised by individuals who do not hold the required qualifications (Article 178), geological works are conducted without an approved plan (Article 179), the decision of a geological administrative authority is not carried out (Articles 180 and 188), or when the management or supervision of the operation of a mining facility is performed by individuals without the required qualifications (Article 181) or without an approved plan of operations (Article 182). This same penalty may be imposed on an individual who performs activities in the operation of a mining facility in a manner that may lead to a threat to the health or life of people, fails to perform the obligation to train people in the relevant regulations and rules of workplace health and safety, or

184. Dz. U. 2017, item 2126 with amendments.

allows an individual without the required qualifications to work in a mining facility (Article 184). Failure to perform duties in respect of maintaining a record of mineral deposits is also punishable by fine (Article 183). A fine may also be imposed on an individual who fails to perform his/her obligation to create a fund, to collect money for a fund, or to present on the demand of the appropriate authorities recent bank statements related to the account in which the fund's money is kept along with information about the manner in which the money is being used (Article 187).

§8. Criminal Liability in the Ozone Layer Depleting Substances Act

624. Criminal liability for infringements involving the ozone layer are addressed in section 11 of the Act of 15 May 2015 on Ozone Layer Depleting Substances and Certain Fluorinated Greenhouse Gases.[185] A fine, non-custodial sentence or imprisonment for a period of up to two years may be imposed on an individual who, in violation of the restrictions or failing to maintain the conditions set forth in Articles 4–13, 15, 17, 20 and 24 of the Regulation (EC) of the European Parliament and of the Council of 16 September 2009 on substances that deplete the ozone layer (OJ L 31.10.2009, No. 286, p. 1) produces, imports, exports, places on the market or uses substances depleting ozone layer, as well as products, equipment and installations containing controlled substances. The one who issues a certificate for staff or entrepreneurs (Article 52 and Article 53) is subject to the same penalty. If the aforementioned is done unintentionally, punishment may be in the form of a fine or non-custodial sentence (Article 47a (1–2)).

§9. Criminal Liability in the Extractive Waste Act

625. Criminal liability regulations are also to be found in the Extractive Waste Act of 10 July 2008,[186] in which section 9 contains provisions under which all activities harmful to the natural environment are punishable by a fine of up to PLN 100,000 or short-term imprisonment. Among the acts penalized in this manner are the generation of extraction waste without the required decision confirming the plan for management of extraction waste, operating a facility neutralizing extraction waste without the required permit, or storing extraction waste in a place not intended for such activity (Article 45). The same punishments are applicable to cases of operating an extraction waste neutralizing facility without examining the conformance of accepted waste with the information contained in the waste transfer record, as well as for the absence of monitoring of an extraction waste neutralizing facility in the course of its operation (Article 46). In addition, an individual who shuts down an extraction waste neutralizing facility without the required permission of the appropriate public authority or contrary to its conditions is also subject to similar penalties (Article 47).

185. Dz. U. 2017, item 1951 with amendments.
186. Dz. U. 2017, item 1849 with amendments.

§10. Criminal Liability in the Waste Act

626. A significant number of provisions concerning criminal liability in matters of environmental protection are contained in the Waste Act of 14 December 2012.[187] Violating the Act's provisions is punishable by short-term imprisonment or by a fine; those potentially incurring such penalties include individuals performing household waste management in a manner that fails to provide proper protection to human health and life and to the environment (Article 171, in conjunction with Article 16). The same penalty may be imposed on an individual who neutralizes contaminated medical or veterinary waste outside the province in which it was generated or introduces such waste into another province (Article 172(1–2)). Similar criminal provisions apply in the event of processing household, mixed and green waste outside the region in which it was generated, as well as introducing such waste into another region (Article 173(1–2)). Short-term imprisonment and a fine may also be imposed for the transport and storage of waste in violation of the provisions of the Act (Article 174(1 and 3)), assigning the management of waste to entities that have not received the required decisions and/or required entry into the appropriate register (Article 175), and for processing waste in a manner causing a threat to human health or life and to the natural environment (Article 176). The same punishment is faced by an individual who gathers waste without concluding the required contract or engages in waste management contrary to information contained in the register (Articles 177 and 178). Failure to maintain records of waste, failure to maintain such records in a timely manner or maintaining them with false data is punishable by fine. Short-term imprisonment and a fine may be imposed in the event of burning polychlorinated biphenyls (PCBs) on ships or submitting it for recycling, mixing waste oils with other dangerous waste substances, including those containing PCB, and submitting for recycling medical and veterinary waste products whose recycling is forbidden (Articles 181, 182 and 183). Transferring municipal sewage sludge for its use to an individual or entity in control of land and failure to inform the provincial inspector for environmental protection is punishable by short-term imprisonment and a fine (Article 184). The same punishment may be imposed on an individual who acts in violation of restrictions to use municipal sewage sludge or, prior to its use, does not conduct testing on municipal sewage sludge nor the ground on which such sludge is to be used (Article 185). Removing to the sea and storing on the seabed waste derived from titanium oxide production and from the processing of such waste (Article 187), as well as accepting metallic waste at waste collection centres without verifying the identity of the individual passing the waste (Article 188) is punishable by the same penalty. Equivalent liability may be borne by an individual managing a waste storage facility who accepts waste without performing such obligations as preparing a basic description of the waste, gathering and storing samples of waste, examining containers and certificates required for the storage of metallic mercury waste, and informing the provincial inspector for environmental protection and the provincial sanitary inspector of changes detected in the observable parameters of a waste storage facility (Article 189). Also subject to penalty is the employment of a waste storage or incineration

187. Dz. U. 2018, item 992 with amendments.

facility of a person who does not possess confirmation of waste management qualifications (Article 190), thermal transformation of waste outside of a waste incineration facility (Article 191) and accepting waste for thermal transformation by a waste incineration facility without determining its mass and/or without reading the description of dangerous waste (Article 192).

§11. Criminal Liability in the International Waste Transport Act

627. Trans-border issues of waste and associated criminal liability are addressed by the International Waste Transport Act of 13 June 2013.[188] Section 8 of the Act provides for penalties of short-term imprisonment or a fine for an individual's failure to carry out a decision ordering the return of waste brought into the country to the country from which it was transported, or establishing the manner in which such waste is to be managed within the country. A fine may be imposed on an individual or organizational entity participating in the international transport of waste which fails to perform its obligation to present to authorized public authorities and officials documents and/or information required in the international transport of waste (Article 31(1–2)).

§12. Criminal Liability in the Packaging and Packaging Waste Act

628. Another source of criminal law in environmental protection is the Packaging and Packaging Waste Management Act of 13 June 2013,[189] in which section 11 provides a financial penalty for the activities harmful to the natural environment. Under this Act subject to a penalty are those who disrupt control by the authorized person, by thwarting or impeding the performance of activities, or the one who does not report the commencement of activity consisting in the manufacture, import or intra-Community acquisition of products in packaging or products, recovery or recycling of packaging waste or waste from products, export or intra-Community supply of packaging waste or waste from products in order to be recovered or recycled or acted as a recovery organization or organization for the recovery of packaging. The one who does not report the change of data contained in the notification is subject to the same penalty. Similarly, the person who, being a user of a dangerous substance which a substance for plant protection, does not return packaging waste at the centre of the entrepreneur running a retail or wholesale unit that sells dangerous substances in packaging (Article 59 – Article 61).

188. Dz. U. 2018, item 296 with amendments.
189. Dz. U. 2018, item 150 with amendments.

§13. Criminal Liability in the Used Electric and Electronic Devices Act

629. Section 14 of the Electronic and Electrical Waste Act of 11 October 2015[190] provides fine penalties. The provisions on the fine penalty apply to the person who does not return used household equipment to the collector of used equipment (Article 96), puts used equipment against the prohibition, together with other wastes (Article 95), does not accept used equipment from households or accepts such equipment for consideration (97).

§14. Criminal Liability in the Recycling End-of-Life Vehicles Act

630. Finally, it is necessary to point out provisions concerning criminal liability contained in the Recycling End-of-Life Vehicles Act of 20 January 2005.[191] Section 8 of the Act provides for a fine in the event of bringing to market materials or parts of motor vehicles containing lead, mercury, cadmium or hexavalent chromium (Article 44), fails to provide labelling of motor vehicle accessories and parts (Article 45), fails to forward information to an entrepreneur operating a disassembly facility concerning the manner of disassembly of a new type of motor vehicle and fails to provide an entity introducing a motor vehicle and/or entrepreneur operating a disassembly facility with information concerning the manner of disassembly, storage and/or testing of reusable motor vehicle equipment or parts (Article 46).) Failure to forward an end-of-life vehicle to an entrepreneur operating a disassembly facility or entrepreneur operating a motor vehicle collection point, as well as failure to forward used lead-acid motor vehicle batteries to the operator of a used-battery processing facility (Article 48 and 48a). The same penalty may be imposed on an individual who fails to accept an end-of-life vehicle at a disassembly facility or motor vehicle collection point (Article 49(1–2)), and an individual who fails to fulfil an obligation to provide the owner of a motor vehicle with a certificate attesting to the disassembly of the vehicle or fails to forward that certificate to the appropriate registration authority for the place in which the vehicle was last registered (Article 51).

190. Dz. U. 2018, item 1466.
191. Dz. U. 2018, item 578 with amendments.

Chapter 3. Civil Liability

§1. Legal Bases

631. The primary legal act containing the foundations of civil liability for damage caused to the natural environment is the Civil Code of 24 April 1964.[192] The Environmental Protection Act, referring to the Civil Code, also introduces some provisions. In addition, fragmentary regulation can be found in the Water Act (Articles 185–188), the Genetically Modified Organisms Act (Article 57), the Atomic Energy Act (Articles 100–108) and the Geological and Mining Act (Articles 91–100).

632. 'Damage caused by environmental impact' is understood in the civil law fashion as every loss incurred by the injured party, whether such loss affects property or another good. It may take the form of damage to property or damage to a person. The cause of such damage should be the activity of a person which has an impact on the environment.

633. Tortious civil liability (the primary form of liability in environmental protection law) and contractual liability (less frequent in this area of law) essentially constitute private law liability, as such forms of liability are traditionally associated with the protection of a private interest rather than a public one; the entity entitled to initiate proceedings leading to the imposition of civil sanctions is a person (natural or juridical) bearing loss or the threat of loss, while such sanctions can be imposed by a common court. In respect of civil liability as it refers to environmental protection, the scope of such liability has been broadened in a certain sense as the environment is protected due to its status as a 'common good'. As a result, an action under Article 323(1) of the Environmental Protection Act can be brought by the State Treasury, local self-government authorities and ecological organizations.

§2. Principles

634. The primary principles for incurring civil liability set forth in the Civil Code are those of fault and of risk. Cases involving environmental protection will most often involve liability based on risk.

635. The principle of fault means that only an entity who can be assigned fault may be held liable. This principle is formulated in Article 415 of the Civil Code: 'Any person who through his fault has caused an injury to another person shall be liable to make it good'. The conditions for establishing liability on the basis of fault are: (1) the existence of injury (potential for injury); (2)objective unlawfulness of the responsible person's behaviour, understood as incompatibility of his behaviour

192. Dz. U. 2018, item 1025 with amendments.

with the law; unlawfulness is interpreted broadly as not only a violation of legal provisions but also of other principles, particularly those of social coexistence or of safety (prudence);(3) guilt of the responsible person in the form of ill will or carelessness; (4) a normal causal nexus between the behaviour of the responsible person and the injury or threat thereof.

636. Liability in risk (objective liability) is characterized by the absence of the requirement to demonstrate fault on the part of the responsible entity. The obligation to provide restitution results from the very fact of a given event's occurrence (e.g., activity conducted by a facility and the causing of damage by that activity). The primary regulation of relevance to environmental protection forming the risk principle is Article 435(1) Civil Code: 'A person who runs on his own account an enterprise or an establishment set in motion by natural forces (steam, gas, electricity, liquid fuels, etc.) is liable for any personal or property damage caused by the operation of the enterprise or the establishment unless the damage is due to force majeure or solely to a fault on the part of the aggrieved party or a third party for whom he is not responsible.' Article 324 Environmental Protection Act extends the scope of Article 435 of the Civil Code to other enterprises and establishments than those set in motion by natural forces insofar as they can be classified as enterprises and establishments of significant or increased risk of occurrence of a serious industrial event.

637. The conditions for liability in risk are:

(1) the existence of injury (or potential for injury);
(2) a normal causal nexus between the activity of the responsible entity (e.g., the functioning of an enterprise or installation) and the injury or potential thereof;
(3) the absence of exonerating circumstances expressly foreseen in statute: force majeure, fault solely on the part of the aggrieved party or solely on the part of a third party for which the liable party is not responsible.

§3. Compensatory Liability and Preventative Liability

638. Independently of the differentiation between liability based on fault and risk, the Civil Code also provides a basis for discerning compensatory liability and preventative liability in the context of environmental protection.

639. Compensatory liability concerns situations when damage has already arisen. Examples of provisions addressing compensatory liability are the aforementioned Articles 415 and 435 of the Civil Code. The aggrieved party, in demanding compensation for damage, may select between restitution and monetary compensation in accordance with Article 363 of the Civil Code. However, if restitution is impossible or would result in excessive difficulties or costs for the liable party, the aggrieved party is limited to accepting monetary compensation.

Article 325 of the Environmental Protection Act establishes a principle addressing compensatory liability under which 'Liability for damage caused by impact on the environment shall not be excluded by the circumstance that the activity leading to the damage is conducted on the basis of a decision and within the restrictions established therein.' This provision indicates that the activity of an entity liable for damage may also be unlawful when it is conducted on the basis of a permit and within the boundaries set forth by it. This affects the interpretation of the provisions of both the Civil Code and the Environmental Protection Act.

640. Preventative liability refers to situations in which damage has not yet occurred but there is a direct threat that it will. In such circumstances it is permissible to demand that the entity responsible for the threat cease the activities causing it. Preventative liability is grounded in Article 439 of the Civil Code, which declares that: 'Anyone who, as a result of another person's behaviour, especially due to a lack of proper supervision of the operations of an enterprise or establishment run by that person or of the condition of a building or other facility in his possession is directly threatened by damage, may demand that the person undertake measures necessary to avert the imminent danger and, if needed, that he give appropriate security.' Another provision establishing a basis for preventative liability is Article 222(2) in conjunction with Article 144 of the Civil Code, which gives the owner of real property the right to bring a negatory action. Under the provision cited above, 'An owner is entitled to claim restitution of the lawful status and for violations of the law to be ceased, against a person who violates his ownership otherwise than by depriving him of actual control of the thing.' Also worthy of note is Article 24(1) of the Civil Code, which provides protection to the rights of personality.

§4. Civil Liability in the Environmental Protection Act

641. An additional basis for claims for damages accompanying those contained in the Civil Code (compensatory and preventative) concerning damage caused by environmental impact is Article 323(1) of the Environmental Protection Act. This liability is based on the principle of risk. Conditions for the existence of liability are: (1) unlawful impact of an activity on the environment; (2) the existence of damage or imminent threat of damage; (3) a normal causal nexus between the unlawful behaviour and the damage.

642. This provision may serve as the basis for demanding that a court order the responsible party to:(1) perform restitution; it must be noted that this differs from the Civil Code in that it is restitution to a lawful condition and not restitution of the previous condition; (2) undertaking appropriate preventative measures, in particular by installing devices or equipment providing protection against potential damage; (3) ceasing activity that is responsible for causing damage or the threat of it – in the event that the application of preventative measures is impossible or unreasonably difficult.

Actions may be brought both by the aggrieved party and by entities which have not incurred direct loss nor are under the threat of loss: the State Treasury, local self-government authorities or ecological organizations (the environment being a common good).

643. As a rule, the costs of repairing damage are borne by the entity responsible for causing it. If another entity, in fact, repairs damage to the environment by way of natural restitution, Article 326 Environmental Protection Act provides a basis for an action against the party responsible for the damage, but the amount of the claim is limited to justified costs incurred in the process of restoring the environment to its previous state.

644. An additional basis for claims can be found in Article 328 Environmental Protection Act, which provides ecological organizations with the right to bring an action demanding the cessation of an advertisement or other form of promotion of a product or service in conflict with the provisions of Article 80, which states that such activity should not promote a model of consumption incompatible with the principles of environmental protection and sustainable development, particularly by using images of wild nature for promoting products and services which exert a negative impact on the natural environment.

645. The Environmental Protection Act also contains provisions addressing evidentiary matters. A complainant bringing a claim foreseen under the Environmental Protection Act may demand that the court impose an obligation on the individual whose activity is linked with the claim being pursued to provide information necessary for determining the scope of liability (e.g., production undertaken, substances used).

Part V. Juridical Actions of Individuals

Chapter 1. Administrative Remedies

§1. Introduction

646. Environmental protection, as an interdisciplinary field, is characterized by a large proportion of public law mechanisms and solutions, and matters involving environmental protection are administrative matters resolved by way of individual decisions issued in the course of standard administrative proceedings.

647. The broadly-defined participation of interested entities in taking decisions concerning the protection of the natural environment encompasses such participation regulated in the Code of Administrative Proceedings (CAP) of 14 June 1960,[193] which grants particular privileges to parties to the proceedings, social organizations joined as a party to proceedings or making use of other procedural privileges, and individuals submitting appeals and motions based on section VIII CAP. Other prerogatives are set forth in the Act on the Sharing of Information on the Environment and its Protection, Public Participation in Environmental Protection and Environmental Impact Assessments, which sets out the principles for public participation in environmental protection in the context of particular types of proceedings.

§2. Administrative Procedure

I. Parties to Proceedings and Entities Joined to Proceedings as Parties

648. Pursuant to Article 28 CAP, anyone whose legal interest or duty is affected by proceedings, or who demands action from a public authority due to his or her legal interest or duty, may be acknowledged as a party. The concept of a legal interest must be understood as an objective, real need for a remedy. This interest must be personal, one's own, individualized and specific, and it must be both objectively perceivable and present rather than a future interest.[194] A duty, as in the case of a legal interest, should be individualized, present, objectively provable, supported by

193. Dz. U. 2017, item 1257 with amendments.
194. Verdict of the Supreme Administrative Court of 20 April 1998, IV SA 1106/97.

factual circumstances suiting the conditions for application of a provision of substantive law, and it must be ruled on or ascertained in the course of administrative proceedings by the issuance of an administrative decision.[195] In matters of a special nature, regulations reduce the scope of potential parties to proceedings having in view the object of such proceedings, such as in the case of a water law permit or construction permit.

649. Social organizations, including ecological organizations, may participate in proceedings regulated by CAP as parties joined to the proceedings.[196] An entity joined to proceedings as a party has neither a legal interest nor a duty as defined under Article 28. Such an entity is also not entitled to dispose of proceedings, nor of the rights and/or duties those proceedings concern; it will not be the addressee of the decision resolving the matter, and may only make use of procedural prerogatives that a party to administrative proceedings may avail itself of (e.g., submit evidentiary motions, submit an appeal against a decision). Pursuant to Article 31 CAP, a social organization may submit a motion to commence proceedings or to be admitted to proceedings in a manner concerning another person, on condition that this is justified by the statutory objectives of that organization and when there is a social interest in its doing so. A social organization may make use of those prerogatives in order to provide support to a party, or to oppose its demands and interests; it may also work on behalf of one party, or it may avoid linking its procedural actions with the interests of any of the parties, looking only to satisfy the general social interest. Procedural initiative may be undertaken independently by a social organization, or it may be evoked by notification addressed by an administrative authority to a social organization due to the former's conviction that it may be interested in participating in proceedings with regard to its statutory objectives and there is a social interest in that organization doing so (Article 31(4) CAP).

650. A public administration authority that holds a social organization's demands to be justified shall initiate proceedings ex officio, or will issue a decision permitting the organization to participate in the proceedings. A decision refusing the initiation of proceedings or permission for a social organization to participate in proceedings may be appealed against.

651. Other means by which a social organization may express its point of view in a matter are through presenting its opinion as recorded in a resolution or statement by a statutory authority of that organization upon obtaining the consent of the public administration authority conducting proceedings (Article 31(5) CAP), and also by participating in an administrative hearing or by submitting a statement and/or evidence upon receiving notification from an administrative authority on the basis of Article 90(3) CAP.

---

195. B. Adamiak, J. Borkowski, *Kodeks postępowania administracyjnego. Komentarz* (CH Beck 2013).
196. Entities joined *ex lege* to proceedings as parties are also the public prosecutor, Human Rights Defender and Childs' Rights Ombudsman.

II. The Procedural Position of Parties

652. In the CAP there are numerous provisions that determine the procedural position of parties to proceedings, beginning with general principles and finishing with detailed provisions regulating both ordinary and extraordinary proceedings.

653. The general principles of administrative procedures are: legality, taking into account the public interests and just interests of citizens ex officio, resolving doubts in favour of the party, cooperation, objective truth, stimulating the trust of citizens to the state authorities, proportionality, impartiality, equal treatment, protection of legitimate expectations, furnishing the parties and other participants with information, active participation (hearing) of the parties in the proceedings, convincing the parties (explaining the grounds for rulings), prompt and simple proceedings, amicable resolution of matter, written proceedings, two-instance proceedings, durability of final administrative decisions, court review of legality of administrative decision.

654. The procedural position of parties is based on the principle of active participation (hearing) of the parties in the proceedings. The party has the right to access to the case files, and make notes and copies. This right can also be exercised after the proceedings are concluded (Article 73(1)). When it comes to proceedings in which the foreigner participates, a problem arises in connection to the exclusions contained in Article 74(1) of the CAP, limiting the foreigner's right to case files protected as classified secret information with clause 'confidential' or 'strictly confidential' and to other files which the public administration authority excluded due to important state interest. A refusal to enable the party to review the case files, make notes and copies, to certify such copies or issue certified copies shall be effected by means of an order which shall be subject to complaint. The effects of these proceedings also affect proceedings before the administrative courts handling cases of using administrative acts which are marked as confidential.

655. The party has right to submit evidentiary motions. A demand of a party concerning admission of evidence shall be allowed if the object of the evidence is material to the matter. A public administration authority may refuse to allow the demand which has not been submitted in the course of evidentiary proceedings or during the hearing if the demand concerns circumstances already proven by other evidence unless such circumstances are material to the matter. According to Article 79 each party should be notified at least seven days in advance as to the venue and date of evidentiary proceedings involving examination of witnesses, experts or inspection. A party has the right to participate in evidentiary proceedings, may ask questions to the witnesses, experts and parties, and may submit explanations. In proceedings initiated at the request of the party, while informing the party of the possibility of making statements as to the collected evidence and material, as well as the demands made, the administrative authority is obligated to indicate the requirements made of the party which were not met as at the day of sending the information, which might result in the issuance of a decision contrary to the party's demands.

656. One of the most important procedural prerogatives of parties is the right to appeal against decisions and rulings issued by authorities in the first instance, as administrative proceedings are, as a rule, comprised of two instances, unless a special provision states otherwise. An exception to the principle of two-instance proceedings, which owes its existence to constitutional considerations, is contained in Article 127(3) CAP, which states that decisions issued in the first instance by a minister (understood to include central governmental administration authorities) or a self-government appeals boards are not subject to appeal; in migration matters this exceptional procedure applies also to certain decisions issued by a consul in visa matters. However, a party dissatisfied with a decision may apply to the issuing authority to reconsider the matter. Provisions concerning appeals against decisions apply to such applications accordingly.

657. Article 17 of the CAP generally specifies which bodies constitute higher authorities in relation to those ruling in administrative proceedings in the first instance.

658. The essence of two-instance proceedings is the right to two substantive reviews of an administrative matter and two substantive decisions resolving the issue. The provisions of the CAP grant higher authorities the power to re-examine and settle a matter in the course of the second instance (Article 127(2)) and to review decisions under extraordinary administrative proceedings (Articles 150(2), 154(1), 155, 157(1), and 161(1–2)).

659. Appeals proceedings are entirely based on the principle of accusatorial procedure. They are initiated upon the submission of an appeal by an entitled entity – a party to the proceedings. In order for this procedural act to have legal effect, it must fulfil specific requirements as to the form, content, time and mode of its performance; the CAP applies the principle of limited formalism to appeals. An appeal need not be submitted in any particular form, nor need it be justified in detail. It is sufficient if the appeal indicates that a party is dissatisfied with the decision. In addition to an expression of dissatisfaction with the decision, an appeal should meet the requirements for submissions (Article 63). In order for an appeal to have legal effect, it must be submitted within the appropriate deadline, which is a strict deadline and one which, under certain circumstances, can be restored by the authority hearing the appeal. As a rule, this deadline is fourteen days from the date on which the decision is duly served (announced). While the prescribed time for making an appeal is running, the party can renounce the right to appeal against the decision. The day the administrative authority is served with the (last) party's statement renouncing the right to appeal, the decision becomes final, which means that it cannot be appealed against to the administrative court.

660. The CAP adopts an indirect mode of submitting an appeal – *via* the authority which issued the decision in the first instance. The legal construction of an appeal can thus be said to be based on the principle of relative devolution, meaning that the power to examine and settle a matter under appeal is transferred to a higher authority only when the authority ruling in the first instance does not find grounds to reverse its own decision following self-review (within seven days). Relative devolution in appeals constitutes an exception to the general principle of an authority being bound by its own decision in the first instance. The possibility to conduct self-review by the authority of the first instance is based on two primary criteria: submission of an appeal by all parties to given proceedings, or submission of an appeal by one of the parties accompanied by the consent of the remaining parties to the reversal or amending of the decision in a manner consistent with the demands contained in the appeal, together with acceptance of the party's demands in full. Parties are entitled to appeal against the new decision.

661. Appeals proceedings before the authority of the second instance can be divided into three phases: introductory proceedings, examination proceedings and the decision-making phase.

662. The authority in the second instance may only – as a rule – conduct complimentary evidentiary proceedings. However, if the decision was issued in violation of the laws governing proceedings, and the aspect of the case that has to be thoroughly considered has an essential impact on the result of the proceedings, at the joint request of all the parties included in the appeal, the appeal organ carries out evidentiary proceedings to the degree that it is necessary to properly conclude the case and issues a decision in which it affirms the contested decision or a decision in which it quashes the original decision and rules as to the substance of the matter within that scope. It is also possible to apply Article 138(4) of the CAP.

663. The types of decisions that can be taken by the appeals authority are set forth in Article 138(1–2 and 4) of the CAP. The following substantive decisions can be taken: (1) a decision to uphold the contested decision; (2) a decision quashing the original decision – the authority hearing the appeal abrogates the contested decision either in whole or in part, and rules as to the substance of the matter within that scope; the content of the new substantive decision may not constitute *reformationis in peius*.

664. The second type of decision that can be issued in the second instance is a cassation decision. There are two varieties of cassation decisions: (1) standard cassation – concludes the examination of the matter, whereby the appeals authority rescinds the decision of the authority in the first instance while refraining from ruling as to the substance of the matter; this type of decision may only be issued in cases when there was no legal basis for examining the matter in general, or by way of standard or special administrative proceedings; (2) cassation and referral of an individual matter to re-examination of the matter by the authority of the first instance; this decision rescinds the contested decision in whole and sends the matter back to the authority of the first instance for re-examination, as in order to make a substantive determination it is necessary to first conduct evidentiary proceedings either in whole or in a significant part; the appeal organ indicates the circumstances which need to be taken into consideration when reconsidering the case and provides guidelines on interpreting the laws that are applicable in the case; a variation of this kind is a cassation decision based on Article 138(4) of the CAP: 'If the provisions specify issuing decision on official form, including issuing by means of electronic communication, and if there are basis to amend the decision appealed, the appellate authority shall quash the decision and shall require the authority of first instance to issue decision with specified content'.[197]

665. Appeal proceedings may also end with the issuance of a decision to discontinue the appeal proceedings. The authority of the second instance issues such a decision when the proceedings have become groundless for any reason.

666. Before the deadline for submission of an appeal, the decision is non-final and is not subject to execution. Submission of an appeal before the deadline elapses results in suspension of the decision's execution. There are two exceptions to this foreseen in the CAP: when the decision has been appended with an order of immediate enforceability, and when it is subject to immediate enforceability under statute. In such situations the appeals authority can suspend the immediate enforcement of the decision if it feels doing so would be justified.

667. The CAP also foresees extraordinary modes for challenging administrative decisions: (1) reopening of the proceedings; (2) declaring a decision invalid; (3) proceedings in respect of quashing or amending a decision afflicted with a non-qualified defect or a proper decision. The object of extraordinary proceedings is to review the validity of a decision issued in the course of ordinary proceedings (proceedings before authorities of the first and the second instance). Extraordinary proceedings are subsidiary to ordinary proceedings. A condition of those modes being activated is the issuance of a final decision in a matter (Articles 145(1), 154, 155, and 161 of the CAP). Only in the case of administrative procedure has the application of the sanction of nullity not been restricted by the condition of finality of the administrative decision (Article 156(1) CAP).

668. The system of extraordinary modes is based on the principle of non-competition, which stems from the separate object of each extraordinary mode. Proceedings to reopen proceedings creates the legal possibility of a second examination and resolution of a matter resolved by a final decision if the proceedings in which the original examination and resolution of the matter were afflicted with a serious, qualified procedural defect. Serious, qualified procedural defects are enumerated in Article 145(1) and 145a(1) of the CAP. Proceedings in respect of declaring a decision invalid create the legal possibility of quashing a decision (ruling) afflicted by a serious, qualified defect of a primarily substantive nature (Article 156(1) of the CAP). Proceedings in respect of quashing or amending an administrative decision afflicted with a non-qualified defect or a proper decision provide the potential for another examination and resolution of a matter in the event of defective interpretation of the law or of a change in assessment of a resolution in cases where a provision of law grants the authority the right to reduce legal consequences on grounds

---

197. Translation Maja Bińkowska, Andrzej Chełchowski, Bartosz Kopik, Richard A. Walewander, The Code of Administrative Proceedings. Kodeks postępowania administracyjnego. Bilingual edition (Warsaw 2014).

of a social interest or the equitable interest of a party. This separate object of review results in the modes described above being based on the principle of exclusivity, thus eliminating competitiveness.

§3. *ACTIO POPULARIS*

669. The right enshrined in the Constitution of the Republic of Poland to submit petitions and grievances to state authorities, local self-government authorities and bodies, and to social organizations and institutions is exercised on the basis of the provisions of section VIII of the CAP. Petitionary proceedings are treated as an instrument of social oversight over public administration.

670. Petitions and grievances may be submitted in the public interest, in one's own interest or in that of another person upon his/her consent. Petitionary proceedings are conducted independently only in cases when the petitioner is not a party to any administrative proceedings, and the petition does not address matters resolved by way of issuing an administrative decision.

671. The simplification of petitionary proceedings is expressed in the fact that there are no parties to proceedings, and that the petitioner is not the addressee of any decisions but rather is only informed by the administrative authority of actions taken internally to clarify the circumstances constituting the basis for the grievance; there is no second instance, nor avenues for appeal. However, it is a rule that such proceedings are conducted within the jurisdiction of a given authority appropriately established on the basis of the subject of the grievance; the principles of objectivism and of a full elucidation of the matter constituting the subject of the grievance are to be followed. Judicial review by administrative courts does not extend to the activities of public administration in matters of petitions and grievances.[198]

§4. PROCEEDINGS REQUIRING THE PARTICIPATION OF SOCIETY

672. Particular prerogatives linked with the participation of entities with an interest in resolving matters concerning environmental protection are foreseen in the Act of 3 October 2008 on the Sharing of Information on the Environment and its Protection, Public Participation in Environmental Protection and Environmental Impact Assessments. The Act does not specify in which types of proceedings concerning environmental protection the public is guaranteed the right to participate in – it provides neither a definition nor an enumeration. The provisions of particular statutes regulating the rules for proceedings in a given matter of environmental protection determine whether proceedings fulfil the criteria for social participation.

673. The Act distinguishes two types of procedures: the participation of society in taking decisions, and the participation of society in composing documents. The

198. Adamiak, Borkowski, *Kodeks postępowania administracyjnego.*

procedural form of social participation in matters of environmental protection consists of the possibility of submitting remarks and petitions; the universality of the right to submit such remarks and petitions is a generally applicable principle. In providing particular prerogatives to society in respect of environmental protection, the legislator uses the term 'anyone': anyone given the right by statute to participate in proceedings (Article 5); similarly, anyone has the right to submit remarks and petitions in proceedings requiring the participation of society (Article 29). This term should be understood to include all entities that find themselves under the authority of the Republic pursuant to Article 37(1) of the Constitution. It is necessary to differentiate between 'anyone' (society) from participants in administrative proceedings which hold the status of a party. In other words, individuals constituting 'society' may participate in proceedings pursuant to the principles set forth in statute when they do not have their own legal interest.[199] If they possess a legal interest, pursuant to the CAP they will participate in proceedings as parties to it. In such cases they will enjoy all of the procedural prerogatives provided for in the CAP, thus it cannot be said that the Act under discussion violated the rights of parties in administrative proceedings.

674. A characteristic of proceedings is the precedent nature of social participation: administrative authorities are required to ensure the possibility of participation by society prior to issuing or amending decisions, as well as prior to the adoption or amending of documents. Activation of the procedure for social involvement is independent of the particular rules applicable for a given proceeding, whether an individual matter or one involving documents (programmes, plans).

675. In order to ensure that social participation is substantive, it must be provided with access to information important for the specific proceedings in question. The provisions of section II of the Act under discussion regulate associated matters. Provisions of the Act related to the refusal to provide requested information are applied in proceedings involving social participation (Articles 16–20). Additionally, the provisions of the Act are without prejudice to the provisions of the Confidential Information Protection Act of 5 August 2010.

676. Remarks and petitions submitted during proceedings requiring the participation of society are not subject to the provisions of section VIII of the CAP, which regulate procedure in matters of remarks and petitions.

I. Participation of Society in Taking Decisions

677. Among administrative proceedings requiring social participation are those whose subject is the issuing of an integrated permit or a decision on amending an integrated permit concerning a significant change to an installation (Article 218 of the Environmental Protection Act); proceedings concerning the issuing of a decision on environmental conditions, in conjunction with which an environmental

199. Verdict of the Warsaw Provincial Administrative Court of 27 January 2010 (VIII SA/Wa 625/09).

impact assessment of an enterprise is carried out (with the possibility of excluding enterprises conducted in closed areas if the application of regulations could have a negative impact on national defence and security – Article 79 of the Act on the Sharing of Information on the Environment and its Protection, Public Participation in Environmental Protection and Environmental Impact Assessments); and proceedings whose subject is the issuing of a permit for the closed use of GMO (Article 29 of the Genetically Modified Organisms Act).

678. The first stage of social participation involves providing information in publicly available directories online and made available in Public Information Bulletins. Next, the authority issuing the decision must make publicly available and without delay information concerning:

(1) the commencement of an environmental impact assessment;
(2) the commencement of administrative proceedings;
(3) the subject of the decision to be taken in the matter;
(4) the authority responsible for issuing the decision and authorities responsible for issuing opinions and coordination;
(5) possibilities for accessing relevant documentation concerning the matter and the location where such documentation is available for review (an application for a decision along with required attachments; the following are required by statute: determinations of the authority responsible for issuing the decision and the opinions of other authorities, if those opinions are available, during the period for submitting remarks and petitions; an environmental impact assessment report);
(6) the possibility of submitting remarks and petitions;
(7) the manner and location for submitting remarks and petitions, simultaneously indicating a twenty-one-day deadline for doing so;
(8) the authority responsible for reviewing remarks and petitions;
(9) the time and location of an administrative hearing open to the public, insofar as one is to be held;
(10) proceedings in respect of trans-border environmental impact, if conducted.

679. The next element of the procedure is becoming familiar with documentation in the matter, followed by the submission of remarks and petitions. They may be submitted in writing, orally for the record, or *via* electronic means of communication without the requirement to affix a secure electronic signature.

680. Statute also foresees the possibility of conducting an administrative hearing open to the general public. Article 89 of the CAP sets forth the conditions necessitating that a hearing be conducted: when it will speed up or simplify proceedings, when it is required by law, when it is necessary to balance the interests of parties, and when it is necessary for clarifying the matter through the participation of witnesses and experts or through conducting inspections. The CAP itself does not, however, provide for hearings open to the general public, which is why separate regulation is necessary.

681. Remarks and petitions submitted after the twenty-one-day deadline has elapsed are not reviewed. The authority conducting proceedings is required to review remarks and petitions submitted in a timely manner and to respond to them. It does so in the justification of its decision closing the proceedings, in which – independently of the requirements set forth in the CAP – it provides information about the participation of society in the proceedings and about the manner and scope of consideration given to remarks and petitions submitted in conjunction with social participation.

682. The submission of remarks and petitions is not equivalent to participation in proceedings as a party. The prerogatives afforded to parties are not given to every participant in proceedings, but statute does give the right to learn about the content of a decision by requiring authorities to provide information to the general public about decisions issued and the means in which it is possible to familiarize oneself with their content.

II. Prerogatives of Ecological Organizations

683. Regulation of the prerogatives of ecological organizations[200] in proceedings requiring social participation constitutes *lex specialis* in respect of general regulations governing the participation of social organizations in administrative proceedings contained in Article 31 of the CAP.

684. Ecological organizations that make reference to their statutory objectives when declaring their desire to participate in proceedings requiring social participation are joined to the proceedings as parties. In contrast to general statutory principles there is no condition concerning a social interest; the public authority thus needs only to determine whether the formal condition for such an organization to participate in proceedings has been fulfilled, that of realizing a statutory objective. Ecological organizations are not obliged to submit remarks and petitions when announcing their desire to participate as a party to proceedings; they may join proceedings at any stage, and there is no deadline for them to do so. Ecological organizations have the right to appeal a decision refusing them participation in proceedings. As an entity joined to the proceedings as a party, an ecological organization enjoys the procedural prerogatives of a party with the exception of those that are emanations of the principle of disposition in administrative procedure, such as the right to demand suspension or the discontinuation of proceedings. Such an organization does, however, have the right to submit an appeal and grievance to an administrative court under more favourable terms than those in the CAP. An ecological organization has the right to appeal against a decision issued in proceedings requiring social participation if it is concurrent with that organization's statutory objectives, including in cases when it did not participate in proceedings conducted by the authority of the first instance. Submission of an appeal is equivalent in its

200. Ecological organization: a social organization whose statutory objective is protection of the natural environment (statutory definition).

effects to declaring a desire to participate in proceedings. An ecological organization has the right to submit an appeal to an administrative court against a decision issued in proceedings requiring social participation if such activity is justified by that organization's statutory objectives, even in cases when it did not participate in given proceedings requiring social participation.

III. Social Participation in the Drafting of Documents

685. Statute provides for the requirement of social participation in procedures for adopting such documents as provincial, county and communal environmental protection programmes – drafted by the executive authority of the relevant administrative unit (Article 17 of the Environmental Protection Act), the action program aiming at reducing water pollution by nitrates from agricultural sources and prevent further pollution (Article 106 of the Water Act), draft program for the protection of marine waters (Article 161 of the Water Act), waste management plans (Article 36 of the Waste Act), the plan of protection for a national park, nature reservation or landscape park (Article 19 of the Nature Protection Act), the plan of protection for a Natura 2000 area and/or its part (Article 29 of the Nature Protection Act).

686. As in the case of proceedings in respect of issuing a decision, the procedure is composed of several elements. The first is the informational requirement which consists of placing data (information) in a publicly accessible location. Next, the authority drawing up a draft document must provide public opinion information without delay concerning:

(1) the commencement of drawing up the draft document and its subject matter;
(2) the ways in which members of the public may familiarize themselves with the relevant documentation and the place in which it is available for review (assumptions or the draft document, required attachments and the opinions of other authorities if they are available within the timeframe for submitting remarks and petitions);
(3) the possibility of submitting remarks and petitions;
(4) the manner and place of submitting remarks and petitions, together with an indication of a deadline for their submission of not less than twenty-one days;
(5) the authority responsible for reviewing remarks and petitions;
(6) proceedings in respect of trans-border environmental impact, if conducted.

687. Remarks and petitions may be submitted in the same manner as in the case of participation in proceedings in respect of administrative decisions. Remarks and petitions submitted after the deadline are not subject to review.

688. The authority drafting a document requiring social participation reviews submitted remarks and petitions; it then affixes information to the adopted document concerning social participation in the proceedings and about the manner and scope in which remarks and petitions submitted in conjunction with social participation. Information is provided to the public on the adoption of the document and ways in which its contents, justification and summary may be examined in the case of documents requiring the drawing up of a strategic environmental impact assessment.

Chapter 2. Judicial Remedies

§1. Introduction

689. Environmental protection is an interdisciplinary field, and matters arising within it can be reviewed not only by administrative authorities but also by common courts, both criminal and civil. A separate but related issue is that of judicial review of public administration, conducted primarily by administrative courts which are not authorized to issue substantive decisions.

690. The right of recourse to a court of law is set forth *expressis verbis* in Article 77(2) of the Constitution, which states that 'Statutes shall not bar the recourse by any person to the courts in pursuit of claims alleging infringement of freedoms or rights,' and Article 45(1) of the Constitution provides the standards to be met by declaring 'Everyone shall have the right to a fair and public hearing of his case, without undue delay, before a competent, impartial and independent court.' Another significant principle is contained in Article 176(1), which establishes the rule that court proceedings have at least two stages.

691. The types and principles of liability in environmental protection law have been discussed in Chapter 4. The division between civil, criminal and administrative liability is reflected in the division of court proceedings: civil and criminal cases are heard by common courts, while administrative courts are the forum for cases involving administrative law.

§2. Civil Proceedings

I. Legal Bases

692. Civil proceedings are conducted on the basis of the Code of Civil Proceedings of 17 November 1964.[201] The objective of civil proceedings is to implement the norms of civil law through compulsion. This task defines the concept of civil proceedings as a set of activities regulated in law, aimed at the concretion and enforced implementation of legal norms in civil cases, in a legally determined form.

693. In respect of some types of injury, the right to pursue court proceedings is dependent on the prior exhaustion of administrative measures. For example, at the request of the injured party, damages for some types of injury in waters are determined by the authority issuing the water law permit; if the injury is not the result of a water law permit, damages are determined in an administrative decision by the marshal of the province in which the injury occurred. Such a decision is non-actionable through administrative channels, but a party dissatisfied with the level of damages set may appeal to a common court. The right to bring an action is also

201. Dz. U. 2018, item 1360 with amendments.

available in the event of failure by the appropriate authority to issue a decision within three months of submission of a claim by the injured party.

II. Substantive and Territorial Jurisdiction

694. The Code of Civil Proceedings differentiates substantive and territorial jurisdiction. As a rule, civil cases are heard in the first instance by district courts. The substantive jurisdiction of regional courts is an exception and must be explicitly established by statute. Regional courts exercise substantial jurisdiction as courts of the first instance for proceedings involving, for example, disputes over property rights with a value in excess of PLN 75,000 and over damage resulting from the issuance of a binding verdict in contradiction with the law. A regional court may choose to hear any case in which an issue of law giving rise to serious doubts has arisen during proceedings before a district court, providing the regional court substantive jurisdiction over such matters in the first instance.

695. The basis for determining geographical jurisdiction is the place of domicile (seat) of the respondent. Regulations on alternative jurisdiction provide a choice of court before which an action may be pursued. The objective of such regulations is to provide for easier access to the courts, to make proceedings more efficient and to aid in fulfilling the postulate of directness by making it easier for courts to perform their procedural duties. An example of this is the provision stating that an action for a claim in tort may be brought before the court in whose district the event giving rise to injury occurred. The Code of Civil Proceedings also provides for the possibility of parties concluding an agreement as to the jurisdiction of a court, allowing for a written agreement appointing a Court of First Instance that does not have the geographical jurisdiction to hear disputes having arisen or potentially arising in the future out of a specified legal relationship.

III. The Principle of Amicable Resolution of Civil Cases

696. One of the principles of civil proceedings is the principle of amicable resolution of civil cases. In cases where it is permissible to conclude a settlement, the court should attempt to induce the parties to do so during every phase of proceedings. The parties may also conclude a settlement before a mediator. The essence of mediation consists of an outside mediator acting to assist (to mediate) the parties in resolving their dispute. The desirability of resolving disputes in this way lies in the fact that, once confirmed by a court, a settlement concluded before a mediator takes on the legal force of a settlement concluded before the court itself. Additional benefits include making it easier for parties to pursue claims in civil cases, their quicker conclusion and reduced costs of proceedings.

697. A settlement may be concluded at various stages of proceedings. Prior to the submission of an action, conciliatory proceedings provide an opportunity for parties to conclude a settlement in civil matters whose character allows for such.

Conciliatory proceedings can be participated in by all entities participating in civil proceedings, without any restrictions. The court reviews the settlement and declares it impermissible if its content contradicts the law or the principles of social coexistence, or if it is intended to circumvent the law. The court exercises identical powers in respect of a settlement concluded during the course of judicial proceedings (after an action is brought). The will of the parties should, however, be decisive, in accordance with the dispositive principle. In the event it determines a settlement to be impermissible, the court issues a ruling that can be appealed against.

698. A court settlement is both a juridical act and a procedural act (concluding a dispute). The contents of the settlement are recorded in the records of the proceedings, and the parties affix their signatures to it. A settlement concluded before the court constitutes an enforcement title, and in this sense may be equated with a judicial verdict. From a procedural perspective, the effect of concluding a settlement is the discontinuation of the proceedings.

IV. A Trial

699. Cases concerning issues of civil liability and environmental protection are heard at trial. A civil trial is initiated by an action. This is the first pleading of a party, submitted to the court with substantive and geographical jurisdiction for a given case. The action is a qualified pleading, meaning that aside from the requirements placed on every submission (incl. specifying the court, the name and surname or name of the parties, their attorneys, indication of the object of the dispute, evidence in support of any claims made, the signature of the submitting party and/or that party's attorney, a list of attachments), it should additionally contain a precisely formulated demand, the value of the object of the dispute (unless it is a specified amount of money) and reference to the factual circumstances justifying the demand made. The action may include a motion to secure the claim, as well as evidentiary motions. The parties are responsible during civil proceedings for presenting evidence, and the burden of proof regarding facts of importance for resolving the dispute rests on the party which infers legal effects from those facts.

700. Applying the above to the principles of liability in tort, it may be pointed out that in the case of liability based on culpability the injured party bringing the action must prove that all necessary conditions have been met. The situation of the injured party in such proceedings is thus less advantageous than in the case of liability based on the risk principle, which provides a softer evidentiary regime neither guilt nor unlawfulness on the part of the potentially liable party (the respondent) need be demonstrated. It should be recalled here, however, that in environmental protection law one of the conditions for unlawfulness of an act is formulated differently: 'Liability for damage caused by impact on the environment shall not be excluded by the circumstance that the activity leading to the damage is conducted on the basis of a decision and within the restrictions established therein'. Not only does the legislator completely ignore the violation of general and abstract legal norms but, in addition, he prevents the respondent from raising a defence that the activity was conducted on the basis of a permit and within the limits established by it. Even in the event the respondent was to prove such a circumstance, it is meaningless when assessing liability.[202]

701. The court assesses the reliability and significance of evidence according to its own convictions, on the basis of a comprehensive weighing-up of all the material. The catalogue of permissible forms of evidence is not closed.

702. After closing the trial, the court issues its verdict. A party dissatisfied with the verdict may lodge an appeal: appeals to district court verdicts are heard by regional courts, and when a regional court serves as the court of the first instance, appeals to its verdicts are heard by appeal courts. Appeals proceedings retain their substantive aspect in spite of serving primarily as a review process. Binding verdicts of courts of the second instance may be the object of a cassation action, heard by the Supreme Court.

V. Secure Claims

703. The Code of Civil Proceedings also regulates proceedings to secure claims, the objective of which is to provide a temporary remedy to parties or participants in proceedings if they are able to provide evidence that their claim is justified together with proving a legal interest in such a remedy. Security of a claim may be granted in every civil matter that is subject to review by a common court or court of arbitration. The court may grant such security both before the commencement of proceedings and during their course. Both monetary and non-monetary claims may be secured, the former of which are generally secured by the seizure of specified chattels, bank accounts, other rights in property or receivables.

§3. Criminal Proceedings

704. Criminal proceedings are a regulated activity intended to lead to the realization of substantive criminal law. Criminal proceedings are intended to determine if an illegal act (crime) has been committed, then to establish the perpetrator and impose criminal liability on him/her.[203] Criminal proceedings are an emanation of the constitutional principle of court implementation of the administration of justice contained in Article 175(1) of the Constitution. Courts exercising jurisdiction in criminal matters are the common courts, military courts and the Supreme Court.

705. District and regional courts are the courts of the first instance in criminal proceedings. District courts rule in the first instance in all matters with the exception of those placed by statute under the jurisdiction of another court (regional

202. B. Rakoczy, *Ciężar dowodu w polskim prawie ochrony środowiska* (Wolters Kluwer 2010).
203. W. Grzeszczyk, *Kodeks postępowania karnego, Komentarz* (Warszawa 2008).

courts under to Article 25(1) of the CCP), and is thus the main court in criminal matters. District courts also exercise jurisdiction in matters of tax-related offences pursuant to Article 114(2) of the Fiscal Criminal Code, and in cases concerning petty offences, regulated under Article 9 §1 of the Code of Proceedings in Matters of Petty Offences. Pursuant to Article 24 CCP, district courts rule in the first instance in all matters with the exception of those placed by statute under the jurisdiction of another court and also rule in matters of appeal as designated by statute.

706. Pursuant to Article 25(1) CCP, regional courts rule as courts of the first instance in matters concerning the following crimes: felonies under the CC and in other statutes, misdemeanours defined in sections XVI and XVII of the CC and Article 140 CC – an attack on a unit of the Polish Armed Forces, Article 141 CC – service in a foreign army, Article 142 CC – recruitment for a foreign army, Article 148(4) CC – murder under the influence of an intense emotion justified by the circumstances (crime of passion), Article 149 CC – murder of a child by its mother, Article 150(1) CC – compassionate murder, Article 151 CC – inducing a suicide attempt, Article 152 CC – termination of a pregnancy in violation of the law with the consent of the woman, Article 153 CC – termination of a pregnancy in violation of the law against the will of the mother, Article 154 CC – death of a pregnant woman as a result of illegal termination of a pregnancy, Article 158(3) CC – aggravated participation in a brawl or assault, Article 163(3) CC – aggravated intentional causing of an event imperilling human life or the health of many persons, Article 163(4) CC – unintentional causing of an event imperilling human life or the health of many persons, Article 165(1) CC – intentional causing of a general danger, Article 165(3) CC – aggravated intentional causing of a general danger, Article 165(4) CC – aggravated unintentional causing of a general danger, Article 166(1) CC – hijacking of a waterborne or airborne vessel, Article 173(3) CC – causing of a catastrophe in land, water or air traffic, Article 173(4) CC – aggravated unintentional causing of a catastrophe in land, water or air traffic, Article 185(2) CC – aggravated pollution of the natural environment, Article 189a(2) CC – preparation for engaging in human trafficking, Article 210(2) CC – aggravated abandonment of a person under 15 years of age or a person helpless by reason of mental or physical condition, Article 211a CC – organizing the adoption of children in contradiction of statute, Article 252(3) CC – conducting preparations for taking a person hostage, Article 258(1) CC – participation in an organized group intended to engage in the commission of a crime, Article 258(2) CC – participation in an armed organized group intended to engage in the commission of a crime, Article 258(3) CC – directing the activity of or founding an organized group or armed organized group intended to engage in the commission of a crime, Article 265(1) CC disclosure or use of information constituting a state secret and labelled as 'secret' or 'top secret' in violation of the State Secrets Act, Article 265(2) CC – aggravated disclosure or use of information constituting a state secret and labelled as 'secret' or 'top secret' in violation of the State Secrets Act, Article 269 KK sabotage of electronic information having particular significance for national defence, transport safety or operation of government authorities, Article 278(1) and (2) CC in conjunction with Article 294 CC – theft of property of considerable value, Article 284(1) and (2) CC in conjunction with Article 294 CC – appropriation of property of considerable value, Article 286(1) CC in conjunction with Article 294 CC – fraud concerning property of considerable value, Article 287(1) CC in conjunction with Article 294 CC – computer fraud concerning property of considerable value, Article 296(3) CC – aggravated abuse of authority, Article 299 CC – 'money laundering', and misdemeanours assigned to the jurisdiction of regional courts by statute.

707. In addition, under Article 25(2) CCP on the motion of a district court an appeals court may assign any case concerning a crime to a regional court as the court of the first instance owing to the particular significance or complicated nature of the case.

I. Parties to Criminal Proceedings

A. *Public Prosecutor*

708. The state authority designated to fulfil the role of the public prosecutor before all courts is the state prosecutor. The public prosecutor brings and pursues indictments for crimes prosecuted ex officio. This authority is also a party to proceedings representing the public interest. As an official of the state prosecutorial service, the state prosecutor is responsible for protecting the rule of law and overseeing the pursuit of criminals.

B. *The Victim*

709. The statutory definition of the victim in a criminal offence is contained in Article 49(1) and (2) CCP. A victim is a natural person, juridical person or state, local self-government or social institution with or without legal personhood whose legal interest has been directly violated or threatened. These interests include property rights and rights of personality. In preliminary proceedings the victim is a party owing to the sole fact of the harm. During a trial, the victim may choose to function as a party to proceedings as a subsidiary or private prosecutor or may make use of the prerogatives granted by statute in a particular procedural situation such as participation in pre-trial hearings (Article 341(1), Article 343(5) CCP). The rights of the victim may also be exercised by authorities of state control who uncovered the crime or filed for the initiation of proceedings in the course of the performance of their activities.

C. *Subsidiary Prosecutor*

710. In matters of indictable offences, the aggrieved party may participate as a party to proceedings as a subsidiary prosecutor either alongside the public prosecutor or instead of him. This provision sets forth two forms of participation by the victim as a party: alongside the public prosecutor as an auxiliary prosecutor, or 'instead of' the public prosecutor as an accessory subsidiary prosecutor. The status of auxiliary prosecutor is achieved upon the submission of a statement declaring the intent to join to proceedings following the submission of an indictment by the public prosecutor, while that of subsidiary prosecutor is granted when he/she submits an indictment in respect of an indictable offence.

D. Private Prosecutor

711. A private prosecutor is an aggrieved party that brings and supports an indictment for a privately prosecuted offence. In doing so, he/she becomes an active party to the proceedings that may initiate proceedings by bringing an indictment to the court or by lodging a written or oral complaint to the Police.

E. The Accused

712. Article 71 CCP contains the terms 'suspect' and 'accused'. A suspect is a party to preliminary proceedings and is the individual against whom an investigation is directed through an order to bring charges. An accused person is one against whom an indictment has been brought to court, and also an individual with respect to whom the state prosecutor has submitted a motion to conditionally suspend proceedings.

§4. ADMINISTRATIVE COURT PROCEEDINGS

I. The Role of Administrative Courts in Implementing Environmental Law

713. Because the provisions of environmental protection law are implemented primarily by authorities of public administration through the issuance of individual and normative acts, a particularly important role is played by the direct judicial control exercised by administrative courts which was restored on 1 January 1980. This is determined in the Constitution, which vests administrative courts (provincial/voivodeship administrative courts and the – SAC) with the power to review the activities of public administration (Article 184). An administrative court matter is thus defined as a matter concerning judicial review of the activities of public administration, and other matters to which the provisions of the Administrative Court Proceedings Act of 30 August 2012[204] apply on the basis of other statutory provisions. The review shall be performed from the point of view of conformity with the law unless otherwise provided by statute.

204. Dz. U. 2012, item 270.

714. Provincial administrative courts examine all administrative court cases with the exception of those reserved for the jurisdiction of the SAC. The SAC shall exercise supervision over the activity of provincial administrative courts within the scope of adjudicating cases according to the procedure specified by statute and, in particular, shall hear means of appeal against the decisions of these courts and adopt resolutions explaining legal issues and shall hear other matters falling within the jurisdiction of the SAC.

715. The limited range of judicial review and defined types of judicial rulings are the result of an entrenched conception according to which a court may not replace public administration in the constructive stimulation of social relationships.[205] The administrative court system is, however, a certain form of administration when considering the specificity of the mechanism by which administrative law is applied.[206] Courts exert a direct influence on the activities of public administration because a court's decisions introduce modifications to an act of law performed by public administration. Judicial review can be considered as a sort of quasi-second instance in administrative proceedings. This role of administrative courts was clearly strengthened by the granting of provincial administrative courts (since 15 August 2015) the right to adjudication in appeals against administrative decisions and resolutions where they concern the most common administrative flaws. Where the circumstances of the case so justify, the court shall oblige the authority to render a decision or order within a specified time limit, indicating the manner in which the case should be handled or determined, unless the determination was left to the discretion of the authority.

716. Jurisprudence is considered a sui generis source of administrative law.[207] It is said to be 'judge-made law' due to its character, authority and expertise,[208] with attention drawn to the lawmaking effects of rulings on the activity of public administration authorities. The function of judicial rulings in the context of recognizing them as a source of law is particularly important, as determining the interpretation of an ambiguous or poorly-constructed norm in one particular case, then later applying that interpretation in the review of other, similar cases, in effect leads to new normative content. The jurisprudence of administrative courts thus plays a very important role in determining the proper interpretation of environmental protection law; it has an anticipatory, preventative function. While it is true that the legal evaluation and indications as to how to proceed contained in a court's ruling are only binding on the authority whose activity, inactivity or undue delay in conducting proceedings were contested (in a specific matter), court rulings influence both their own future verdicts and the manner in which public authorities resolve disputes in future cases, making them de facto binding in other cases. Of particular importance in this respect are resolutions of the SAC intended to clarify provisions of the law which have given rise to discrepancies in the jurisprudence of administrative courts

205. Boć, *Prawo administracyjne*, 393.
206. J. Zimmermann, *Prawo administracyjne*, 359 (Wolters Kluwer 2008).
207. Boć, *Prawo administracyjne*, 124.
208. *See* D. Dąbek, *Prawo sędziowskie w polskim prawie administracyjnym* (Wolters Kluwer 2010).

(abstract resolutions), as well as resolutions containing solutions to legal dilemmas causing deep uncertainty in a particular matter before an administrative court (material resolutions). These resolutions are passed by the SAC either by a panel of seven justices, by an entire Chamber, or by the entire court.

II. The Cognition of Administrative Courts

717. The cognition of administrative courts is based on a general clause, and deviations from this principle are exceptional (negative enumeration). There are no matters excluded from the jurisdiction of administrative courts based on subject matter that would fall under the category of matters concerning environmental protection law.

718. Taking it generally, the cognition covers both individual and general acts, activity and lack of action or excessive length of proceedings. The review of the activity of public administration by administrative courts shall include adjudicating on complaints against:

(1) administrative decisions;
(2) orders made in administrative proceedings, which are subject to interlocutory appeal or those concluding the proceeding, as well as orders resolving the case in its merit;
(3) orders made in enforcement proceedings and proceedings to secure claims which are subject to an interlocutory appeal, with the exclusion of the orders of a creditor on the inadmissibility of the allegation made and orders dealing with the position of a creditor on the allegation made;
(4) acts or actions other than the acts or actions referred to in subparagraphs 1–3, falling within the scope of public administration and relating to the rights or obligations arising from the provisions of law, with the exclusion of the acts or actions taken in the course of the administrative proceedings referred to in the CAP and proceedings referred to in sections IV, V and VI of the Tax Ordinance Act as well as proceedings to which the provisions of the abovementioned Acts apply;
(5) written interpretations of tax law provided on individual cases;
(6) local enactments issued by local government authorities and territorial agencies of government administration;
(7) enactments issued by units of local government and their associations, other than those specified in point 6, in respect of matters falling within the scope of public administration;
(8) acts of supervision over activities of local government authorities;
(9) lack of action or excessive length of proceedings in the cases referred to in points 1–4 or excessive length of proceedings in the case referred to in point 5;
(10) lack of action or excessive length of proceedings in cases relating to acts or actions other than the acts or actions referred to in subparagraphs 1–3, falling

within the scope of public administration and relating to the rights or obligations arising from the provisions of law, taken in the course of the administrative proceedings referred to in the CAP and proceedings referred to in sections IV, V and VI of the Tax Ordinance as well as proceedings to which the provisions of the above-mentioned Acts apply.

Administrative courts shall also adjudicate in respect of objections against decisions issued on the basis of Article 138(2) of the CAP (cassation decisions) and matters where provisions of specific statutes provide for judicial review and shall employ means specified in those provisions.

719. Administrative courts also resolve jurisdictional disputes between local self-government bodies and between local self-government appeals chambers, as well as competence disputes between those bodies and bodies of central government administration.

720. Practically the sole criterion for judicial review is lawfulness. This is not, however, a simple criterion, which is demonstrated by such controversies as those surrounding the possibility of judicial review of administrative discretion.

721. From the above assumptions regarding the system for review of the activities of public administration, it results that the primary function of administrative courts is to protect the rights of the individual. In respect of reviews of normative acts (acts of local law), the protection of an objective legal order is also provided. Indeed, in such cases the verdict of a court differs from rulings in individual matters: the non-specified group of addressees and the derogation of the act appealed against allow for such verdicts to be considered lawmaking. For this reason they are similar to verdicts of the Constitutional Tribunal, which is authorized to review the normative acts of central administrative authorities.

III. Court Proceedings and Verdicts

722. The capacity to appear before an administrative court as a party have: a natural person, a legal person, a public administration body, the state and local government organizational units not having legal personality, as well as social organizations not having legal personality. Other organizational units not having legal personality shall also have capacity to be a party in court, if provisions of law allow the possibility of imposing obligations, or conferring rights, on those units or making them the subject of orders or bans, as well as acknowledging or recognizing rights or duties resulting from provisions of law. Social organizations, even if not having legal personality, shall have the capacity to be a party in court within the scope of their statutory responsibilities in matters relating to legal interests of other persons.

723. A complaint may be lodged after the exhaustion of the means of review which have lied with the complainant in proceedings before an authority competent in the matter. A complaint shall be lodged within thirty days from the day of service of the determination of the case on the complainant. The Act adopts an indirect mode of submitting a complaint. It shall be lodged *via* the authority which issued the final decision.

724. Administrative court proceedings are based on the following principles: two instances of proceedings, legality, provision of assistance to parties, openness, procedural efficiency, contradictoriness and the ex officio principle, the right to access to court.[209]

725. Court proceedings can essentially be divided into three phases: the pre-trial phase, the trial phase and the adjudication phase.

726. The process is initiated when an entity with standing brings an action. Entities with standing are any individual which has a legal interest in the matter, the Human Rights Defender, the Children's Rights Ombudsman, and social organizations whose statutory activity includes matters concerning the legal interests of other individuals insofar as that organization took part in prior administrative proceedings. Statutes also give the right to bring an action to other entities, such as Article 101 of the Communal Self-Government Act which authorizes every entity whose legal interest or rights have been violated by a resolution or ordinance passed by a communal authority and within the scope of public administration to bring an action against the resolution, on condition that the complainant had previously and unsuccessfully summoned the communal authority to reverse its position. This provision is also applicable to situations in which the communal authority fails to act (Article 101a),[210] such as in situations when a communal authority fails to respond to an application or to remarks submitted on the basis of Article 40 of the Act on the Sharing of Information on the Environment and its Protection, Public Participation in Environmental Protection and Environmental Impact Assessments. An individual submitting such an application or remark has the right to submit an appeal, then a complaint to an administrative court.[211]

727. The pre-trial phase includes determining jurisdiction in the matter, reviewing the complaint in respect of formal requirements, completing documentation, selecting the justices to hear the case, and issuing a decision in regards to an injunction suspending the performance of the contested act or activity.

728. Where the complaint has been lodged against an (administrative) decision – the authority which has issued the decision or order, may suspend, on its own motion or at the request of the complainant, their execution in whole or in part, unless there are grounds which in administrative proceedings makes the decision

209. M. Jaśkowska, M. Masternak, E. Ochendowski, *Postępowanie sądowoadministracyjne*, 75 (Warszawa 2004).
210. Analogical provisions are contained in statutes on county and provincial self-government.
211. Verdict of the Poznań Provincial Administrative Court of 16 June 2010 (II SA/Po 214/10).

immediately enforceable or where specific statute excludes staying of their execution. A refusal to stay the execution of an act or action by the authority shall not preclude the complainant from applying to the court. After the complaint has been transferred to the court, the court may, at the request of the complainant, issue an order staying in whole or in part the execution of an act, if there is danger of serious damage or hardly reversible consequences, unless a specific statute excludes the staying of their execution.

729. After the pre-trial phase, the proper trial begins. It is focused on examining the matter at hand, meaning a review of the legality of the contested act, activity or lack of action or excessive length of proceedings. The court shall determine a case within its limits while not being bound by the charges and requests of the complaint and the legal basis invoked.

730. Upon the submission of a motion prior to the appointment of a trial date by the complainant or the authority, conciliatory proceedings may be conducted aimed at clarifying and deliberating the factual and legal circumstances of the case as well as at encouraging the parties to accept a solution for resolving the matter within the confines of the law. Such proceedings may be conducted even if none of the parties has applied for them. Following conciliatory proceedings, the communal authority either revokes or modifies the contested act or engages in another activity appropriate to the circumstances surrounding the case, within the boundaries of its jurisdiction and powers. If the parties are unable to come to agreement as to how the matter should be resolved, it becomes the subject of judicial review.

731. Parties have the right to examine case files as well as to receive transcripts, copies or excerpts from the files. The services of an interpreter is guaranteed to the foreigner.

732. The court shall resolve the case by a judgment. Voivodeship administrative courts and the SAC are vested generally with the power of cassation when ruling on compliance with the law of acts (activities) of public administration. Depending on the type of act (activity) and the seriousness of the abuse of law, the court may: set aside the decision or order in whole or in part, find that the decision or order is invalid in whole or in part or find the decision or order to be issued in violation of law. In the case the court rules in favour of a complainant bringing an action against inactivity or undue delay in proceedings by an authority in matters listed in Article 3(2)(1–4a), it obliges that authority to issue an act or interpretation, perform an activity or recognize a right or duty arising out of the law. The court also declares whether the inactivity or undue delay in conducting proceedings was accompanied by a gross violation of the law, which then leads to questions concerning liability on the part of the authority (civil servant).

733. Parties dissatisfied with the ruling of a voivodeship administrative court may bring a cassation claim to the SAC.

Selected Bibliography

Adamiak, B., Borkowski, J., Kodeks postępowania administracyjnego. Komentarz, C.H. Beck 2017.

Bar, M., Bukowski, Z., Jendrośka, J., (red.), Jerzmański, J., Urban, S., Leksykon prawa ochrony środowiska, Wolters Kluwer 2012.

Barczak, A., Zadania samorządu terytorialnego w zakresie ochrony środowiska, Wolters Kluwer 2006.

Bieluk, J., Łobos-Kotowska, D., Ustawa o ochronie gruntów rolnych i leśnych. Komentarz, C.H. Beck 2015.

Boć, J., Nowacki, K., Samborska Boć, E., Ochrona środowiska, Kolonia Limited 2008.

Boć, J., Wybrane zagadnienia prawnej ochrony środowiska, Kolonia Limited 2013.

Bucińska, J., Górski, M., Niedziółka, M., Stec, R., Strus, D., Administracja publiczna – człowiek a ochrona środowiska. Zagadnienia społeczno-prawne, Wolters Kluwer 2011.

Bukowski, Z., Czech, E., Karpus, K., Rakoczy, B., Prawo ochrony środowiska Komentarz, LexisNexis 2013.

Bukowski, Z., Rakoczy, B., (red. nauk.), Szuma, K., Prawo wodne. Komentarz, Wolters Kluwer 2013.

Ciechanowicz-McLean, J., Bukowski, Z., Rakoczy, B., Prawo ochrony środowiska, LexisNexis 2008.

Ciechanowicz-McLean, J., Nyka, M., Environmental Law, Wydawnictwo Uniwersytetu Gdańskiego 2016.

Danecka, D., Radecki, W., Ustawa o ochronie przyrody. Komentarz, Difin 2018.

Filipowicz, T., (red.), Plucińska-Filipowicz, A., (red.), Wierzbowski, M., (red.), Ustawa o udostępnianiu informacji o środowisku i jego ochronie, udziale społeczeństwa w ochronie środowiska oraz o ocenach oddziaływania na środowisko Komentarz, Wolters Kluwer 2017.

Górski, M., Odpowiedzialność administracyjna w ochronie środowiska, Oficyna 2008.

Górski, M., Rynkiewicz, K., Ustawa o opakowaniach i odpadach opakowaniowych. Komentarz, Wolters Kluwer 2009.

Górski, M., Pchałek, M., Radecki, W., Prawo ochrony środowiska. Komentarz, C.H. Beck 2011.

Górski, M., Pchałek, M., Radecki, M., Jerzmański, M., Bar, M., Urban, S., Jendrośka, J., Prawo ochrony środowiska. Komentarz, C.H. Beck 2014.

Selected Bibliography

Górski, M., Miłkowska-Rębowska, J., Prawo ochrony różnorodności biologicznej, Wolters Kluwer 2013.

Górski, M., (red.), Prawo ochrony środowiska, Wolters Kluwer 2018.

Gruszecki, K., Ustawa o udostępnianiu informacji o środowisku i jego ochronie, udziale społeczeństwa w ochronie środowiska oraz o ocenach oddziaływania na środowisko. Komentarz, Presscom 2009.

Gruszecki, K., Prawo ochrony środowiska. Komentarz, Wolters Kluwer 2016.

Gruszecki, K., Ustawa o ochronie przyrody. Komentarz, Wolters Kluwer 2016.

Habuda, A., Radecki, W., Ochrona przyrody w systemach prawnych ochrony środowiska Polski, Czech i Słowacji, Difin 2017.

Iwańska, B., Koncepcja 'skargi zbiorowej' w prawie ochrony środowiska, Wolters Kluwer 2013.

Jendrośka, J., Bar, M., Prawo ochrony środowiska. Podręcznik, Centrum Prawa Ekologicznego 2005.

Kałużny, M., Prawo wodne. Komentarz, Wolters Kluwer 2016.

Karski, L., System handlu uprawnieniami do emisji gazów cieplarnianych. Komentarz do ustawy, Wolters Kluwer 2012.

Kaźmierska-Patrzyczna. A., (red. naukowy), Korzeniowski, P., (red. naukowy), Stahl, M., (red. naukowy), Problemy pogranicza prawa administracyjnego i prawa ochrony środowiska, Wolters Kluwer 2017.

Kenig-Witkowska, M., Międzynarodowe prawo środowiska. Wybrane zagadnienia systemowe, Wolters Kluwer 2011.

Lipiński, A., Prawne podstawy ochrony środowiska, Wolters Kluwer 2010.

Mazur-Wierzbicka, E., Ochrona środowiska a integracja europejska. Doświadczenia polskie, Difin 2012.

Paczuski, R. Prawo ochrony środowiska, Bydgoszcz 2000.

Pchałek, M., (red.), Rakoczy, B., Wybrane problemy prawa ochrony środowiska, Wolters Kluwer 2010.

Radecki, W., Opłaty i kary pieniężne w ochronie środowiska. Komentarz, Difin 2009.

Radecki, W., Prawna ochrona przyrody w Polsce, Czechach i Słowacji, Studium prawnoporównawcze, Wolters Kluwer 2010.

Radecki, W., Ochrona walorów turystycznych w prawie polskim, Wolters Kluwer 2011.

Radecki, W., Ustawa o ochronie gruntów rolnych i leśnych. Komentarz, LexisNexis 2012.

Radecki, W., Utrzymanie czystości i porządku w gminach. Komentarz, Wolters Kluwer 2015.

Radecki, W., Ustawa o lasach. Komentarz, Wolters Kluwer 2017.

Radecki, W., Ustawa o odpadach. Komentarz, Wolters Kluwer 2016.

Rakoczy, B. Ciężar dowodu w polskim prawie ochrony środowiska, Wolters Kluwer 2010.

Rakoczy, B., Wybrane problemy prawa leśnego, Wolters Kluwer 2010.

Rakoczy, B., Ustawa o lasach. Komentarz, Wolters Kluwer 2017.

Rakoczy, B., Wybrane problemy prawa wodnego, Wolters Kluwer 2013.

Rakoczy, B., Prawo wodne. Praktyczny przewodnik, Wolters Kluwer Polska 2018.

Rakoczy, B., Prawo ochrony środowiska. Zagadnienia podstawowe, Wolters Kluwer 2018.
Stec, R., Uprawianie łowiectwa i prowadzenie gospodarki łowieckiej. Uwarunkowania administracyjne, cywilnoprawne i organizacyjne, Wolters Kluwer 2012.
Stelmasiak, J., (red.), Prawo ochrony środowiska, LexisNexis 2010.
Trzcińska. D., Prawo planowania i zagospodarowania przestrzennego z perspektywy środowiska i jego ochrony, Wolters Kluwer Polska 2018.

Selected Bibliography

Index

The numbers here refer to paragraph numbers.